The Manual

We encourage shelter managers and direct care workers to duplicate the Fact Sheets for use by their clients.

The Manual of Common Communicable Diseases in Shelters is an original publication of the Boston Health Care for the Homeless Program.
For further information, contact Boston Health Care for the Homeless Program,
723 Massachusetts Avenue, Boston, MA 02118.

Distributed by The Fund for the Homeless and The Boston Foundation,
One Boston Place, Boston, MA 02109.

Project Editors: James J. O'Connell, M.D. and Janet Groth, R.N., M.S.
Editorial assistance by David Eddy, Editorial Services of New England, Inc.
Design and Production Coordination by Patricia Mullaly, Circle Graphics.

Typeset by Discovery Graphics, Boston, MA
Color Transparencies by Spectragraphic N.E., Inc., South Boston, MA
Printed by Noonan-Leyden Press, Plymouth, MA

Photography credits: David Comb, pp. iv, x, xviii, xxiii, 30, 38, 78, 129, 186, 202; Richard Howard, p.8; James J. O'Connell, M.D., pp. xiii, xxiv, 25, 26, 27b, 41, 85, 91, 148, 156; Melissa Shook, pp. 27a, 31, 159; Janet Groth, R.N., M.S., p. 34; Centers for Disease Control, Atlanta, Georgia, pp. 56, 58, 81a, 81b, 118, 130, 151, 162, 207; Irwin Freedberg, M.D. and the Department of Dermatology at New York University, pp. 62, 65, 101, 103, 142a, 155, 160, 163, 187, 188, 189, 194, 210, 211; Howard Koh, M.D., pp. 86, 95, 100, 132, 137, 138, 142b, 142c, 152, 153, 154, 157, 191, 195; Reed & Carnrick Pharmaceuticals, p.145; National Pediculosis Association, p. 147; Nicholas Fiumara, M.D., pp. 175, 176, 197

ISBN 0-9629478-0-6

Library of Congress Cataloging-in-Publication Data
The Manual of common communicable diseases in shelters / edited by
James O'Connell and Janet Groth.
p. cm.
Includes bibliographical references.
1. Communicable diseases--Handbooks, manuals, etc. 2. Shelters for the homeless--Health aspects--Handbooks, manuals, etc. 3. Homeless persons--Health and hygiene--Handbooks, manuals, etc.
I. O'Connell, James, 1948- . II. Groth, Janet, 1958- . III. Boston Health Care for the Homeless Program.
[DNLM: 1. Communicable Diseases. 2. Communicable Diseases--prevention & control. 3. Homeless Persons. WA 110 M294]
RA643.M36 1991
616.9--dc20
DNLM/DLC 91–13542
for Library of Congress CIP

The Manual

of Common Communicable Diseases in Shelters

Edited by James J. O'Connell, M.D.
and Janet Groth, R.N., M.S.

Boston Health Care for the Homeless Program • 1991

Distributed by The Fund for the Homeless
and The Boston Foundation, One Boston Place, Boston, MA 02109

BHCHP nurse practitioner Jennifer Burroughs and family advocate Jocelyn Beverly perform a well-child examination at the Milner Hotel.

Table of Contents

Alphabetical Listing of Communicable Diseases

Sister Margaret Leonard, L.I.C.S.W., L.S.A., Executive Director of Project Hope Family Shelter in Dorchester.

Sister Margaret studies the plans for the new Magnolia Cooperative Housing Project with a young aspiring architect.

Dedication

Sister Margaret Leonard, the Executive Director of Project Hope, has been an inspiration to the Boston Health Care for the Homeless Program, teaching us gently the lessons of poverty. Homelessness is an extreme manifestation of poverty and will be solved by our society only with the creation of affordable housing.

Sister Margaret has worked with impoverished families in East Harlem and Dorchester for almost thirty years. After receiving an MSW from Fordham University, she became the Director of Family Health Services for the Little Sisters of the Assumption in New York. In 1975 she became the Chief Executive Officer for the United States Province of the Little Sisters, presiding over the boards of nine home health agencies.

Just as the fledgling BHCHP began clinical services in 1985, Sister Margaret arrived in Boston to become the Executive Director of Project Hope, a family shelter in Dorchester that has emphasized the community dimensions of family health while providing aftercare and support groups for all family members. Sister Margaret and Project Hope have created housing ownership opportunities through Magnolia Cooperative Housing, cited by Mayor Raymond L. Flynn as one of Boston's most imaginative and innovative attempts at permanent affordable housing for economically disadvantaged families.

An outspoken and courageous advocate of the poor and forgotten, Sister Margaret has been a leader in the Massachusetts Shelter Providers Association and a member of the Board of Directors of Pine Street Inn. She has been an invaluable resource to our Program, always available with words of encouragement to guide us through difficult times and lead us back to our mission of service to homeless individuals and families.

We dedicate this book to Sister Margaret Leonard, LICSW, LSA, for her courage, compassion, and commitment to those who have so little. Her patience and guidance have shown us the strength and heroism of those families struggling to survive and provide decent lives for their children despite abject poverty. Through Sister Margaret we also dedicate this book to those families whose courage in the face of homelessness has been a gift to all of us who have had the privilege of working and sharing with them.

Homeless mother comforts her child despite the hardships of sparse living in a welfare hotel.

Acknowlegements

This manual is a testament to the generous benefaction of:

The Boston Foundation

Comic Relief

The Fund for the Homeless

The Harvard Community Health Plan Foundation

Jordan Marsh Company

The Robert Wood Johnson Foundation

Acknowledgements

We are deeply grateful to our many friends and colleagues whose vision, support, and encouragement made this book possible.

John Ramsey of The Boston Foundation and Ruth McCambridge and Lisette Rodriguez of the Fund for the Homeless provided the venue for our first meetings in the Fall of 1988. Sr. Margaret Leonard of Project Hope, Jill Larcombe of Families in Transition, Patricia Brennan of Pathways Family Shelter, Mark Baker of Pine Street Inn, and many other members of the Massachusetts Shelter Providers Association have given us constant guidance and direction and a special awareness of the harsh realities of a world without enough affordable housing.

The photographs in this book have been wonderful gifts, and we owe a special thanks to Dr. Irwin Freedberg, Chairman of the Department of Dermatology of the New York University School of Medicine, for an extraordinary contribution. Dr. Freedberg was a gracious teacher who answered our call for help and devoted much time and energy to our efforts.

Dr. Howard Koh of the Dermatology and Oncology Departments of the Boston University School of Medicine has been an inspiration to our clinicians. He has generously given his time and considerable expertise throughout the evolution of the BHCHP, and we can hardly find the words to express our gratitude. His contribution of remarkable photographs has enlivened this manual just as his indomitable spirit has enriched our Program.

Jon Fuller, S.J., M.D., who has long astounded us with his legendary clinical and teaching skills, made the charts in the HIV and Gonorrhea chapters. He and Dr. Howard Libman have welcomed our staff as an integral part of the AIDS Clinic at Boston City Hospital.

Several of the photographs of the sexually transmitted diseases have been given by Dr. Nicholas J. Fiumara, who responded without hesitation to our call for assistance. Dr. Fiumara is Clinical Professor of Dermatology at Tufts University School of Medicine and Adjunct Professor of Dermatology at Boston University School of Medicine.

David Comb has contributed superb black and white photographs throughout this book. Melissa Shook has been a constant friend whose keen eye has enlivened our Program. Other photographs have been contributed by the Centers for Disease Control in Atlanta or were taken from our own BHCHP collection.

Boston Celtic Larry Bird and an exultant Billy Crystal trade foul shots while preparing a Comic Relief announcement. BHCHP, one of 19 projects begun by the Robert Wood Johnson Foundation in 1985, has received generous support from Comic Relief since 1988.

Dr. Anita Barry, the Director of the Communicable Disease Control of the Department of Health and Hospitals of Boston, embraced our embryonic efforts in the summer of 1988. She has given direction and guidance through innumerable hours of planning and editing. We thank her for an unwavering belief in the importance of this project. We could not have done this without her.

Several others have provided professional guidance: Nancy Harrington, regional epidemiologist of the Massachusetts Department of Public Health; Dr. Donald Craven, Director of Clinical AIDS Programs at Boston City Hospital; and Dr. Jerome O. Klein and Dr. Joanne Harris of the Department of Pediatrics at Boston City Hospital. Dr. Noreen Hynes took time from a Florida vacation to review our first draft, offering many suggestions which have considerably improved this work. Their advice and guidance, cajoling and editing, have been most appreciated.

Drs. John Noble, Robert Witzburg, James Heffernan, Kenneth Freedberg, John Rich, and Jeffrey Samet of the Section of General Medicine of Boston City Hospital have become trusted and supportive colleagues. Drs. John Potts, Albert Mulley, and Britain Nicholson of Massachusetts General Hospital have provided personal and institutional support to the BHCHP mission.

Dr. Ross Neisuler and other volunteer staff and clinicians from the Alliance for the Homeless of the Harvard Community Health Plan were invaluable sources of information and assistance, and have continued to be wonderful colleagues in our shared mission.

David Eddy of Editorial Services of New England, Inc. has been a patient and caring editor, willing to brave the styles of many contributors and the foibles of our frequent uncertainty and indecision.

A very special thanks is due Patricia Mullaly of Circle Graphics. Captured and conscripted at the very first meeting, she has formed and crafted these contents from unimaginably humble and scattered beginnings. She has suffered through innumerable changes and delays, and we cannot thank her enough for such gentle persuasion and direction. We cannot forget the journeys to the Hull seashore through many changing seasons, and the warm smell of coffee in her cozy office.

Many thanks to Stan Erck and Mary Riggin of Procept in Cambridge for the use of the Macintosh during those snowy Saturday afternoons.

We have been blessed by the support of many others. John Christian, Stuart Goldstein, Dennis Neighbors, Karen Tefft, and William Dunsford of the Trustees of Health and Hospitals of Boston, Inc., have been stalwart friends whose firm and caring guidance has been responsible for the success of the BHCHP. Dr. George Lamb and the Advisory Board of BHCHP forged the original coalition that conceived the Program's innovative model. They have proved steadfast in their commitment, having spent literally hundreds of hours nurturing an infant project toward maturity. The Robert Wood Johnson Foundation provided the original BHCHP grant, overseen with remarkable patience and wisdom by Dr. Philip Brickner and Stephen Wobido of St. Vincent's Hospital in New York City. Raymond L. Flynn, Mayor of Boston, Judith Kurland, Commissioner of Health and Hospitals, Alonzo Plough, Ph.D., Deputy Commissioner, and Ann Maguire of the Emergency Shelter Commission have championed the mission of the Program and assured the integration of the BHCHP into the fabric of the city's health care system. The Commonwealth of Massachusetts has provided generous support to BHCHP since 1985, and the United States Public Health Service has been a critical component of the success of the BHCHP since 1988 through the McKinney funds.

BHCHP has 34 staff members, creative and energetic professionals who have been willing to devote their days and evenings to the service of homeless individuals and families. The talent of these nurses, doctors, and social workers is truly staggering, and the success of this Program is due to this most unusual group. We cannot thank them enough, and we only wish that the readers of this book could share in the fun and competence that abound at our meetings.

We thank the shelter staffs who have so willingly allowed us to share feelings and frustrations. Their commitment and dedication have been a profound inspiration to all of us.

Most of all, we offer thanks to the heroic families whose strength and character have continually proved indomitable in a struggle against the ravages of poverty while deprived of the basic right to housing.

John Christian, **Vice President and General Manager, Trustees of Health and Hospitals of Boston, Inc.**

Advisory Board Members, 1985 - 1991

George A. Lamb, M.D., *Chair*
Alison Abdu, M.B.A.
Sarah Anderson, J.D.
Rand Bailey, R.N.
Edrick Bain
Sister Sue Beaton, M.A., M.S.
Barbara Blakeney, R.N., M.S.
Joseph Cohen, M.D.
Barbara Davidson, R.N.
Peter Dreier, Ph.D.
Stuart Goldstein
Ira Greif
Mary Ann Hart, R.N.
Robert Johansen, R.N.
Ann Kibbrick, R.N., Ph.D.
Judith Kurland
Irene Lee
Gerry Morrisey
Eileen McGee, R.N.
John O'Brien
Gloria Oldsman
Marjorie Perry
Alonzo Plough, Ph.D.
Robert Richards, M.S.W.
Kip Tiernan
Basil Tommy
Julie Vaughn

Staff Members, 1985 - 1991

Marsha Adderly
Michelle Audet, M.S.W.
Robin Avery, M.D.
Betty Bell
Thomas Bennett, M.D.
Migdalia Berrios
Joceyln Beverly
Michael Bierer, M.D., M.P.H.
Linda Brown
Barry Bock, R.N.
Naomi Bock, M.D.
Aljernon Bolden, D.M.D.
Joan Boland, L.P.N.
Eileen Brigandi
Jennifer Burroughs, R.N.,C., M.S.N.
Ka Ling Cheung
Molly Clark
Paula Cushman, R.N.,C., M.S.
Lyn Dionne
Alan Drabkin, M.D.
Socrates Francis, M.D.
Lori Friedman
Janet Groth, R.N., M.S.
Geanessa Gonzalez
William Goodwin
Robert Harrington, D.M.D.
Nicholas Herold
Rosemarie Kenney, R.N.,C., M.S.
Barbara King
Joan Lebow, M.D.
Margaret Lewis, R.N.,C.
Rika Maeshiro, M.D.
Coleman Mansfield
John Mazzulo, M.D.
Marc Miletsky
Veronica Miletsky
Jean Molloy, R.N.,C., M.S.
John Montgomery, L.I.C.S.W.
Ruth Moran
Maya Mundkur, R.N.,C., M.S.N.
Maureen Murray
Mark McGovern, M.S.W.
Maureen McLaughlin
Margaret McNamara, R.N.,C., M.S.
Terry O'Brien, R.N.
Mary O'Brien
James J. O'Connell, M.D.
Millie Owen, L.P.N.
Roberta Padua
Katie Pellett, R.N.,C, M.S.
Maria Pitaro, M.D.
Joan Quinlan, M.P.P.
Kieth Radcliffe, M.P.H.
Sylvia Roman
Jacqueline Santiago
Deborah Sarson, R.N.,C.
Robin Scott
Ben Siegel, M.D.
Ann Slattery
Betty Snead
Greg Stoute, D.M.D.
Dargis Valdez
Maria Valentin, R.N.
Yoshiko Vann, R.N.,C.
Morris Walker
C.C. Williams
Mark Yoder, R.N.,C., M.S.
Mary Michelle Young

The Boston Health Care for the Homeless Program

A non-profit entity of the Trustees of Health and Hospitals of the City of Boston, Inc., BHCHP was originally funded by a grant from the Robert Wood Johnson Foundation and the Commonwealth of Massachusetts. Current funding is received from the United States Public Health Service, the Commonwealth of Massachusetts, the City of Boston, Comic Relief, and many individual, foundation, and corporate donations. The Program is affiliated with the Department of Health and Hospitals of the City of Boston.

Foreword

The Commonwealth of Massachusetts has been a leader in the promotion of public health, beginning with the first state board of health established in 1869. The twentieth century has seen major epidemics of tuberculosis, syphilis, rheumatic fever, polio, and measles, among many others, virtually eradicated by advances in medicine and public health.

Unfortunately, these communicable diseases continue to surface in the midst of the poverty of many of our neighborhoods and inner cities. The litany of illnesses in this manual is disturbingly reminiscent of the health problems of last century, with the addition of the tragic epidemic of AIDS. The protection of human health has become the shared mission of public health agencies and a network of public and private agencies concerned with the environment, education, housing, and public safety.

The Boston Health Care for the Homeless Program has become a national model for the delivery of quality health care to individuals and families who must struggle for survival without the safety and security of homes. This innovative public health approach utilizes multidisciplinary teams of doctors, nurses, and case workers integrating the primary and specialty clinics of Boston's major teaching hospitals with direct outreach services in over 40 sites. This remarkable network of health care and social services has resulted from the efforts of committed providers willing to challenge existing systems, and the collaboration of many public and private agencies in Massachusetts.

This manual offers a practical approach to the health risks facing the guests, staff, and health care providers in shelters for homeless persons throughout the country. The Massachusetts Department of Public Health is proud to share in this innovative endeavor.

COMMONWEALTH OF MASSACHUSETTS DEPARTMENT OF PUBLIC HEALTH

David Mulligan

Commissioner
Department of Public Health
Commonwealth of Massachusetts

Foreword

The Boston Board of Health, established in 1799 with Paul Revere as President, was one of the first public health boards in the nation. Since that time, Boston has continued a proud tradition of leadership in preserving the health of the city's neighborhoods through the prevention of communicable diseases.

Many of the triumphs of public health over such epidemics as tuberculosis, syphilis, gonorrhea, and measles have begun to crumble during this past decade. Persistent poverty and the loss of affordable housing stock in our inner cities have caused growing numbers of citizens to seek emergency shelter. At the same time, the AIDS epidemic has engulfed many neighborhoods in Boston and other major cities throughout our country, compromising the immune systems of those infected and facilitating the spread of tuberculosis and many other communicable diseases.

The twin challenges presented by homelessness and the AIDS epidemic are daunting. To meet those challenges, Boston's Department of Health and Hospitals collaborated with the Boston Health Care for the Homeless Program and the Massachusetts Department of Public Health to produce a manual for those who need help and guidance in combating and preventing illness in a shelter setting. This manual provides practical guidelines for shelter providers, staff, and guests and is an important step toward the prevention and management of these often devastating illnesses. Mayor Raymond L. Flynn and I salute the efforts of the dedicated clinicians whose work makes this all possible.

We hope that you will enjoy this manual and find it helpful in alleviating the suffering of so many of our citizens who must cope with survival without the comfort and safety of a home.

Judith Kurland

Commissioner
Department of Health and Hospitals
City of Boston

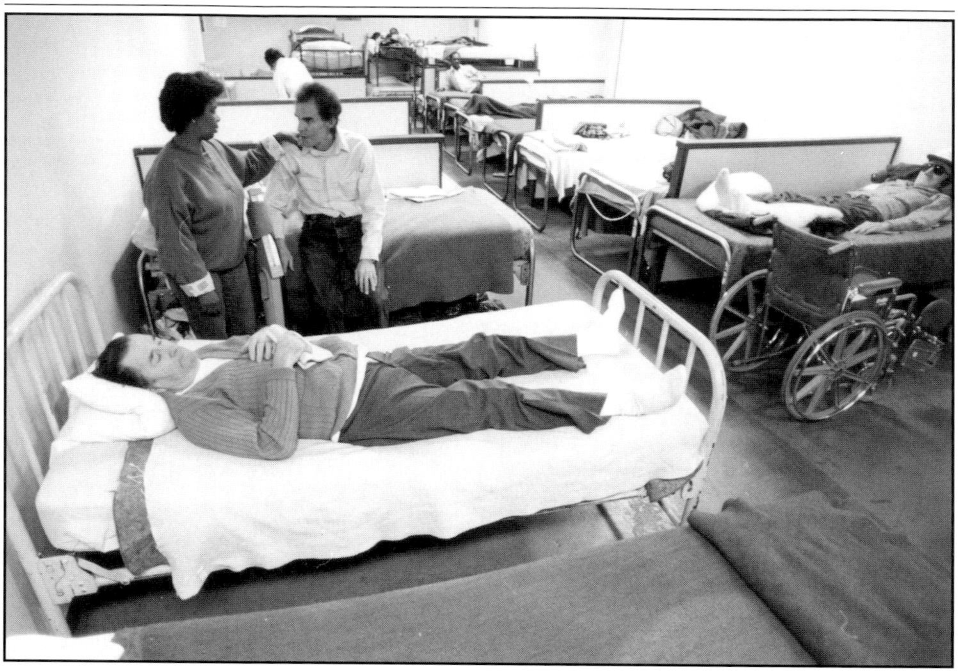

The 25–bed Medical Respite Unit of the BHCHP at the Lemuel Shattuck Shelter provides comprehensive health care and social services for persons ready for discharge from acute care hospitals but not yet ready to withstand the rigors of survival on the streets. This innovative and cost-effective model of care has been particularly helpful in relieving the suffering of homeless persons with symptomatic HIV infection.

Contributing Authors

George Alliegro, M.D., is a Visiting Physician in Infectious Diseases at Boston City Hospital and a staff physician at New England Deaconess Hospital and New England Baptist Hospital. He is also an Instructor in Medicine at Harvard Medical School. After finishing a residency in Medicine at Thomas Jefferson University Hospital in Philadelphia, Dr. Alliegro was a Fellow in Infectious Diseases at Boston City Hospital from 1986 until 1989. He was of invaluable assistance to the BHCHP during an outbreak of *Haemophilus influenzae* type b among adult men in a large Boston shelter.

Robin K. Avery, M.D., completed her residency in Medicine at Massachusetts General Hospital in June of 1988 and spent the next year with the Boston Health Care for the Homeless Program, developing a primary and specialty care network for homeless persons with AIDS and HIV infection. She is now a Fellow in the Infectious Diseases Unit at Massachusetts General Hospital and an Instructor in Medicine at Harvard Medical School.

Johnye Ballenger, M.D., completed her residency in Pediatrics and a fellowship in Ambulatory Pediatrics at Boston City Hospital. She is currently an Assistant in Medicine at Children's Hospital in Boston and an Instructor in Pediatrics at Harvard Medical School. She was also the pediatrician for Project Better Health, a program funded by the Better Homes Foundation that served families in motels on the North Shore of Boston from 1989 until 1990.

M. Anita Barry, M.D., M.P.H., Director of the Communicable Disease Control for the Boston Department of Health and Hospitals, has organized many public health prevention and treatment programs for homeless individuals and families throughout the city. She completed a residency in Medicine and a fellowship in Infectious Diseases at Boston City Hospital. She is an Assistant Professor of Medicine and Public Health at Boston University.

Joel Bass, M.D., completed his residency in Pediatrics at Children's Hospital in Boston and is currently Director of Ambulatory Pediatrics at Framingham Union Hospital and Clinical Professor of Pediatrics at Boston University. He has provided care for family shelters in the Framingham area and is the principal author of "Pediatric Problems in a Suburban Shelter for Homeless Families" which appeared in *Pediatrics* in January 1990.

Thomas M. Bennett, M.D., joined the Boston Health Care for the Homeless Program in the summer of 1987 after completing his residency in Medicine at Boston City Hospital. He served as Clinical Director until 1990, helping to develop the Medical Respite Unit at the Shattuck Shelter and the St. Francis House Clinic. He is now a physician at the Fenway Community Health Center.

John Bernardo, M.D., a part-time Volkswagen mechanic and cell-sorter operator extraordinaire, doubles as the Director of the Tuberculosis Clinic at Boston City Hospital. He trained in Medicine at New York Hospital and Boston City Hospital, and then did research at NIH. He is an Associate Professor of Medicine at Boston University. He has written widely on the subject of tuberculosis among homeless populations, conducts a weekly tuberculosis screening clinic at Pine Street Inn, and has been an invaluable resource to the clinicians of the BHCHP.

Michael Bierer, M.D., M.P.H., completed a residency in Medicine at Massachusetts General Hospital in 1988 and an M.P.H. at Harvard in 1989. He has been a physician with the BHCHP since 1988, working at Pine Street Inn and St. Francis House, while supervising the weekly clinic for homeless persons at Massachusetts General Hospital, where he is an Assistant in Medicine. He is an Instructor in Medicine at Harvard Medical School.

Barry Bock, R.N., was a nurse and Director of Pine Street Inn's Nursing Clinic from 1986 until 1990, the nation's oldest independent nurses' clinic that had over 110,000 visits in three facilities during 1990. In October of 1990, he became the Clinical Director for the Boston Health Care for the Homeless Program, where he has established an active Quality Assurance Program while continuing to integrate the BHCHP's clinical services with those of Boston's major teaching hospitals and shelter clinics.

Diane Duffy, R.N., is a graduate of the Boston City Hospital School of Nursing and holds a B.S.N. from Salem State College. She was a staff nurse in the Surgical Unit and Recovery Unit at BCH, and became the Head Nurse of the Surgical Unit in 1980. In 1985 she began work in the Public Health Clinic at Boston City Hospital and was Head Nurse in this state-funded clinic specializing in the treatment of sexually transmitted diseases from 1987 to 1990. She is currently the Director of Operations in the Division of Community Affairs of the Boston Department of Health and Hospitals.

Lori Fantry, M.D., finished her residency in Medicine at the University of Massachusetts Medical School in 1988 and was the Medical Director for the Homeless Outreach and Advocacy Project in Worcester until the summer of 1990. She is now the Director of the General Internal Medicine Residency

Program at Francis Scott Key Hospital in Baltimore and an Assistant Professor of Medicine at Johns Hopkins School of Medicine. She also serves as a physician for the Baltimore Health Care for the Homeless Program.

Janet Groth, R.N., M.S., was a public health nurse managing the care of homeless persons with tuberculosis for the Boston Department of Health and Hospitals for two years before joining the Boston Health Care for the Homeless Program in the fall of 1988. She has collaborated with the city and state health departments to develop strategies for the prevention and control of communicable diseases in both adult and family shelters throughout the Boston area. She received her M.S. at Boston College in May of 1991.

M. Kathleen Hennessy, has been the Director of the Food Sanitation Training Program of the Boston Department of Health and Hospitals since 1988. Previously, she had been the Director of Labor Relations for the City of Boston, the Mayor's Advisor on Women's Issues, and the Executive Director of the Women's Commission. She has also worked as a teacher and a social worker in the Boston school system.

Noreen A. Hynes, M.D., M.P.H., completed her internship in Medicine at Massachusetts General Hospital in 1986. She served as an Epidemic Intelligence Officer at the Centers for Disease Control (CDC) in Atlanta, Georgia, in the Influenza Branch from 1986 until 1988. She then completed a residency in Medicine and a Clinical Fellowship in the Infectious Diseases Unit at Massachusetts General Hospital. She is currently a research medical officer in the Molecular Virology Section of the Division of Vector-borne Infectious Diseases, CDC, Fort Collins, Colorado, and an Assistant Professor of Medicine at the University of Colorado School of Medicine.

Joan Lebow, M.D., completed a residency in Medicine at The Bowman Gray School of Medicine of Wake Forest University and joined the BHCHP in the summer of 1989. As the Program's Director of AIDS and HIV Services, she oversees the primary and specialty care of more than 300 homeless persons with HIV infection. She is an Assistant Attending Physician at Boston City Hospital and an Assistant Professor of Medicine at Boston University.

Barbara McInnis, R.N., has been the public health nurse at Pine Street Inn's Nursing Clinic since 1973. Although her primary role has been the management of tuberculosis in the shelter, her commitment and expertise have been the cornerstone and inspiration for those delivering health care to homeless persons in Boston. Whenever in doubt, we have all simply asked Barbara.

Jean E. Molloy, R.N., C., M.S., has been a Family Nurse Practitioner with the Boston Health Care for the Homeless Program since the summer of 1988.

She earned her M.S. at the University of Virginia after working for several years as a community health nurse in Connecticut. She is the Director of the Family Program of the BHCHP.

Maya Mundkur, R.N., C., M.S.N., worked as a Family Nurse Practitioner with the Boston Health Care for the Homeless Program from the spring of 1988 until 1990. She received her M.S.N. at Yale University. She is currently on the staff of the Fenway Community Health Center.

James J. O'Connell, M.D., joined the Boston Health Care for the Homeless Program after completing his residency in Medicine at Massachusetts General Hospital in 1985. He has been the Program's Director since 1988 and is also the Director of the Homeless Families Program of the Robert Wood Johnson Foundation.

Maria Pitaro, M.D., joined the BHCHP after completing her residency in Medicine at Boston City Hospital, where she was President of the House Officers' Union. She has been a leader in issues concerning the health care of homeless women and has been the Program's representative on a task force to assure universal health insurance in Massachusetts. She is an Assistant Attending Physician at Boston City Hospital and an Assistant Professor of Medicine at Boston University.

Ben Siegel, M.D., has been the Pediatric Consultant for the BHCHP since clinical services began in the summer of 1985. His vision has been primarily responsible for the development of the Family Program. He completed his residency in Pediatrics at Boston City Hospital and Montefiore Hospital, and is an Associate Professor of Pediatrics at Boston University. He has been nationally prominent in the evolution of pediatric residency training programs and has a special interest in the development of multidisciplinary teams in the delivery of primary health care to underserved populations.

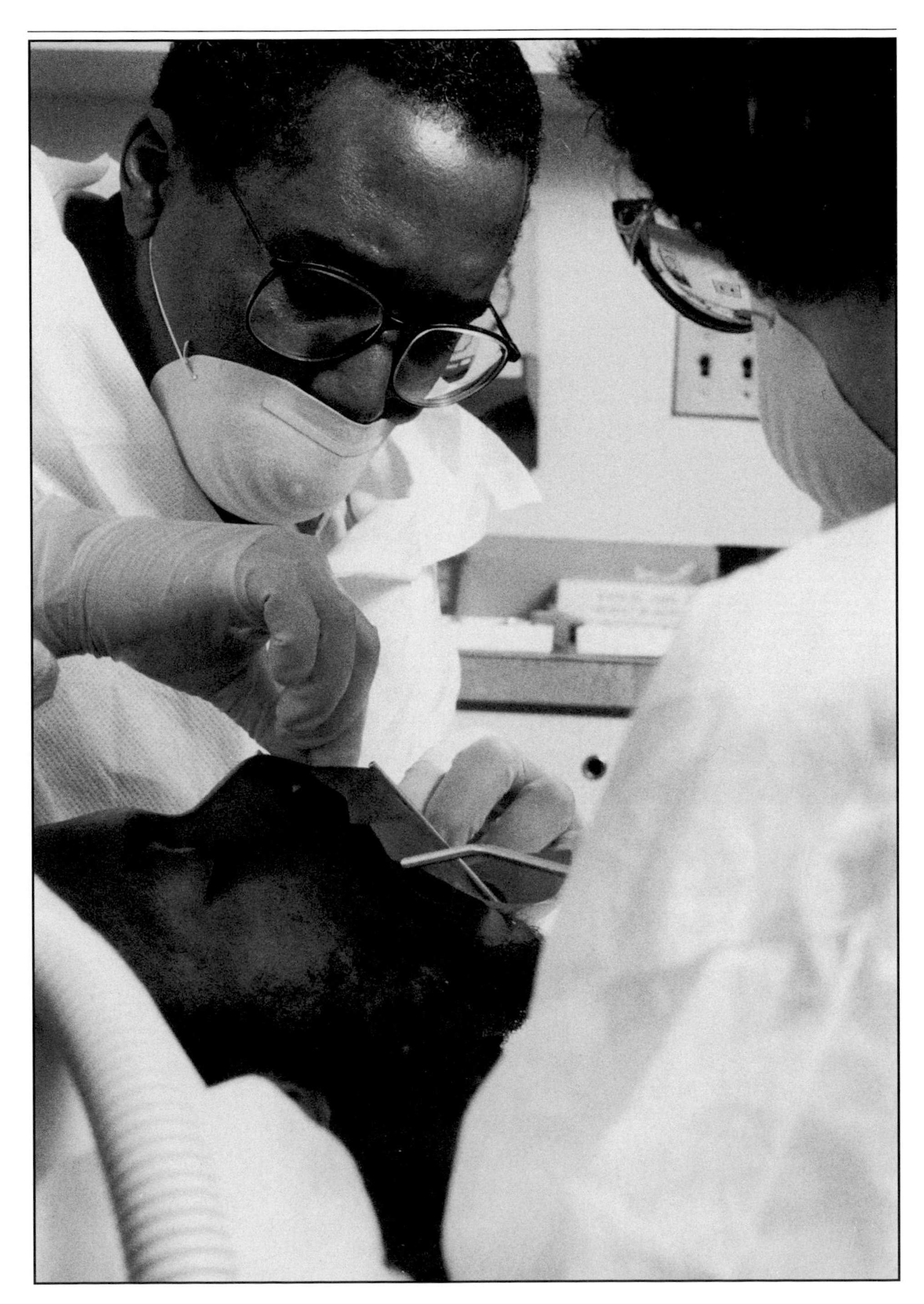

BHCHP dentist Al Bolden and dental assistant Sylvia Roman bond a fractured tooth at St. Francis House Clinic.

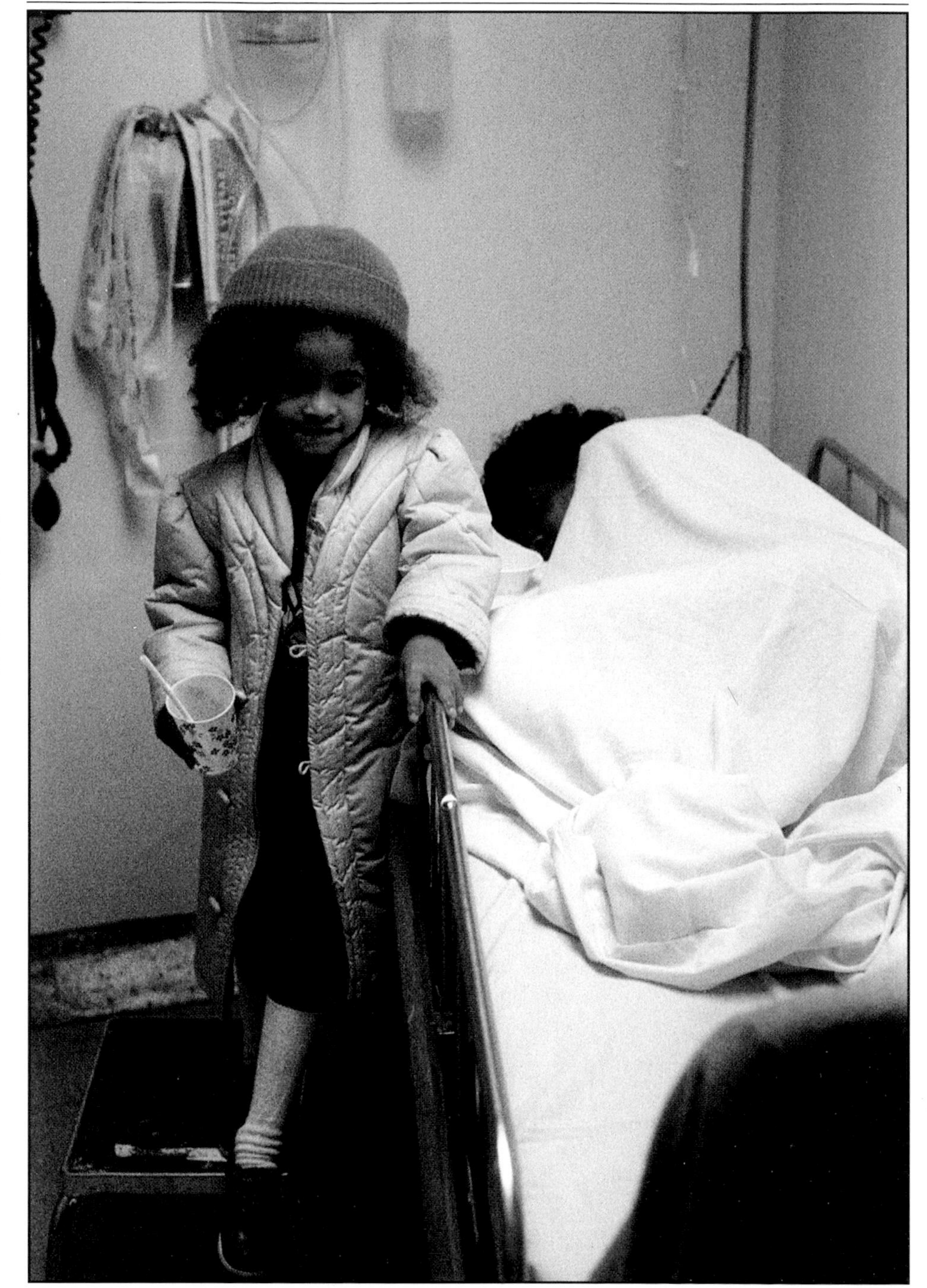

A young girl guards her mother's bedside in a local emergency room, fearing the separation she has experienced so often during the chronic illness that has led to their homelessness.

Part One: Introduction

History

This manual has been over two years in the making. What began as a brief collection of protocols has blossomed into a compendium of common communicable diseases, seen from the viewpoint of health care professionals working in the shelters and soup kitchens that serve persons struggling to survive without homes.

The Boston Health Care for the Homeless Program (BHCHP) was originally funded by the Robert Wood Johnson Foundation and the Commonwealth of Massachusetts, and given the mission of assuring access to quality health care to homeless persons in Boston. Clinical services began in the summer of 1985, and teams of physicians, nurses, and case workers have cared for over 25,000 homeless men, women, and children since that time. Primary care clinics are held daily at Boston City Hospital and twice weekly at Massachusetts General Hospital. Direct care services are delivered at over 40 outreach sites in the greater Boston area, including most large adult shelters as well as family shelters, shelters for battered women, soup kitchens and day centers, and hotels and motels.

Boston City Hospital, located in the city's South End, provides almost 25 percent of the free care delivered in Massachusetts, and is the hub of the BHCHP clinical activity.

BHCHP physicians and nurses also hold several sessions each week in the AIDS Clinic at Boston City Hospital to provide continuous and specialty care for homeless persons with HIV-infection. Inpatient rounds are held twice each week for all homeless persons admitted to Boston City Hospital and Massachusetts General Hospital. The Medical Respite Unit at the Lemuel Shattuck Shelter, staffed by the BHCHP, has 25 beds for persons recovering from acute illnesses but unable to withstand the rigors of survival on the streets. The Dental Program offers comprehensive care at St. Francis House, a day center for homeless persons located in the Combat Zone of Boston. Bicultural and bilingual services are available for Hispanic persons.

The Family Program provided the seeds for the growth and development of this manual. Boston is blessed with several small family shelters that offer an array of services to help families transition to permanent housing. When these shelters are full, new families are sent to hotels and motels in the metropolitan area. Unfortunately, these latter families are geographically uprooted from neighborhood and community supports and must cope within the confines of a bland room, often without refrigeration or cooking facilities.

The Milner Hotel in Boston's theater district provides emergency shelter for families. The average length of stay is between two and three months.

The BHCHP Family Team, assisted by Dr. Ben Siegel of the Pediatric Department of Boston City Hospital, collaborated with the staffs of the shelters to understand the special health care needs of homeless families. A persistent plea for help emerged: how to cope with the periodic outbreaks of infectious and communicable diseases that invariably wreaked havoc, fear, and confusion within the shelters. Indeed, this plea only further underscored our own ineptitude at managing the frequent outbreaks (usually late Friday afternoons!) of illnesses such as chickenpox or infectious diarrhea.

To address this concern, we decided upon two practical goals: find a public health professional who would work with us to develop strategies for preventing and managing communicable diseases within shelters, and write a manual of protocols that might be helpful to shelter staff, guests, and providers. To that end, Janet Groth, a community health nurse who had been organizing the outreach program of the Boston Department of Health and Hospitals for homeless persons with tuberculosis, began working with us in the fall of 1988. This manual is a testament to her boundless energy and dogged efforts.

The Manual

We have attempted to make this book easy to navigate and read. Occasionally we have oversimplified, particularly with the modes of transmission. Many illnesses are spread in several ways, and we have chosen the most obvious for the sake of simplicity and organization.

This manual is divided into six parts. Following this introduction, Part Two discusses the ways in which diseases can spread from one person to another and offers guidelines for the prevention of communicable diseases in general as well as methods for controlling the transmission of specific types of illnesses. We have attempted to categorize communicable diseases into four groups by mode of transmission: airborne, fecal-oral, direct and indirect contact, and blood and sexual contact. Such categorization is necessarily simplistic and belies the bewildering complexity of many organisms. For example, chickenpox is familiar to most of us as a rash in childhood. The varicella virus that causes chickenpox is transmitted through the respiratory tract, although the virus can also be spread by direct contact with the lesions of chicken-pox. This virus then becomes dormant and may appear later in life as shingles or herpes zoster, which can be transmitted by direct contact. So we beg the reader's indulgence in understanding the organizational need to straighten a few crooked pathways.

Standing in interminable lines is a daily routine for homeless persons, often exposed to the extremes of temperature and weather. These men are waiting for the doors of a local shelter to open in the late afternoon.

TB outreach worker Ursula Kelly and BHCHP case worker Marc Miletsky celebrate the completion of an 18-month course of daily medications with this elderly poet who prefers the streets to the crowded shelters.

Part Three contains discussions of 26 common communicable diseases, each of which was written by a person familiar with the problems associated with the prevention and control of these illnesses in shelter settings. An attempt has been made to inform health care providers while making these chapters readable to a more general audience. Each chapter briefly discusses the prevalence, transmission, diagnosis, treatment, and prevention of a particular illness. A brief summary written specifically for the shelter staff concludes each chapter. A few references are included for those who wish more in-depth knowledge. The chapters are grouped according to mode of transmission; for those unsure of the mode of transmission and those seeking a quick reference, an alphabetical listing of diseases and page numbers appears after the Table of Contents on page vii.

Part Four discusses immunization schedules for children and adults, as well as some of the illnesses rendered rare by widespread vaccination programs, such as polio, diphtheria, mumps, rubella, and tetanus. Other resurgent or persistent vaccine-preventable infections, such as measles, pertussis, *Haemophilus influenzae* type b, and hepatitis B, are included with the common communicable diseases in Part Two.

Part Five includes practical suggestions for the proper handling and preparation of food in shelters. Our own experience with an outbreak of hepatitis A nudged our concern in this area.

Fact Sheets for shelter guests are compiled in Part Six. These pages are simple instructions for families and individuals. They are intended to be photocopied and passed to shelter guests during outbreaks of these illnesses. This idea came from many of the shelter staff and guests who were involved in the conception of this book, and we hope you will find these as useful as we have.

Throughout this manual we have chosen to refer to "injection drug use" to include subcutaneous "skin-popping" as well as intravenous (IV) drug use, both of which are efficient means of transmitting several infections.

Our recommendations and suggestions are not dogma. Most of our approaches are practical and have worked well in the shelters. We fully acknowledge that there are other approaches, many of which are perhaps better. We understand that shelters differ in size, layout, staffing, and a host of other variables. Our hope is that this book will generate an open discussion among the growing numbers of providers in this field and will lead us all to more effective strategies for preventing and managing these illnesses in shelters.

The pace of medicine is rapid, and inevitably new treatments and approaches will supercede many of our recommendations. We urge you to maintain a dialogue with your local health departments, hospitals, and community health centers in order to keep abreast of the most current methods of prevention, control, and treatment of communicable diseases in your cities and neighborhoods.

— JJO'C *Boston, January 1991*

Part Two: A Primer of Communicable Diseases

I. Introduction

Communicable or infectious diseases include those illnesses caused by bacteria, viruses, parasites, and fungi that can spread directly or indirectly from one person to another. These diseases may spread wherever groups of people live or work together. The risk of transmission is especially high in the crowded settings typical of schools, nursing homes, and shelters for homeless persons.

Certain measures can help reduce the risk of transmission in shelters. As with any effort to improve public health, these measures depend on three key elements:

1) knowledge: each communicable disease has characteristic signs and symptoms, specific modes of transmission, and ways of prevention, control, and treatment. While staff and guests do not need detailed knowledge of the specific aspects of each disease, a general understanding of the principles of transmission and control is most useful. Awareness of one's history of childhood illnesses is invaluable and allows a determination of the immune status of each guest and staff member well before an outbreak of any vaccine–preventable disease.

2) attitudes: people often have strong feelings and emotions about communicable diseases. When informed by knowledge rather than rumor or prejudice, attitudes that help promote the conditions necessary for controlling and preventing the transmission of disease can be nurtured.

3) behavior: health-promoting habits depend on knowledge and attitudes. Good personal habits can dramatically reduce the risk of spread. When individual staff and guests practice these habits, an environment is created in which the health of all is protected. Shelters should be sure to keep staff and guests informed about the dangers of particular diseases and effective ways to control their spread. Each shelter should have access to a health consultant who is familiar with the special problems of public health in group settings. Local and state health departments can be vital sources of information and support for the control of infectious diseases.

II. Early Warning Signs of Illness

The prevention and control of communicable diseases depend very much on the ability of staff and guests to recognize the early stages of such illnesses. Health care providers should be alerted whenever an adult or child in the shelter experiences any of the following signs and symptoms:

fever of 101° F (38° C) or higher
change in normal behavior
loss of appetite
loss of weight
coughing: severe, persistent, or bloody
difficulty with breathing
sore throat or trouble swallowing
headache, especially with neck stiffness
vomiting
diarrhea
yellowish skin or eyes
dark, tea-colored urine
gray or white stool
pink or draining eye(s)
skin patches that ooze or become crusted
itchiness of the scalp, skin, or groin
unusual spots or rashes of the skin

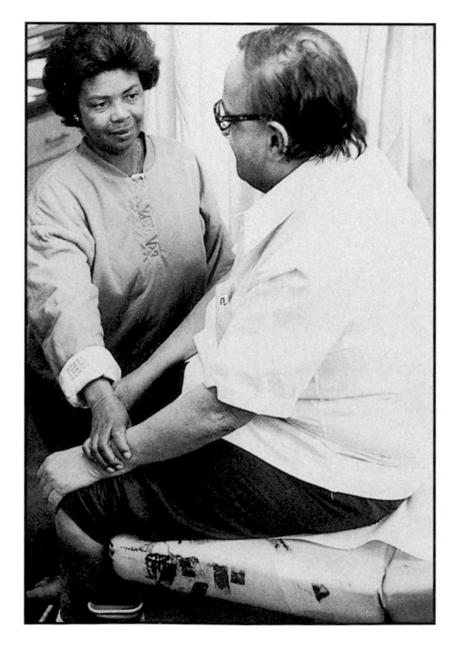

Aide Betty Snead tends to the concerns of this patient with chronic lung disease in the BHCHP Medical Respite Unit at the Lemuel Shattuck Shelter.

III. The Four Modes of Transmission.

Communicable diseases can be classified by the ways in which they spread. The four principal modes of transmission and the associated diseases include the following:

- **airborne transmission**, spread via secretions from the lungs, throat, nose, or eyes, e.g. chickenpox, influenza, tuberculosis, strep throat;

- **fecal-oral transmission**, spread via infected feces that enter the digestive tract through the mouth, e.g. pinworm, hepatitis A, *Salmonella, Giardia;*

• **direct and indirect contact** with the site of infection on another person, e.g. impetigo, ringworm, lice, scabies;

• **blood and/or sexual contact**, which includes the sexually transmitted diseases (STD's) such as gonorrhea, syphilis, and chlamydia, as well as those STD's which are also spread through contact with an infected person's blood or blood products, as occurs with hepatitis B and the human immunodeficiency virus (HIV).

Crowded conditions in many shelters make the control and prevention of infection very difficult. However, a few basic measures can dramatically reduce the risk of communicable disease in shelters. Many apply to all types of diseases and are included in the section on General Guidelines. Other measures are specific to each mode of transmission and can be found in the appropriate sections under Specific Guidelines.

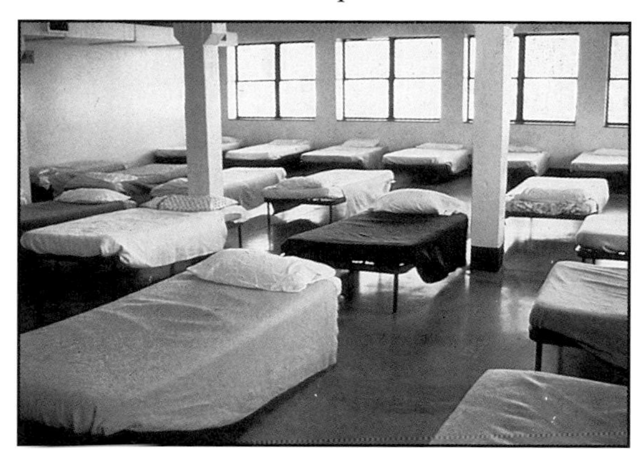

The close proximity of the dormitory beds in most adult shelters facilitates the spread of many airborne infections, including tuberculosis and influenza.

Unfortunately, financial constraints may make some of the suggestions seem unrealistic. For example, we recommend that shelters stock adequate supplies of paper towels and tissues for all guests. This can be very costly and must be weighed against the potential benefit of reducing risk and preventing such illnesses. However, most of these measures rely on common principles of hygiene, and creative solutions can be found that work within the limits of each shelter's budget.

IV. The Reportable Diseases

Providers are required to report many of these communicable diseases to the local health department because of the dangers of rapid transmission and widespread epidemics. In Massachusetts, the diseases listed below should be reported immediately by telephone or in writing to the health department in the community where the case has been diagnosed. In addition, an outbreak in any community (including shelters) of a similar illness involving two or more persons within a two-week period, including those which do not appear on this list, should be reported to the local health department. Those reportable diseases included in this book are in bold letters:

Reportable Diseases in Massachusetts

Amebiasis
Animal bite
Anthrax
Babesiosis
Brucellosis (Undulant Fever)
Chickenpox (Varicella)
Cholera
Diphtheria
Encephalitis (specify type, if known)
Epidemic Staphylococcal Infection of Newborn (onset within 30 days after birth)
Foodborne Intoxications:
- a. Botulism
- b. Mushrooms and other poisonous vegetables and animal products
- c. Mineral or inorganic poisons such as arsenic, lead, etc.
- d. Staphylococcal
- e. Paralytic shellfish poisoning
- f. Other

Giardiasis
Haemophilus influenzae systemic infection (without meningitis)
Hepatitis, Viral
- **a. Type A**
- **b. Type B**
- c. Type C (non-A, non-B)
- d. Type D (delta)
- e. Undetermined

Kawasaki Disease
Legionnaires' Disease (Legionellosis)
Leprosy (Hansen's Disease)
Leptospirosis
Listeriosis
Lyme Disease
Malaria
Measles
Meningitis: bacterial, viral, other
Meningococcal infection (without meningitis)
Mumps
Pertussis (Whooping Cough)
Plague
Poliomyelitis
Psittacosis
Rabies (human or animal)
Reye's Syndrome
Rickettsial Disease
- a. Rickettsialpox
- b. Typhus
- c. Rocky Mountain Spotted Fever
- d. Other

Rubella (German Measles)
- a. Congenital
- b. Non-congenital

Salmonellosis (including Typhoid and Paratyphoid Fever)
Shigellosis (Bacillary Dysentery)
Tetanus
Toxic Shock Syndrome
Toxoplasmosis
Trichinosis
Tuberculosis
Tularemia
Yersiniosis

In addition, the following diseases and syndromes are reportable directly to the Massachusetts Department of Public Health:

Acquired Immune Deficiency Syndrome (AIDS)
Chancroid
Chlamydial infection (Genital)
Gonorrhea
Granuloma inguinale
Herpes neonatal (onset within 30 days after birth)
Lymphogranuloma venereum
Ophthalmia neonatorum
 a. Gonococcal
 b. Other agents
Pelvic Inflammatory Disease (PID)
 a. Gonococcal
 b. Other agents
Syphilis

Handwashing is the single most important measure for preventing the spread of communicable diseases in most environments, especially in shelters with infant children.

V. Prevention of Communicable Diseases

A. General Guidelines
A few simple habits and precautions are the most important tools we have to prevent the spread of these infections. Like all habits, they must be practiced and repeated so that they are performed routinely. We realize how difficult this may be, but we cannot emphasize how important these procedures are if we hope to protect ourselves and others living in the shelters. These guidelines are divided into personal hygiene and care of the shelter environment.

1. Personal Hygiene
a. Handwashing
This is perhaps the single most important measure for the prevention of the spread of communicable diseases in any environment and especially in shelters with infant children. Adults and children should wash their hands regularly with soap and warm water. Careful handwashing is especially important:

BEFORE handling food (eating, preparing, serving, or storing);
feeding or breastfeeding a child;

AFTER using the toilet;
diapering an infant;
contact with any body secretions.

Washing hands after using the toilet is especially important, and every parent should carefully teach and monitor toilet-trained children in the bathroom to wash their hands after using the toilet. This lifelong habit is best taught carefully in these early years.

Pre-packaged handwipes are very useful for guests who may spend much of their time away from sanitary facilities. If possible, handwipes that contain alcohol should be provided, such as Wet Ones™ or Wash 'n Dries™. Diaper wipes for babies are usually oil-based and do not inhibit the growth of bacteria and other micro-organisms.

Clean sanitary facilities for staff and guests encourage handwashing, and are vital to good health. Bathrooms should be stocked with soap, paper towels, and toilet paper. Staff should monitor the supply of these items and replenish them regularly.

Soap from a dispenser is ideal, although bar soap is fine as long as it is allowed to drain.

Cloth handtowels should never be used for community sanitary facilities. Always use paper towels.

Signs encouraging handwashing should be placed in all kitchens and bathrooms.

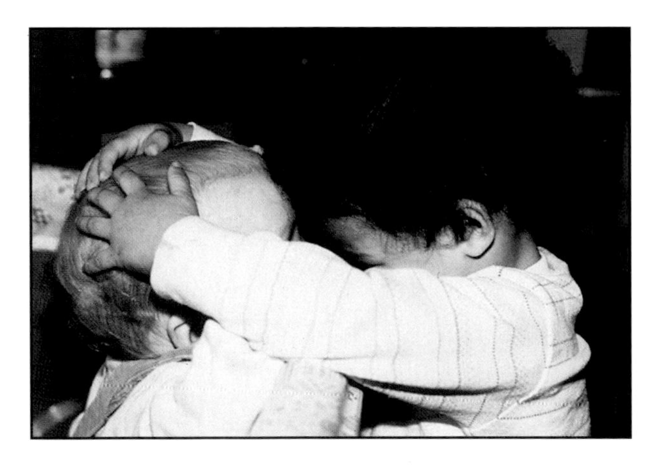

These toddlers share friendship and germs in a family shelter.

b. Shared Objects

Discourage children from sharing toys and other objects that may be mouthed or chewed. Such items should be washed regularly in warm, soapy water, and then disinfected in a dilute bleach solution (1/4 cup bleach to 1 gallon water). This solution, which must be mixed fresh each day, is also recommended for disinfecting dishes. Cleaning toys during the general kitchen cleanup is a convenient and practical habit.

Discourage the sharing of clothing and personal items such as combs, brushes, razors, and toothbrushes.

c. Laundry
Clothes and linen soiled with body fluids should be disinfected by washing with detergent and bleach (1 cup per load) in hot water for cotton and colorfast articles. Items that are not colorfast can be washed in warm water with detergent and a phenolic disinfectant such as Lysol™. A second wash and rinse without Lysol™ will remove the residual chemicals.

2. Care of the Shelter Environment

a. Bathrooms
Bathroom surfaces, especially the toilets and sinks, should be washed with warm soapy water or a household cleaner. Once a day these surfaces should be disinfected with a dilute bleach solution (1 part bleach to 10 parts water). This solution loses potency rapidly, and a new batch must be mixed every day.

Children should be discouraged from playing in the kitchen, bathroom, or eating areas.

Bathroom floors, shower stalls, benches, and tubs should be washed once or twice a week with a disinfectant agent (e.g. Lysol™, Pine-Sol™).

Children should never be allowed to play in bathrooms.

Tubs and shower drains, favorite places for bacteria and fungi to grow, should always be clean and free of standing water.

Disposable razors should be placed in a safe place and kept well out of the reach of children. One suggestion is using coffee cans. When the cans are three-quarters full, bake them in an oven at 350° F for 10 minutes or until the razors have melted. Once cooled, the cans should be covered, sealed in a plastic bag, and placed in a covered trash container.

b. Kitchen and General Areas
Children should be discouraged from playing in the kitchen or eating areas.

Dishwashers are preferred to the handwashing of dishes, utensils, pots, and pans. When a dishwasher is unavailable, first wash the dishes in hot soapy water, then dip them in a warm or hot rinse, and finally soak them in a disinfectant. A fresh mixture of 1/4 cup bleach to one gallon of water is sufficient for this purpose.

Counters, tabletops, and all other frequently used surfaces in the shelter should be washed and disinfected daily or more often if needed. We strongly recommend that this routinely follow the general kitchen cleanup. These areas should be washed with hot soapy water and then disinfected with a fresh solution of 1/4 cup bleach to 1 gallon water. Many people have had success using a spray bottle containing a mixture of 1 tablespoon of bleach per quart of water.

Rugs should remain dry to avoid the growth of fungi.

Waste cans and diaper pails should be lined with plastic and covered, and always kept out of the reach of children.

B. Specific Guidelines

The guidelines detailed above should be the basis of good health prevention and promotion at all times. In addition, several specific guidelines apply to those illnesses that are spread through each of the four modes of transmission. This section offers suggestions that we have found to be most helpful in preventing and controlling outbreaks of each classification of communicable diseases commonly seen in the shelters.

1. Airborne Transmission

Diphtheria
Haemophilus influenzae type b (Hib)
Influenza (flu)
Measles
Meningococcal infections
Mumps
Pertussis (whooping cough)
Rubella (German measles)
Group A streptococcal infections
    (strep throat, scarlet fever)
Tuberculosis (TB)
Upper respiratory infections
    (URI/common cold)
Varicella (chickenpox)

a. General Comments. Infectious droplets secreted from the nose, eye, or throat can spread certain illnesses. Whenever people with respiratory tract illnesses cough, sneeze, talk, or breathe, infectious secretions are sprayed and dispersed into air that others may inhale. These tiny droplets can also spread disease when they land on objects that come into contact with the mucous membranes of another person's eyes, nose, or mouth. In this way, food and toys can become contaminated. For example, infectious secretions can be left on a tissue after blowing one's nose. When a healthy person later picks up the tissue while cleaning and happens to rub his eyes or eat some food without remembering to wash his hands, he risks becoming sick.

Unfortunately, not all classifications are pure. You will notice that we have included varicella in this category of airborne illnesses. The varicella-zoster virus (VZV) causes both chickenpox and shingles. Chickenpox is passed via respiratory secretions or by direct contact with infected lesions. Persons who have had chickenpox can later develop shingles. However, those persons who develop shingles do NOT pass this illness to others, but can pass chickenpox to others by direct contact with open blisters.

b. Specific Suggestions. Here are a few simple measures to reduce the risk of airborne illnesses in a shelter:

1. Ventilation. Rooms should be thoroughly ventilated at least once a day and more often in very crowded shelters. Smaller shelters can open windows to let air circulate. Larger shelters may have ventilation systems. Fresh air should enter through intake vents, circulate through the room, and then be removed through vents to the outside that are located away from the intake vents. Regular maintenence is important for effective operation.

2. Handwashing. Handwashing is important after any contact with respiratory and other body secretions, as emphasized above in the General Guidelines.

3. Managing Secretions. Encourage staff and guests to cover their mouths when coughing or sneezing. Have facial tissues readily available for all guests, especially those who have runny noses or eyes as well as those who are coughing or sneezing. Provide lined, covered waste cans for the safe disposal of tissues.

4. Bed Location. At least 3 feet of space should be left between each bed. Whenever possible, guests should be assigned to the same shelter bed each night. This will diminish the number of persons exposed to others with respiratory illnesses and may be particularly important for diseases like tuberculosis, for which contact testing can be an essential control measure.

5. Immunizations and Health Screenings. Finally, we want to emphasize that many respiratory illnesses are completely preventable through routine immunizations and periodic health screenings. We encourage all shelters to have the immunization histories of employees evaluated and updated at the time of employment. We also urge all providers to assure up-to-date immunizations for all children and parents living in shelters. Please refer to Part Four for a complete explanation of immunization recommendations and schedules.

At least 3 feet of space should be left between each bed. Whenever possible, guests should be assigned to the same shelter bed each night.

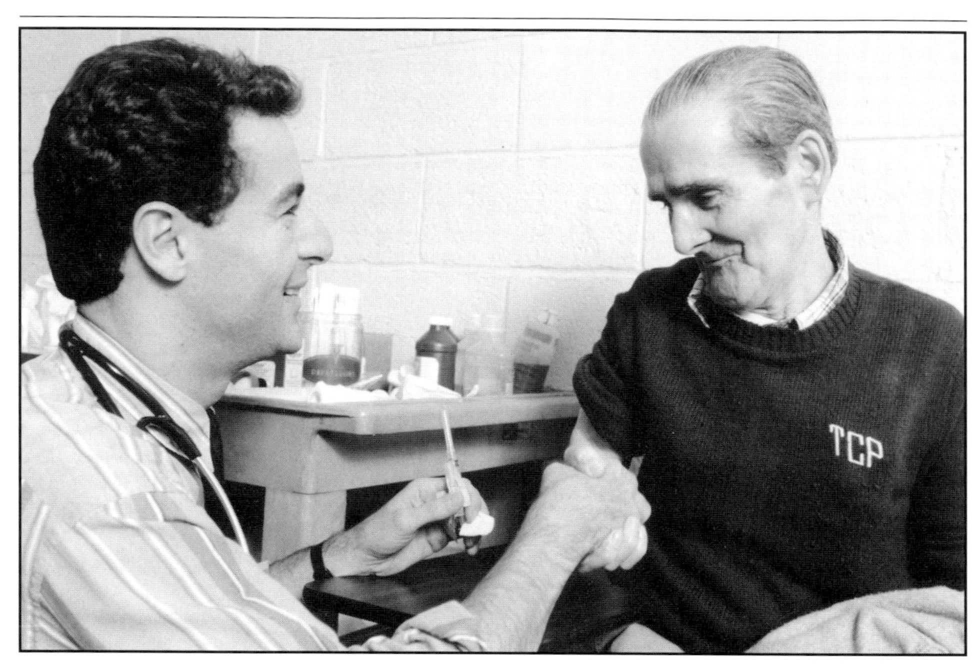

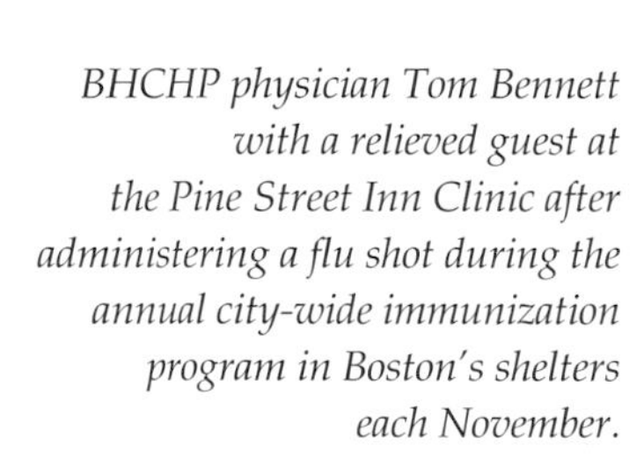

BHCHP physician Tom Bennett with a relieved guest at the Pine Street Inn Clinic after administering a flu shot during the annual city-wide immunization program in Boston's shelters program in Boston's shelters each November.

2. Fecal-Oral Transmission

Diarrhea
Hepatitis A
Pinworm
Polio
Viral meningitis

a. General Comments. Bacteria, viruses, and parasites can cause diseases that are spread through contact with stool. While anyone can acquire these infections, crowded living situations place people at greater risk.

The improper management of food contributes significantly to the spread of this classification of diseases. Part Five discusses ways in which this risk can be diminished.

Crowded shelters may have few sanitary facilities for many people. Maintaining adequate supplies of soap, paper towels, and toilet paper is often a formidable challenge for these shelters.

Children, especially those still in diapers, tend to spread intestinal illnesses easily because they share toys and objects and frequently don't wash their hands. Parents and other caregivers risk infection if they do not wash their hands properly after diapering children.

Organisms from the intestinal tract can survive on the surfaces of toys and other objects for hours to days, and their presence can not be detected by simply looking at the object. Therefore staff and guests should take all possible measures to prevent the transmission of stool from children's hands onto food, toys, and other objects which may end up in the mouths of others in the shelter.

Once again, all of the General Guidelines apply to diseases spread through the fecal-oral route. A few additional measures specific to these diseases may help prevent or limit the spread of these illnesses.

b. Specific Suggestions

1. Handwashing. Not surprisingly, proper handwashing prevents the spread of these organisms to the mouths of adults and children living in the shelter. This is the cornerstone for preventing illnesses spread through the fecal-oral route. Thorough handwashing is absolutely critical: **before** handling, preparing, serving, or eating food; **before** breastfeeding; and **after** using the toilet or diapering an infant. Pre-packaged handwipes such as Wet Ones™ or Wash 'n Dries™ should be provided to persons with limited access to handwashing facilities, especially in those shelters with many people and few bathrooms.

Parents and other caregivers risk infection if they do not wash their hands properly after diapering children.

Toilet-trained children need to be encouraged to wash their hands after using the toilet. We strongly recommend that adults accompany children to the bathroom to practice and monitor good handwashing.

Posting signs in kitchens and bathrooms is a gentle and helpful way to remind all adults and children in the shelter to wash their hands.

Cloth handtowels should never be used for community bathrooms. Always use paper towels.

Gloves may be helpful when handling the stool of children known to have an intestinal infection, although good handwashing will provide a similar degree of protection (unless the hands are cut). Always remember to wash hands after removal of the gloves.

2. Disinfecting Diapering Tables. Designated places should be available for changing diapers. Couches, floors, and other areas should not be used for diapering. Covered pails should be easily accessible for the disposal of soiled diapers. After each changing of a child's diapers, the surface of the diapering table should be washed and disinfected. A spray bottle containing 1 part bleach to 10 parts water provides a handy and inexpensive way to disinfect these areas. However, the solution must be mixed daily to assure potency, and stored well out of the reach of children. We also encourage parents to diaper and feed only

their own children in order to minimize the risk of spreading intestinal illnesses among families.

3. Persons with Intestinal Illnesses. Persons with nausea, vomiting, diarrhea, or other abdominal (stomach) discomforts should abstain from preparing, serving, or storing food until the symptoms have subsided. Any of these symptoms, especially when accompanied by fevers or lasting three days or longer, should be evaluated by a health care provider.

Individuals with particular bacterial, viral, or parasitic infections and their family members must avoid handling the food of others until: stool cultures turn negative; or the symptoms resolve, if less than one week; or one week after the onset of symptoms.

Children with known intestinal illnesses should be watched very carefully and not allowed to share toys that are mouthed or chewed by other children in the shelter.

3. Direct and Indirect Contact

Conjunctivitis
Cytomegalovirus (CMV)
Herpes simplex virus (HSV)
Impetigo
Lice
Ringworm
Scabies
Tetanus

a. General Comments. Bacteria, viruses, and fungi can cause skin infections such as impetigo, conjunctivitis, or ringworm, respectively. Parasites (lice and scabies) can lead to infestations of the skin. These very common conditions result when people have direct contact to draining skin areas, secretions, or infested areas such as clothes or hair. Children and persons living in crowded situations are at particular risk for these problems.

Herpes simplex virus (HSV) is easily transmitted by direct contact to the blisters, which can include intimate sexual contact. For this reason, we have included HSV under both direct contact and sexual transmission.

b. Specific Guidelines and Suggestions

- All guests and staff should seek medical care for inflamed eyes, new rashes, or draining wounds.
- Use gloves when having contact with any open wounds or draining rashes.
- Keep rashes clean and dry unless otherwise directed by a health provider.
- Wash and cover all wounds with sterile bandages or clean clothing. Larger wounds and rashes such as chickenpox and shingles should be covered with clean cotton clothing.
- Provide tissues to wipe draining eyes. Never share eye ointments.
- Place used bandages in a covered container with a disposable plastic liner. Soiled clothing and linen should be kept separate from other items until washed and disinfected.
- Washcloths, towels, and other linen should never be shared.
- The sharing of personal items such as make-up, mascara, combs, brushes, hats, and clothing should be discouraged.

Personal items such as combs, brushes, and hair ornaments should always be washed before sharing with others. To disinfect personal items, one of the following three methods can be used:

- boil items for ten minutes;
- soak items overnight in a dilute Lysol™ solution; or
- leave items in a dilute bleach solution (1 part bleach to 10 parts water) for 1 hour.

Betsy Kendrick and Barbara McInnis of the Pine Street Inn Nurses' Clinic have found that humor is often the best approach to controlling unwanted infestations.

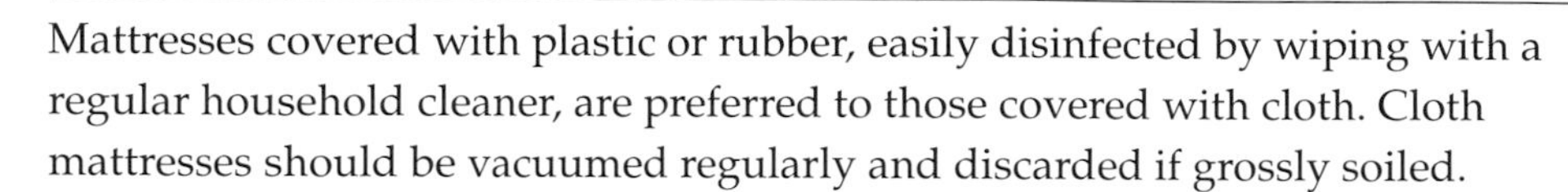

Mattresses covered with plastic or rubber, easily disinfected by wiping with a regular household cleaner, are preferred to those covered with cloth. Cloth mattresses should be vacuumed regularly and discarded if grossly soiled.

Furniture and rugs should be vacuumed regularly.

4. Blood & Sexual Contact

Hepatitis B
Human immunodeficiency virus (HIV)
Chlamydia
Gonorrhea
Syphilis
Herpes simplex virus (HSV)

a. General Comments. This classification includes infections that are transmitted through intimate sexual contact. Some of these diseases are also spread by contact with blood or blood products. Specifically, human immunodeficiency virus and hepatitis B can be transmitted in either way. Because all of these communicable diseases can be transmitted sexually, we have chosen to include them in a single category.

1. Sexual Contact. Sexually transmitted diseases (STDs) are caused by bacteria, viruses, and parasites. These diseases spread when infectious secretions from one person come into contact with the mucous membranes of the eyes, mouth, throat, rectum, or genitalia of another person. Generally, this requires very intimate contact, and these illnesses most often appear in sexually active adults and adolescents.

Infected women can spread sexually transmitted diseases to the newborn infant during a vaginal delivery when the baby comes into contact with an infected birth canal. In some cases, the fetus can become infected in utero through the placenta.

With the exception of mother-to-infant transmission, a diagnosis of a sexually transmitted disease in a child points to the possibility of sexual abuse. Health care providers in Massachusetts must file a Section 51-A report with the Department of Social Services, which mandates an investigation for the protection of the child.

People with STDs are not a risk to the general population, but only to those with whom they have intimate contact. The sexual partner(s) of anyone with a diagnosed STD should receive prompt and confidential assessment, treatment, and follow-up.

2. Contact with Blood. Hepatitis B and HIV are viruses that are spread through sexual activity and through contact with blood or blood products. Not surprisingly, the incidence of hepatitis B and HIV in the USA is growing most rapidly among injection drug users and their sexual partners. Transmission can occur when blood infected with virus comes into contact with the bloodstream of an uninfected person. Accidental or intentional puncture of the skin by a contaminated needle or sharp object can allow the virus to spread.

HIV and hepatitis B can also be transmitted when infected blood or sexual fluid comes into direct contact with the mucous membranes of the mouth, genitalia, rectum, and in rare cases, the eyes or nose. The risk of spreading these viruses is much greater whenever the mucous membrane has been damaged by a cut, rash, or infection. For example, other STDs can cause sores and open lesions, which increase the possibility of transmission of HIV or hepatitis B during subsequent sexual activity.

Infected mothers can pass either virus to a fetus through the bloodstream during pregnancy or at the time of delivery.

b. Specific Suggestions and Guidelines: Sexual Contact

1. Education. Everyone has a right to information regarding the spread and prevention of sexually transmitted diseases. Shelters can be an excellent place to educate people who may not have any other contact with the health care system. In Massachusetts, teaching materials are available through the local and state health departments.

2. Basic Precautions. Examination gloves should be worn during all contacts with mucous membranes, rashes, and open or draining lesions.

Hands should be washed with warm water and soap after every contact with another person's mouth, eyes, or genital area, regardless of whether gloves were worn.

Sexually active adolescents and adults should have regular check-ups that include an evaluation for STDs. In Massachusetts, free diagnosis and treatment are available at the Sexually Transmitted Disease Clinics supported by the Department of Public Health. The local health department and affiliated clinics can provide information on other resources in your area.

3. Safe Sexual Practices. Abstinence is undoubtedly the safest and best way to prevent the spread of sexually transmitted diseases, but hardly a reflection of the real world.

For persons who are sexually active, the use of latex condoms is the best means of avoiding most of these infections:

- condoms must be worn from the beginning of sexual activity until the very end;
- only water-based lubricants should be used (K-Y Jelly™, For-Play™, PrePair™, and Probe™). Oil or petroleum-based lubricants (baby oil, Vaseline™) can damage the condom;
- a readily accessible supply of condoms is essential;
- condoms should always be used for oral or anal penetration as well as for vaginal intercourse.

We had previously recommended that condoms be lubricated with the spermicide nonoxynol-9. However, recent studies have suggested that this may irritate the vaginal and penile mucosa, causing erosions of the mucous membranes that could facilitate the transmission of viruses. Further studies will be necessary to determine the efficacy of this lubricant, but at this time we do not recommend its use.

While condoms are the best means of protection available, they do not always protect against syphilis, herpes simplex virus, and other STDs when the lesions have spread beyond the distal shaft of the penis or the vaginal wall.

Some shelters provide condoms for sexually active guests. Shelters that do not supply condoms can provide guests with information about local distribution sites.

c. Specific Suggestions and Guidelines: Blood

1. Avoid Needle-Sharing. Injection drug users should be urged to avoid sharing needles or "works" (needle, syringe, and cooker). Many persons suffering from "drug sickness" are unable to find a clean set of works, and any shared works should be cleaned with a dilute bleach solution (1 part bleach to 10 parts water) before using. Easy access to bleach and instructions is a very important public health measure in the prevention of the spread of these viruses. We recognize that substance abuse is a chronic, relapsing disease; therefore such interim measures as the use of bleach are necessary even though the cause of the addiction has not been addressed. Treatment-on-demand is a necessary but still elusive goal that requires the ready availability of adequate numbers of substance abuse treatment beds.

Some shelters have chosen to provide condoms and dilute bleach solution to guests who may be at risk for exposure through sexual contact or the use of illegal drugs. Shelters that choose not to supply these materials may opt to refer guests to clinics and community programs that provide education and prevention programs and supply condoms and bleach.

The Pine Street Inn Nurses' Clinic has cared for homeless adults since 1968, and was celebrated on this cover of the American Journal of Nursing in November of 1985. Guests receive a host of services, including footsoaks, dressing changes, and assistance with medications and transportation to hospital appointments. BHCHP teams work in the Clinic four evenings each week.

2. Disposal of Sharp Objects. Needles should never be recapped before disposal.

Razors, toothbrushes, and other objects that have direct contact with mucous membranes should never be shared.

All sharp objects such as razors and needles should be placed in puncture-proof containers. These containers should be available in convenient places (bathrooms or shower rooms) and kept well out of the reach of children.

When puncture-proof needle boxes are not available, coffee cans may be substituted. When the cans are three-quarters full, bake them for 10 minutes in an oven at 350° F, or until the needles and razors have melted. Once cooled, the cans should be covered, sealed in a plastic bag, and disposed in a covered trash container.

3. Disinfecting Surfaces and Objects. All surfaces and objects contaminated with blood or body secretions should be cleaned promptly with a dilute bleach solution. A mixture of 1 part bleach to 10 parts water is sufficient. A fresh batch should be mixed every day as the bleach can lose its potency over time. Gloves should always be worn while cleaning, and hands should be washed carefully after taking off the gloves.

4. Use of Latex Gloves. Latex gloves must be worn whenever there may be contact with blood or bodily secretions that may contain blood or semen. Gloves should always be worn when handling potentially contaminated articles such as soiled linen and laundry, particularly if there is obvious soiling.

5. Proper Wound Care. All open or draining skin areas should be covered with bandages or clean cotton clothing. Soiled bandages should be disposed in a lined and covered container. Soiled clothing should be separated from other items until disinfected, as detailed in the General Guidelines section on page 35.

d. Occupational Exposure to Blood or Body Fluids

Data from the Centers for Disease Control (CDC) in January 1990 suggests that workers exposed to HIV-infected blood (a needle puncture, a cut with a sharp object, etc.) have a 0.4 percent risk of subsequent infection. For every 1000 needle punctures or cuts contaminated with HIV-infected blood, an average of four health care workers will become infected with the virus. Workers who have mucous membrane exposure to infected blood are at even less risk than those exposed through needle puncture or a cut with a sharp object. The risk of occupational exposure to HIV-infected bodily fluids other than blood is presently unknown.

The risk with hepatitis B exposure is considerably higher than with HIV, between 6 and 35 percent.

Each employer should have a clear policy for prompt referral of any employee who has been exposed to potentially infected blood or body fluid. The U.S. Public Health Service recommends obtaining the following information from the health care provider when an exposure happens:

- date and time of exposure;
- job duty being performed by worker at time of exposure;
- details of exposure, including:
  amount of fluid or material,
  type of fluid or material, and
  severity of exposure;
- for percutaneous exposure: depth of injury
  and whether fluid was injected;
- for skin or mucous-membrane exposure: the extent and duration of contact and the condition of the skin (chapped, abraded, intact);
- description of the source of exposure, including whether the source material was known to contain HIV or hepatitis B virus.

The current prophylaxis and treatment protocols for those exposed to blood or blood products potentially infected with HIV or hepatitis B or other blood-borne agents include the use of AZT, hepatitis B immune globulin (HBIG), and the hepatitis B vaccine.

References

Centers for Disease Control. Protection against viral hepatitis. *MMWR* 1990; 39: RR-2.

Centers for Disease Control. Public Health Service statement on management of occupational exposure to human immunodeficiency virus, including considerations regarding zidovudine postexposure use. *MMWR* 1990; 39: RR-1.

Centers for Disease Control. Recommendations for prevention of HIV transmission in health care settings. *MMWR* 1987; 36(25): 35-185.

Centers for Disease Control. Update: universal precautions for prevention of transmission of human immunodeficiency virus, hepatitis B virus, and other blood-borne pathogens in health care settings. *MMWR* 1988; 37(24): 378-387.

Crosson F, Black S, et al. Infections in day-care centers. In: *Current Problems in Pediatrics.* Chicago: Year Book Medical Publishers; 1986: 129-183.

Georges P, Hall CB, Lepow ML, Phillips CF, eds. *The 1988 Red Book: Report of the Committee on Infectious Diseases.* 21st ed. Elk Grove Village, Illinois: American Academy of Pediatrics; 1988: 61-69.

Shapiro-Kendrick A, Messenger K. *Health in Day Care.* Division of Family Services, Department of Public Health, Commonwealth of Massachusetts; 1988.

Part Three: The Common Communicable Diseases

Part Three is a collection of 26 chapters discussing the most common communicable diseases encountered in shelters. For organizational purposes, each disease is categorized by the primary mode of transmission: airborne (blue), fecal-oral (orange), direct and indirect contact (green), and blood and sexual contact (red).

The chapters are generally organized as follows: signs and symptoms, prevalence, transmission, diagnosis, treatment, and prevention and control. A brief summary, designed to be helpful to shelter staff, concludes each chapter.

The simplicity of Part Three belies the complexity of many of these illnesses. While some are transmitted in a variety of ways, we have chosen the most common category. For example, herpes simplex virus is generally considered a sexually transmitted disease, but can be spread by direct contact with active lesions.

To help with any confusion, we have included an alphabetical listing of diseases following the Table of Contents on page vii.

Haemophilus Influenzae Type b (Hib)

George Alliegro, M.D.

Haemophilus influenzae type b (Hib) is a bacterium responsible for serious infections primarily in infants and young children. *Haemophilus influenzae* occurs both as encapsulated and non-encapsulated types. Non-encapsulated types occasionally cause respiratory infections and are commonly found in the upper respiratory passages of people of all ages, particularly smokers with chronic obstructive pulmonary disease (COPD). While there are several encapsulated types of *H. influenzae*, only type b is known to cause serious invasive disease.

Fifty percent of invasive Hib infections lead to meningitis, most of which are in children from 2 months to 5 years of age. Infants from 6 to 12 months are at greatest risk. Other manifestations of the disease in children include bacteremia, epiglottitis, pneumonia, pericarditis, osteomyelitis, septic arthritis, and cellulitis.

Common symptoms of Hib infection in children

In children, infection of the meninges can result in fever, headache, stiff neck, increased irritability, and confusion. Infants may also have seizures and a bulging fontanelle from meningeal infection. Usually meningitis from Hib infection arises quietly after several days of upper respiratory symptoms. On rare occasions, the disease can proceed rapidly, leading to death in only a few hours.

Signs of pneumonia may include a fever (above 101° F or 38.4° C), a cough that produces yellow, green, or blood-tinged sputum, and progressive shortness of breath. Chest pain can occur, often worsening with coughing or deep breathing.

Epiglottis infection produces fever, sore throat, drooling, difficulty in swallowing, swollen neck glands, and a change in the sound of the voice.

Hib in adults

Most adults are immune to serious infections with Hib, probably because they have formed protective antibodies from an exposure to the organism in childhood. Those adults at risk for serious infection with Hib include:

- the elderly;
- alcoholics;
- diabetics;
- persons with poor immune systems due to AIDS, cancer, removal of the spleen, or low immunoglobulins.

Hib infection in adults is unusual but can include pneumonia, with or without infection of the blood stream. Hib can also cause minor infections of the ears, upper airways, and sinuses.

Adults at risk for serious infection with Hib include: the elderly, alcoholics, diabetics, and persons with poor immune systems due to AIDS, cancer, removal of the spleen, or low immunoglobulins.

Transmission

Hib spreads through person-to-person contact. This happens when someone directly touches the nasal secretions or saliva of an infected person. The uninfected person can then carry the bacteria into his or her mouth, nose, or eyes. Hib also spreads by the inhalation of respiratory secretions that have been coughed or sneezed into the air. Kissing or sharing bottles, drinking glasses, cigarettes, toothbrushes, and food may transmit Hib.

As noted above, infected adults generally do not get sick unless they have an underlying chronic illness. However, adults can still carry the organism in the nose and throat and then spread it to others.

Outbreaks of the disease among children usually happen in close settings such as households and day care centers, which suggests that family shelters are especially vulnerable settings.

The incubation period for Hib is unknown.

Diagnosis

Microscopic examination of sputum or other body fluids can reveal *Haemophilus* bacteria. Confirmation of the diagnosis depends on culturing the organism from spinal fluid, pleural fluid, blood, sputum, or other specimens. If *Haemophilus* infection is suspected in the respiratory tract, a laboratory may take additional steps to isolate Hib. The isolation of Hib from throat specimens requires a special culture for optimal growth.

All patients suspected of having meningitis must have a lumbar puncture (spinal tap). The spinal fluid then undergoes the same examination and culturing described above.

Treatment

The outcome of Hib infection, especially in cases of meningitis, depends on the time between infection and treatment with appropriate antibiotics. Hib infection poses great risk of severe complications, including death, in all children as well as adults with underlying diseases such as malignancies or immuno-deficiencies.

Anyone who exhibits the symptoms described in the introductory section should see a doctor or nurse immediately. If diagnosed early, Hib infection responds well to a variety of antibiotics. Most serious infections are initially treated with broad-spectrum antibiotics (ampicillin, chloramphenicol, third-generation cephalosporins) while awaiting the results of antibiotic sensitivity tests. Ampicillin alone effectively treats most minor localized infections such as otitis, sinusitis, pharyngitis, or bronchitis.

All patients hospitalized with suspected Hib meningitis should stay in respiratory isolation during the first 24 hours of antibiotic therapy.

If cultures confirm the presence of Hib, infected individuals older than 1 month are also treated with oral rifampin 20 mg/kg (maximum dose 600 mg PO) once daily for 4 days. The dosage in children less than 1 month is not yet established, but some experts recommend reducing the dose to 10 mg/kg. This ensures the elimination of any remaining Hib organisms in the nasopharynx.

Rifampin is the antibiotic usually chosen to eliminate nasopharyngeal carriage of the organism; however, other antibiotics such as ceftriaxone may be effective.

Chart 1. Rifampin: contraindications and side effects.

Rifampin: contraindications and side effects

Pregnant women and people with active liver problems should not receive rifampin.

Rifampin increases the metabolism of several drugs, including methadone and the anticoagulant warfarin (Coumadin™). Dosages of these drugs may have to be increased during rifampin therapy.

Rifampin may accelerate the clearance of hormones used in oral contraceptives. Women who take birth control pills should use a barrier form of birth control (diaphragm and/or condom for the partner) to avoid pregnancy while taking rifampin.

Sweat, tears, saliva, urine, stool, and semen may become orange-red while taking rifampin. The drug can also stain soft contact lenses permanently, so those receiving treatment should wear glasses during treatment.

Rifampin may cause mild stomach distress.

Prevention and Control

Susceptibility to serious infection with *Haemophilus influenzæ* type b has led to well-developed guidelines for vaccination to prevent Hib disease in children, as discussed below. However, guidelines for prevention of Hib disease among adults are less well established because most adults are likely to be immune to serious Hib infection. Adults with a history of alcoholism, immune deficiency (e.g. AIDS), or splenectomy may be at higher risk for serious infection with Hib.

Vaccination

The Food and Drug Administration (FDA) presently has approved the use of selected Hib vaccines (HibTITER™, PedvaxHIB™) to infants beginning at 2 months of age. Hib vaccine is not recommended for children older than 5 years except for those with chronic illnesses such as sickle cell anemia or those who have lost their spleens. A complete schedule of routine and delayed administration of Hib vaccine is included in Part Four on page 218.

All children under six years old should be vaccinated against Hib.

Caregivers should review the immunization records of all children when assessing a possible exposure. Those not vaccinated should receive the Hib vaccine if they are between the ages of 2 months and 5 years. The American Academy of Pediatrics supports administering Hib vaccine at the same time as other routine immunizations including MMR, OPV, and DT, as appropriate to the age and previous vaccination status of the recipient.

Vaccination is not currently recommended for adults.

Antibiotic prophylaxis for close contacts

Vaccination after exposure does not replace antibiotic prophylaxis for those who have had recent close contact to an active case of Hib. Certain close contacts will require prophylaxis with an antibiotic, usually rifampin.

Close contacts are defined as people who have spent at least 20 hours with the infected person within 7 days of the onset of symptoms. Close contacts also include anyone who has been exposed to the saliva of the infected person. For example, contact may happen with intimate kissing or when children share toys that have been mouthed. Those with less than 20 hours contact may also be at risk of disease and should be followed closely.

If children under 4 years old are in the same household or group setting as the infectious person, everyone in the group should be considered a close contact.

When an adult shelter resident develops a serious Hib infection, such as blood stream infection or meningitis, rifampin prophylaxis should be considered for any close contact with a history of alcoholism, cancer, loss of spleen, sickle cell anemia, AIDS, or other evidence of impaired immunity. In addition, individuals with these underlying illnesses who had intimate contact with the infected patient's oral secretions (kissing or sharing food, beverages, or cigarettes) should also receive rifampin regardless of the duration of their exposure.

Caregivers should closely monitor for 60 days all those considered close contacts for signs of a febrile illness, whether or not they receive rifampin. This applies especially to children under six and people with chronic illnesses. Persons suspected of having Hib disease should be referred immediately to the hospital for evaluation.

Everyone in shelters caring for children, particularly those at high risk, may need to receive rifampin if 2 or more cases of invasive disease occur within 2 months. As indicated above, caregivers must carefully monitor the health of all close contacts for approximately 2 months.

Summary

Haemophilus influenzae type b (Hib) is an infection that can cause serious illness, particularly in children under 5 years of age. Some of the diseases that can result from Hib infection include meningitis (inflammation of the lining around the brain), epiglottitis (swelling of the throat and upper airways), pneumonia, and sepsis (infection of the blood).

The risk of spread of Hib is related to the duration of exposure; prolonged contact (usually more than 20 hours) results in a higher risk of disease. The bacteria are spread when an infected person coughs or sneezes secretions into air that is then inhaled by others. Hib organisms can also be spread by intimate kissing or by infected droplets getting onto objects that are then mouthed or chewed.

A person diagnosed with Hib requires isolation, antibiotics, and close monitoring in an acute care setting. If Hib is confirmed, notify the local or state board of health and a health provider familiar with the shelter without delay. People considered at risk due to exposure to the sick person need to be evaluated for therapy with the antibiotic rifampin as soon as possible to prevent Hib disease.

Preventive therapy with rifampin does not provide complete protection against disease. Therefore, any person who becomes ill following exposure should be promptly referred to a health provider.

In Massachusetts, as in most states, the law requires that cases of invasive *Haemophilus influenzae* type b be reported to the local health department.

References

Fleming DW, Leibernhaut MH, Albanes E, Cochi SL, Hightower AW, Makintubee S, et al. Secondary Hib in day-care facilities: risk factors and prevention. *JAMA* 1985; 254(4): 509-514.

Levin DC, Schwarz MI, Matthay RA, LaForce M. Bacteremic *Haemophilus influenzae* pneumonia in adults: a report of 24 cases and a review of the literature. *Am J Med* 1977; 62: 219-224.

McGowan JE, Klein JO, Bratton L, Barnes MW, Finland M. Meningitis and bacteremia due to *Haemophilus influenzae* : recurrence and mortality at Boston City Hospital in 12 selected years, 1935-72. *J Infect Dis* 1974; 130(2): 119-124.

Patterson JE, Madden GM, Krisivinas EP, Masecar B, Hierholzer WJ, Zerbos J, Lyon RW. A nosocomial outbreak of ampicillin-resistant Hib in a geriatric unit. *J Infect Dis* 1988; 157(5): 1002-1007.

Smith PF, Stricot RC, Shayetgani M, Morse DL. Cluster of *Haemophilus influenzae* type b infections in adults. *JAMA* 1988; 260(10): 1446-1449.

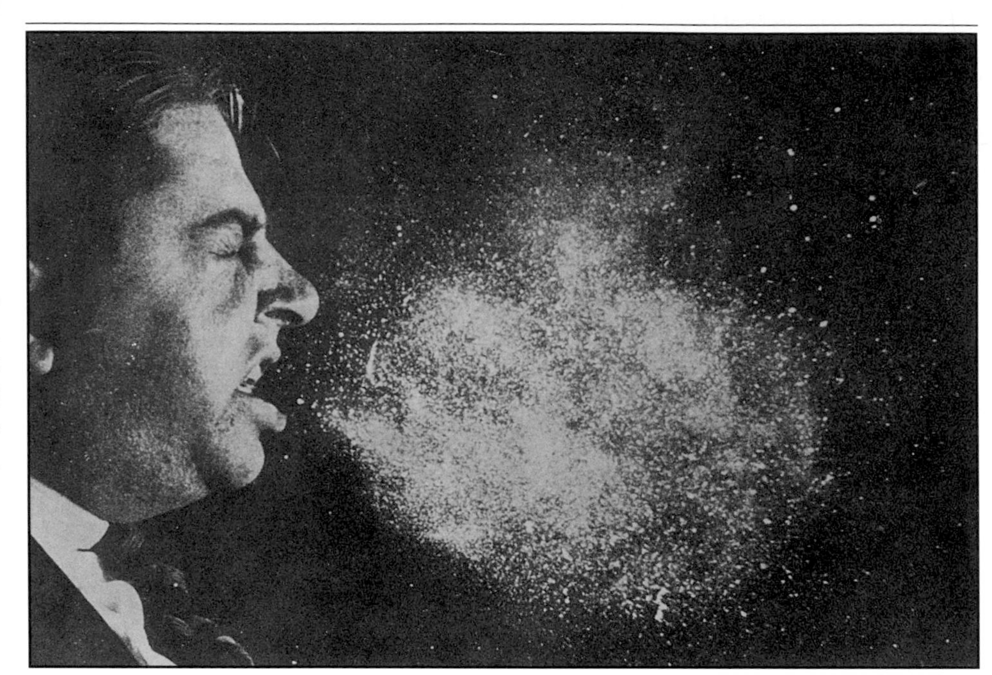

Sneezing is a very efficient way to spread many airborne diseases, such as influenza. The virus is contained in the many small droplets shown by backlighting in this photograph from the CDC.

Influenza (Flu)

Noreen A. Hynes, M.D., M.P.H.

Influenza (flu) consists of two principal types of virus, called A and B. The protein envelope or coat that protects all influenza viruses can mutate from one year to the next. This variation prevents people from developing long-lasting immunity and helps explain why influenza continues to be one of the major epidemic illnesses of humans.

Typical influenza virus infection causes the abrupt onset of a fever, chills, dry cough, sore throat, headache, extreme fatigue, and muscle aches. Other symptoms include joint pain, burning and tearing of the eyes, and anorexia. Unlike most other common respiratory infections, influenza can cause extreme weakness or fatigue lasting several days to weeks.

The arrival of influenza in a community is often associated with outbreaks of acute respiratory illness in people of all ages. Most cases usually improve in 3 to 7 days without any treatment. However, complications such as viral pneumonia, secondary bacterial pneumonia, and exacerbations of underlying chronic diseases are common in certain populations.

High Risk Groups

Certain people are prone to developing complications from influenza that can lead to hospitalization and possible death. These include:

- adults and children with chronic problems of the lungs or the heart, including children with asthma;
- people 65 years and older;
- adults and children who have a history of regular medical care or frequent hospitalizations because of chronic problems such as diabetes mellitus, kidney failure, anemias (including sickle cell), and depression of the immune system (including those infected with HIV);
- children and teenagers who are receiving long term aspirin therapy, placing them at risk of developing Reye's syndrome (a rare but serious disease affecting the brain and liver) after an influenza infection.

Transmission

Influenza usually spreads through direct contact with droplets coughed or sneezed into the air by infected people. These droplets can also contaminate objects that others then put in their mouths.

Symptoms usually appear within 24 to 72 hours of contact with an infected person. Outbreaks in the northern hemisphere are most common in the late autumn and the winter. As much as one quarter of a community may become infected when the influenza virus appears. That may double or even triple among people who live or sleep in group settings, such as students in boarding schools, nursing home residents, and shelter guests.

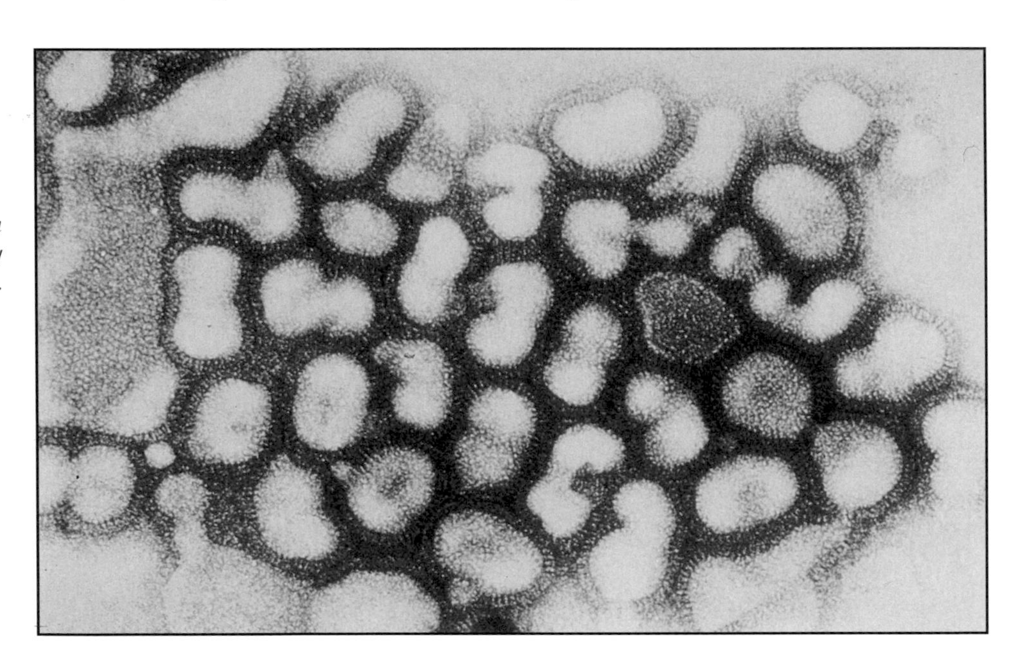

The Influenza Virus. An electron micrograph shows the morphology of this widespread virus.

Diagnosis

The only way to confirm a diagnosis of influenza virus infection is through laboratory tests that either isolate the virus itself or confirm the presence of antibodies against the virus. To find proof of antibodies, 2 blood specimens must be collected 4 weeks apart. To culture influenza virus, special kits must be used which are available in Massachusetts through the Department of Public Health.

Once the public health laboratory confirms the presence of the virus in a community and reports confirm an increase in school and industrial absenteeism caused by respiratory illness, health providers in the affected community can be reasonably sure that most acute respiratory illnesses within the following 3 to 4 weeks are due to the influenza virus. During the influenza season weekly contact with the health department can help identify when to take special measures to control the spread of the virus.

Treatment

Influenza is usually a mild illness in those without chronic medical problems. Affected people should be encouraged to drink plenty of fluids, and those who are very fatigued or have severe muscle aches need bedrest.

Children less than 18 years old should not take aspirin because of an association between the use of aspirin and a rare but serious disease called Reye's syndrome. Acetaminophen (Tylenol™) is a safe alternative.

The annual immunization of shelter guests and staff is the primary means of controlling influenza outbreaks in shelters.

Unless contraindicated, people with medical conditions that put them at high risk for complications should be evaluated for a 10 to 14 day course of the antiviral drug amantadine. When started within 48 hours of the onset of symptoms, amantadine decreases the severity and duration of the illness associated with Type A influenza virus infection. These high risk persons should also receive a routine annual influenza immunization; those unable to be vaccinated may require a several week long course of amantadine.

The most common side effects of amantadine involve the central nervous system and include nervousness, lightheadedness, poor concentration, and insomnia. Antihistamines and anticholinergics may compound these CNS side effects of amantadine. Also, amantadine may induce nausea and lack of appetite.

Amantadine is not helpful against Type B viruses.

Prevention

The annual immunization of shelter guests and staff is the primary means of controlling influenza outbreaks in shelters. Therefore, annual inoculation with influenza vaccine for all shelter guests and staff over the age of 6 months is recommended. Because of the group setting, the virus can easily spread among shelter staff and guests, endangering those at high risk for developing severe complications.

The vaccine is produced from killed organisms and cannot cause influenza. The production process also involves eggs, so anyone with an egg allergy should not receive the vaccine.

People with a fever (100.5° F/38° C or greater) should have the vaccination delayed until the temperature returns to normal. In less than one third of those immunized, the vaccine may cause soreness at the injection site for up to 2 days. In rare instances, people may develop a mild systemic illness (muscle aches and low grade fever) that begins 6 to 12 hours after inoculation and lasts 1 to 2 days.

Amantadine is also approved for use as a preventive agent against influenza, particularly for high-risk people who did not receive vaccine. As mentioned above, amantadine helps supplement protection when used with the vaccine. Its side effects, the sometimes lengthy course, and high cost limit its use.

Timing of influenza vaccination activities

Homeless people must move often among shelters, depending on the availability of beds. To ensure most are protected while minimizing repeat vaccination of the same individuals, vaccination of as many shelter guests and staff as possible on the same day is optimal. The best time for the immunization is early to mid-November. This usually provides enough time for people to develop a full response to the vaccine before the virus begins to circulate in the community.

Vaccination of as many shelter guests and staff as possible on the same day is optimal, preferably in early to mid-November.

Children less than 13 years old who have never received prior influenza immunization need to receive 2 doses of influenza vaccine at least 1 month apart. The second dose should be given before December if possible.

Influenza vaccine can be offered up to and during an outbreak of the virus.

Control

If an outbreak happens in a shelter, those who are ill should ideally be separated from staff and guests with high-risk conditions, particularly those with chronic heart and lung problems. For example, infected guests could sleep on a separate floor or in a separate section of the shelter. However, influenza spreads very rapidly in group settings, and such factors as air flow within the shelter and crowding can limit the effectiveness of attempts to protect those at high risk.

Summary

Influenza (flu) is a highly contagious virus that primarily affects the respiratory system. There are 2 important groups of influenza and within these groups are many strains of flu virus. Every year new strains emerge, making it possible for a person to get the flu annually.

Flu is spread when an infected person coughs or sneezes infected droplets into the air, which are then inhaled by others.

Symptoms of the flu range from very mild to severe with complications. Among those at particular risk for complications are the elderly and people with chronic medical problems, including people infected with the human immunodeficiency virus (HIV).

To prevent the spread of influenza, everyone in a shelter should receive a flu shot once a year. The best time to receive the shot is in the fall. The local board of health or appropriate health agency should be contacted regarding the provision of vaccine for the shelter.

References

Benenson AS, ed. *Control of Communicable Diseases in Man.* 15th ed. Washington, DC: American Public Health Association; 1990: 224-229.

Centers for Disease Control. Prevention and control of influenza: part I, vaccines. *MMWR* 1989; 38(17): 297-298, 303-311.

Kendal AP, Patriarca PA. *Options for the Control of Influenza.* New York: Alan R. Liss, Inc; 1986.

Kilborne ED, ed. *Influenza.* New York: Plenum Medical Book Company; 1987.

Measles

M. Anita Barry, M.D., M.P.H.

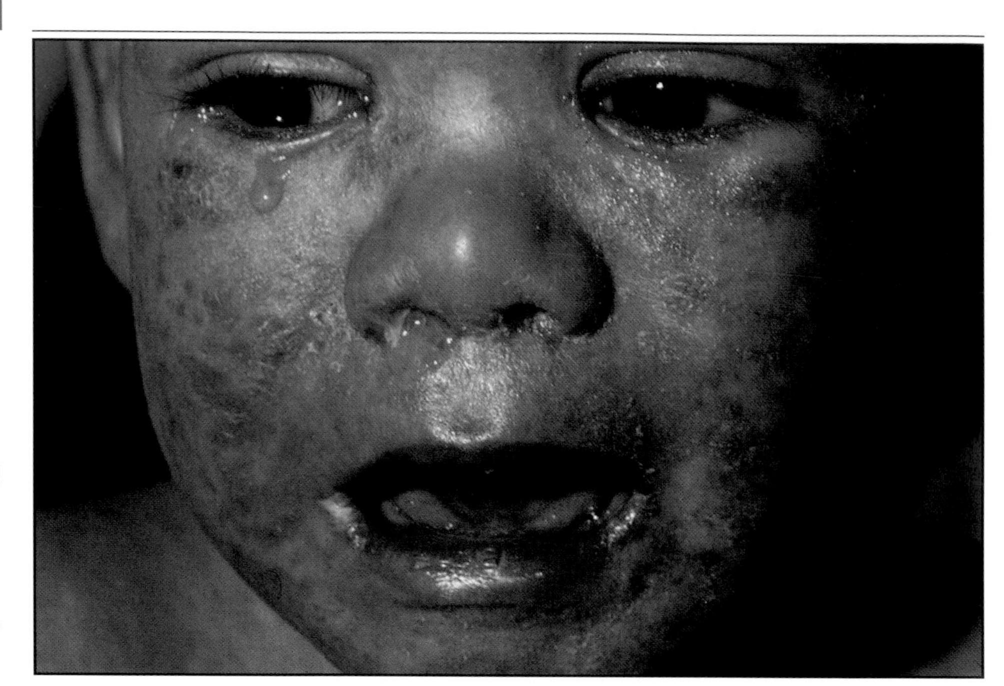

Measles. This child had developed a cough in addition to this red blotchy rash over the entire body. Note the runny nose (coryza) and red, watery eyes (conjunctivitis).

Measles is an acute, highly contagious disease caused by the measles virus. Typical symptoms of measles include fever, cough, runny nose (coryza), a red blotchy rash that usually covers the entire body, and red, watery eyes (conjunctivitis). Koplik spots, tiny blue-white bumps resembling grains of sand, may arise on the mucous membranes of the mouth. Their presence effectively confirms a diagnosis of measles.

Complications of measles include middle ear infections, pneumonia, and inflammation of the brain (encephalitis). Measles during pregnancy increases the probability of spontaneous abortion, premature labor, and low birth-weight infants. In rare circumstances, measles results in a degenerative neurologic illness (subacute sclerosing panencephalitis).

In the USA, 1 of 3,000 measles cases results in death. Infants and those with poor immune systems are at particular risk, although recent deaths have occurred in adults and children with normal immune systems.

Prevalence and Distribution

Measles vaccine became available in the USA in 1963. Prior to the introduction of the vaccine, annual incidence hovered around half a million cases reported throughout the nation. After 2 decades of the vaccine availability, the reported incidence dwindled to 1,497 cases in 1983. Unfortunately, the downward trend has recently reversed. Over 14,000 cases were reported nationally in 1989.

Measles outbreaks have been a particular problem in pre-school aged children and college students. Health care workers have accounted for several cases. Many factors have led to the increase in measles, including:

- a lack of immunization against measles;
- failure to respond to the measles vaccine;
- a waning of the immune response produced by the measles vaccine.

Prior infection with measles seems to provide lifelong protection against later exposures to the disease.

Transmission

Measles spreads when an infectious person disperses droplets carrying the virus into the air by coughing , sneezing, or talking. These droplets land on mucous membranes of other people or are inhaled from the air. Measles virus can last in the air of an enclosed area for up to 2 hours after an infectious person has left the room. Air ventilation in a facility can also disperse the virus from room to room.

The incubation period for measles is 8 to 13 days. Usually, the rash appears 14 days after exposure. Individuals are infectious from 3 to 5 days before the rash and for 4 days after the rash appears.

Diagnosis

Measles should be suspected in anyone who has the following signs or symptoms:

- a generalized rash;
- fever;
- cough, coryza, or conjunctivitis.

Measles should also be suspected if there have been other measles cases in the area, or if the patient has travelled to other countries or areas in the USA where a large number of measles cases have been reported.

Blood tests can confirm the diagnosis by measuring the levels of measles antibody. Usually, only one specimen is necessary; occasionally, two specimens must be drawn 1 to 3 weeks apart. The measles virus can also be isolated in a laboratory, but this is technically difficult and not widely available.

Treatment and Prevention

No specific treatment exists for measles. Prevention is crucial. Because measles virus was widespread before the introduction of measles vaccine, it is likely that most persons born before January 1, 1957, have been exposed to the virus and are probably immune to the disease. Those born after January 1, 1957, are at higher risk for measles infection unless they have one of the following:

1. a history of physician-diagnosed measles;
2. laboratory evidence of immunity to measles;
3. documentation signed by a health care provider that includes the month and year of a measles vaccination on or after 15 months of age, and administered after 1/1/68.

Most persons born before January 1, 1957, have been exposed to the measles virus and are probably immune to the disease.

Anyone who does not fit the above criteria should receive 2 doses of measles, mumps, rubella (MMR) vaccine, administered no less than one month apart. Normal childhood immunization schedules call for the first dose to be administered at 15 months of age in most areas of the country. Certain areas may begin the vaccination schedule as early as 12 months of age. These areas include:

- counties with more than 5 cases among preschool children during each of the previous 5 years;
- counties with a recent outbreak among unvaccinated preschool-aged children.

The second dose is recommended either on entry to kindergarten or first grade, or on entry to middle school. Anyone at risk whose immunization history is incomplete or unknown should be offered 2 doses of MMR no less than a month apart.

Measles vaccine is recommended for children with HIV infection. Unimmunized adults with HIV infection may also be vaccine candidates, depending on measles activity within a particular region.

Measles vaccine is contraindicated in people with specific immune system problems, those with moderate to severe febrile illnesses, and women who are pregnant or considering becoming pregnant within the 3 months following vaccination. It also should not be administered for at least 3 months after receiving antibody-containing blood products, including immune globulin and whole blood. Extreme caution should be used when administering the vaccine to those with a history of severe reactions to eggs, including hives, swelling of the mouth and throat, dyspnea (difficulty breathing), a drop in blood pressure, or shock. In general, the vaccine is not given to infants less than one year old because adequate antibody responses are not reliably produced.

Control

Suspected measles cases must be reported to the local health department immediately. Health officials can then conduct an overall assessment of the risk to others within a shelter. To reduce the possibility of infection, people with confirmed or suspected measles who reside in larger shelters should be separated from guests and staff who may not be immune to the disease. If housing with an immune friend or relative is not an option, admission to an acute care facility may be the only alternative. Many small family shelters house people for many weeks or months. New admissions should have their immunization records carefully reviewed, with measles vaccines updated for each family member as necessary. Shelters should avoid admitting anyone who may not be immune to measles for at least 13 days (one incubation period) following the last possible exposure.

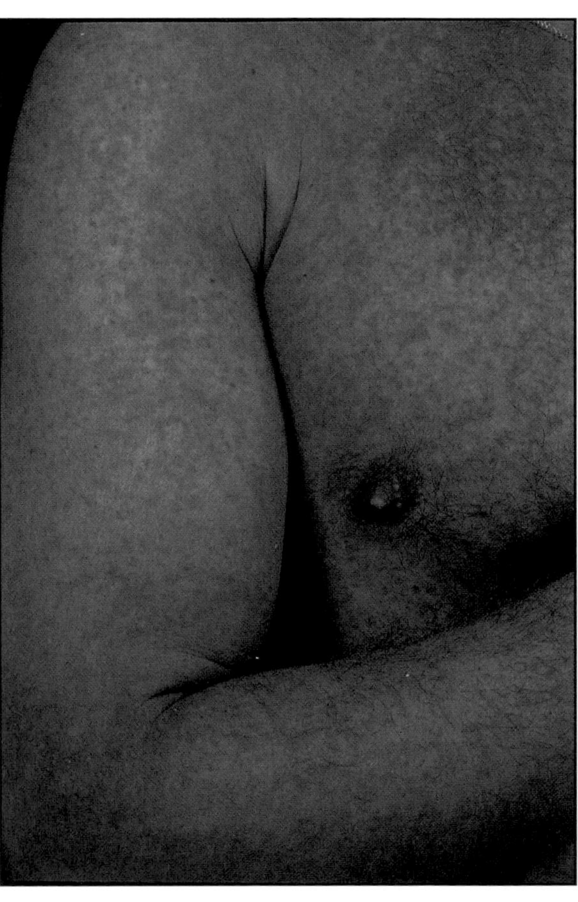

Measles. A generalized rash, typical of many viral illnesses, appears two weeks after exposure to measles. This person is infectious for 3-5 days before and for 4 days after the rash first appears.

Those susceptible to measles who have been exposed to a case may be candidates for post-exposure preventive therapy. Preventive therapy can occur in two forms:

1. A dose of MMR vaccine, if given within 72 hours of the first exposure, may prevent disease.

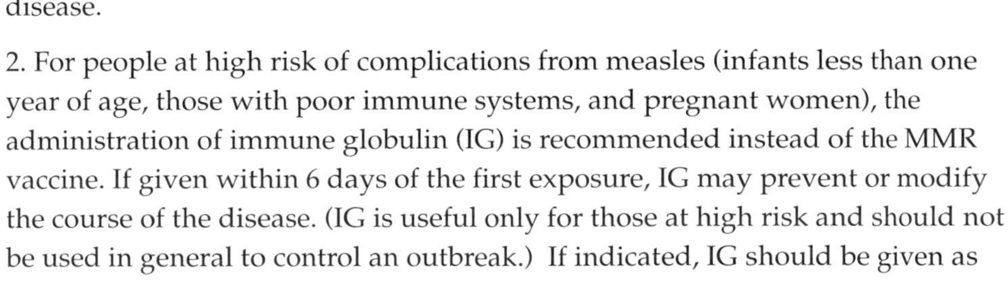

2. For people at high risk of complications from measles (infants less than one year of age, those with poor immune systems, and pregnant women), the administration of immune globulin (IG) is recommended instead of the MMR vaccine. If given within 6 days of the first exposure, IG may prevent or modify the course of the disease. (IG is useful only for those at high risk and should not be used in general to control an outbreak.) If indicated, IG should be given as

soon as possible after exposure to ensure maximum protection. The recommended dose of IG is 0.25 ml/kg body weight given intramuscularly (IM); persons with poor immune systems should receive 0.5 ml/kg IM. The maximum recommended dose is 15 ml.

Summary

Measles is a very serious and highly contagious virus characterized by a cough, runny nose, fever, a rash covering the entire body, and red, watery eyes. Tiny blue-white bumps resembling grains of sand may arise inside the mouth.

Measles spreads when a person with the disease talks, sneezes, or coughs, releasing infected droplets into the air. The droplets are then inhaled by others and can infect a person through the lining of the mouth, nose, or throat.

Measles infection can lead to serious complications, including middle ear infections, pneumonia, and inflammation of the brain (encephalitis). Pregnant women infected with measles risk spontaneous abortions, premature labor, and low birth-weight infants.

The incidence of measles is on the rise in the USA. It occurs most often in preschool aged children or college-age persons.

People at particular risk for infection after an exposure to measles include anyone born after January 1, 1957, unless they meet certain criteria which are outlined in the "Prevention" section of this chapter.

Recent revisions in the vaccine recommendations now call for 2 doses of measles vaccine.

People with unknown vaccine histories should also receive 2 doses of vaccine no less than 1 month apart unless vaccination is specifically contraindicated.

Those suspected of having measles should be referred to a health provider without delay. With this highly contagious disease, the provider should be alerted before the person arrives to diminish risk of exposure to others.

Shelters with suspected or confirmed cases of measles also need to contact the local board of health immediately. Measures for prevention of spread, including the vaccination of people at risk, must be taken quickly to be effective.

References

Centers for Disease Control. Measles prevention: recommendations of the Immunization Practices Advisory Committee. *MMWR* 1989; 38(S-9): 1-18.

Georges P, Hall CB, Lepow ML, Phillips CF, eds. *The 1988 Red Book: Report of the Committee on Infectious Diseases.* 21st ed. Elk Grove Village, Illinois: American Academy of Pediatrics; 1988: 277-289.

Public Health Fact Sheet on Measles. Massachusetts Department of Public Health; 1987.

Meningococcal Infections

Joan Lebow, M.D.

and Janet Groth, R.N., M.S.

Meningococcal disease is a very serious infection caused by the bacterium *Neisseria meningitidis*. These bacteria have a particular affinity for the meninges and blood, with the severity of infection varying from a transient fever and bacteremia to severe, life-threatening disease. Infrequently, meningococcal infection may cause pneumonia or conjunctivitis.

The clinical syndrome of meningococcal disease is similar to that of other types of meningitis. Symptoms may first appear as those of a respiratory tract illness, but often there is an abrupt onset of fever, headache, stiff neck, and vomiting. Changes in mental status may appear, including confusion, drowsiness, stupor, and even coma. Infants may have fever with irritability, poor feeding, vomiting, or a high-pitched cry.

A specific feature in the presentation of meningococcal disease may be the appearance of tiny hemorrhages called petechiae that arise in 3 of 4 patients. These lesions are usually located on the trunk and lower extremities.

In rare cases, meningococcal disease follows a fulminant course known as Waterhouse-Friedrichsen Syndrome. This rapidly progressive disease, marked by hemorrhages into the skin, joints, and internal organs, can lead to septic shock and death even if the patient receives antibiotics immediately.

A positive outcome of meningococcal disease depends on prompt diagnosis, early referral, and rapid treatment with antibiotics.

Prevalence and Distribution

Endemic disease is most common in children under 5 years of age, particularly those in the 6 to 12 month age group. Epidemics may involve older children and adults. Studies of outbreaks in group settings (day care centers, military camps, and colleges) show that close contacts to people with active disease are also at high risk.

Transmission

Neisseria meningitidis organisms spread when carriers cough or sneeze infected secretions into air that others inhale. The disease also spreads through infected nose and throat secretions that come into contact with the mucous membranes of others. The onset of disease usually occurs within 10 days (commonly 3-4 days), although longer intervals are possible.

N. meningitidis inhabits the upper respiratory tract of a significant proportion of individuals without causing illness. It is not known why some who carry the bacteria get ill and others do not. Some speculate that a concurrent viral infection may diminish a person's resistance to *Neisseria meningitidis* that has colonized in the upper respiratory tract, thus allowing illness to develop in someone who had been carrying the organism.

Diagnosis

Anyone suspected of meningococcal disease should have blood cultures and a lumbar puncture without delay. The organism may also be cultured from synovial, pleural, or pericardial fluid.

Treatment

1. Meningococcal Disease

Persons suspected of having meningococcal disease require intravenous antibiotic therapy and close supervision. The disease calls for strict respiratory isolation for at least 24 hours after the beginning of antibiotic therapy. High doses of penicillin G, ampicillin, chloramphenicol, or selected third-generation cephalosporins for 1 to 2 weeks have successfully treated this infection.

2. Colonization

Penicillin G, ampicillin, and chloramphenicol do not reliably reach high enough concentrations in upper respiratory tract fluids to destroy the organism at the site of colonization in the nasopharynx. To eradicate the organism completely, patients treated with these antibiotics should follow parenteral therapy with 2 days of oral rifampin (10 mg/kg with a maximum of 600 mg every 12 hours in those 1 month or older, and 5 mg/kg every 12 hours in infants less than 1 month). For infants, the liquid form of rifampin is easier to administer. If unavailable, the contents of rifampin capsules can be mixed with applesauce.

Rifampin is contraindicated in pregnant women and those with active liver disease.

During rifampin therapy, urine, stool, sweat, tears, and semen may turn orange-red. Rifampin can permanently stain soft contact lenses so patients should wear glasses while taking the medication. Rifampin may also diminish the effects of methadone and the effectiveness of birth control pills. Patients should use a barrier form of contraception (condoms, diaphragm) for the duration of the entire birth-control pill cycle in which rifampin therapy occurs. Please refer to Chart 1 on page 52 for a summary of rifampin's side effects.

Alternative drugs for eliminating nasal carriage of *Neisseria meningitidis* may be available depending on the sensitivity of the organism.

Prevention and Control

Risk of disease in those exposed to a case varies with the duration and closeness of exposure. In general, persons with less than 20 hours of contact in the week prior to illness are likely to be at less risk than those with a longer duration of contact. However, contacts who have had direct mucous membrane exposure to secretions from the infected person's nose and throat are at higher risk. Contact includes:

- mouth-to-mouth resuscitation;
- kissing;
- mouthing toys;
- sharing food, glasses, or bottles.

Identified close contacts should be evaluated for rifampin prophylaxis within 24 hours of exposure. Refer to the treatment section above for dosages. If rifampin cannot be initiated within 1 to 2 weeks of exposure, the efficacy is likely to be markedly diminished.

Identified close contacts should be evaluated for rifampin prophylaxis within 24 hours of exposure.

Because of the possibility of the emergence of rifampin-resistant strains of *Neisseria meningitidis* or the possibility of noncompliance with recommended antibiotic prophylaxis, caregivers should monitor all close contacts for at least 2 weeks following the diagnosis of the initial case, whether or not they have received prophylaxis. We recommend that smaller shelters, where families or adults live for weeks or months, hold any new admissions until all identified persons at risk within the shelter have completed the 2 day course of rifampin. If compliance with therapy cannot be assured, then admissions should be held for 2 weeks following the diagnosis of the last case of meningococcal disease. Any close contact who develops a febrile illness should go to an acute care facility immediately for evaluation. Staff or caregivers should notify the facility ahead of time to ensure that precautions are taken to lessen the risk of exposure to others.

A vaccine is available for certain strains of *N. meningitidis*, but it is not routinely given to the general population.

Massachusetts and most other states require that confirmed cases of meningococcal illness be reported to the local board of health.

Summary

Meningococcal disease is a serious bacterial infection that most commonly causes varying degrees of infection in the blood or meninges (the linings covering the brain). This illness can be life-threatening and occurs most commonly in children under 5 years of age.

Initial symptoms can be similar to an upper respiratory tract illness. The infection may also start suddenly with headaches, fever, stiff neck, vomiting, or a change in behavior. Infants may show a fever, appear irritable, have a high-pitched cry, and feed poorly. Tiny hemorrhages into the skin may appear on the trunk or legs in both adults and children.

The spread of meningococcal disease occurs when infected individuals cough or sneeze into air that is then inhaled by others.

Those suspected of having meningococcal disease must be evaluated as soon as possible in an acute care setting. Respiratory isolation, antibiotic therapy, and close monitoring is required.

Persons likely to be at greatest risk from exposure include those who have spent 20 or more hours with the infected person in the week preceding the illness or who have had contact with the person's nose and throat secretions through activities such as sharing toys, food, glasses, or bottles. These "close contacts" should be evaluated as soon as possible for antibiotic therapy to prevent this illness.

If a suspected or confirmed case of meningococcal disease occurs in a shelter, the local board of health must be notified immediately. This agency can assist the shelter in identifying people at risk and instituting measures to control the spread of this potentially grave disease.

References

Apicella MA. *Neisseria meningitidis*. In: Mandell GL, Douglas RG, Bennett JE, eds. *Principles and Practices of Infectious Diseases*. 3rd ed. New York: Churchill Livingston; 1990: 1600-1612.

Dagbjartsson A, Ludvigsson P. Bacterial meningitis: diagnosis and initial antibiotic therapy. *Pediatric Clinics of North America* 1987; 34(1): 219-230.

Georges P, Hall CB, Lepow ML, Phillips CF, eds. *The 1988 Red Book: Report of the Committee on Infectious Diseases*. 21st ed. Elk Grove Village, Illinois: American Academy of Pediatrics; 1988: 289-291.

Griffiss JM. Meningococcal infections. In: Wilson JD, Braunwald E, Isselbacher KJ, Petersdorf RG, Martin JB, Fauci AS, Root RK, eds. *Harrison's Principles of Internal Medicine*. 12th ed. New York: McGraw-Hill Book Co; 1991: 590-593.

Kaplan SL, Feigin RD. Meninogococcal infections. In: Behrman RE, Vaughan VC, eds. *Nelson Textbook of Pediatrics.* 13th ed. Philadelphia: WB Saunders Co; 1987: 589-591.

Pertussis (Whooping Cough)

Johnye Ballenger, M.D.

Pertussis, commonly known as whooping cough, is a highly infectious disease of the respiratory tract caused by the bacterium *Bordetella pertussis*. In a young child it can be very serious and may cause pneumonia, apnea, seizures, cerebral hemorrhage, and even death. Newborns and infants not yet immunized are at the highest risk for serious infection and complications. Other people at risk include young adults who were not immunized as children or whose immunity from the vaccine routinely given in childhood has waned.

Three stages of pertussis

The course of pertussis involves three stages. Each stage lasts an average of 2 weeks. The usual incubation period is 7 to 10 days.

1. Catarrhal stage

Stage I is the catarrhal or "cold-like" stage. This usually begins with mild cold symptoms: sneezing, runny nose, tearing, and mild conjunctival infection. Later in this phase, a mild cough develops and soon becomes worse. The pertussis bacteria is most easily spread from one person to another during the first stage.

2. Paroxysmal stage

Stage II is the paroxysmal or "coughing" stage. During this stage, the cough becomes harsh, dry, and irritating. Spasms of sudden coughing happen in clusters or repetitive bursts, lasting 10 to 20 seconds. These episodes often end with a deep breath that causes the characteristic "whooping" sound. Vomiting, cyanosis, and exhaustion often follow these bursts of coughing.

Paroxysmal coughing is more common at night but can happen several times a day to several times an hour. External stimuli (cold air and smoke) and internal stimuli (stress) can trigger the episodes. The paroxysmal stage usually lasts 1 to 2 weeks, but may last 4 weeks or longer.

3. Convalescent stage

Stage III is the convalescent or "recovery" stage, normally lasting several weeks. The cough becomes milder and less frequent during this phase. If a person develops an upper respiratory infection such as bronchitis during the third stage, the paroxysms will increase. Despite the cough, people are usually not infectious at this point in the course of the disease.

In older children and adults, the disease may be somewhat milder or atypical, sometimes with only a cough that lingers for several weeks.

Transmission

Pertussis spreads by direct contact with secretions from the nose or throat of an infected person, or by breathing the droplets dispersed in the air when an infected person coughs.

Pertussis most easily passes between people in the initial catarrhal stage of illness, often before diagnosis. While the organism can spread throughout the course of illness, the degree of infectivity decreases with time and depends on environmental conditions, such as crowding and ventilation.

Spasms of sudden coughing often end with a deep breath that causes the characteristic "whooping" sound.

Diagnosis

Diagnosis of pertussis depends on a patient's history and a physical examination. Caregivers should suspect pertussis in anyone with:

- a new cough lasting 14 days or more; or
- a cough followed by vomiting that lasts 7 days or more.

A confirmed diagnosis depends on culturing secretions from the nose and throat in the early stages of the disease. Culturing must be done on media that specifically supports the growth of *Bordetella pertussis* organisms. The local or state health departments can provide information about obtaining these kits. People on antibiotic therapy and those who have been ill for several weeks are less likely to have positive cultures.

In addition, a blood test to detect antibodies to pertussis is available on a limited basis and can be used for diagnosis.

Treatment

A person diagnosed with pertussis needs strict respiratory isolation for 5 days from the initiation of antibiotic treatment. Staff should not admit infected children to a shelter until they have completed 7 days of medication. If antibiotic treatment is impossible, the patient should remain isolated until 3 weeks after the onset of paroxysms.

Young children need careful management, because the paroxysms may make feeding and breathing difficult. Also, thick mucous in the nose and throat can block the airways. Some children may need frequent suctioning to remove the mucous. In cases with severe complications, such as respiratory distress or dehydration, hospitalization may be required.

Antibiotic treatment

For children and adults, the antibiotic of choice is erythromycin. The course of illness may be less severe if the patient receives antibiotic treatment during the incubation period or even early in the catarrhal stage (stage I). However, treatment begun after the paroxysmal stage (stage II) does not change the course of the illness. Antibiotic treatment after stage II will prevent further spread of the disease by killing the remaining bacteria in the body.

Immunization with pertussis vaccine remains the most important measure to prevent the spread of the organism.

The dose of erythromycin is 40 mg/kg/day, orally, divided into 4 daily doses for 14 days. The maximum daily dose is 2 grams. For those unable to tolerate erythromycin, trimethoprim-sulfamethoxasole (Bactrim™, Septra™) is an acceptable alternative.

Prevention

Immunization with pertussis vaccine is the most important measure to prevent the spread of the organism. Immunization is particularly important for young children in whom the disease is likely to be most severe.

The pertussis vaccine is combined with the diphtheria and tetanus toxoids in a single shot called DTP. The recommended immunization series consists of 5 doses. Infants usually receive the first dose between the ages of 6 and 8 weeks. Additional doses are given at 4 months and 6 months of age. The fourth dose comes at 18 months of age, completing the primary series. Children receive the fifth dose between the ages of 4 and 6 years. This schedule may need modification for children who have not followed a normal immunization schedule. (For more information, refer to the immunization schedules in Part Four on pages 216-217.) Pertussis vaccine is not usually recommended for those over 7 years of age.

Serious side effects, including high fever (above 104.9° F or 40.5° C), convulsions, persistent or unusual screaming, shock, encephalopathic manifestations, and serious allergic reactions have been reported in association with pertussis vaccine. However, such incidents may occur in any child at the age that pertussis vaccine is recommended and may solely be a temporal association rather than a causal one. If circumstances point to pertussis immunization causing such an event, further administration of pertussis vaccine is contraindicated. Deferral of pertussis immunization should be considered in certain infants and children with neurological or convulsive disorders or conditions that predispose them to neurological deterioration or convulsions.

Control

Caregivers should report suspected and confirmed cases of pertussis to the local health department, which can provide information about control measures.

When there has been an outbreak of pertussis in a community or shelter, the health department or consulting pediatrician may decide to begin the DTP vaccine schedule as early as 2 weeks of age with subsequent doses given as often as every 4 weeks. Generally, 3 doses will provide protection from the disease in 80 percent of children.

Close contacts under 7 years of age who have had at least 4 doses of vaccine should receive a booster dose unless they received a dose in the past 3 years. Children under 7 years of age with no history of DTP vaccine or with less than 4 doses of DTP should begin the vaccination schedule or continue on schedule.

In addition, a 14-day course of erythromycin in the dosages described above is recommended for all household contacts and other close contacts. This is because vaccine-induced immunity does not prevent disease in all cases. Also, older children and adults may develop a very mild case of pertussis that may still be transmitted to others.

All contacts to a case of pertussis should be watched closely for respiratory symptoms (sneezing, runny nose, tearing, conjunctivitis, and later, a mild cough) for 2 incubation periods (28 days) after the last exposure. New suspected cases should be promptly referred to a health provider for evaluation.

Family shelters

Pertussis can create considerable problems in a family shelter, because children under 12 months are at greatest risk of infection and complications.

Anyone exposed to an infected person for more than one hour in a close setting (play group, dining area, etc.) is a close contact. These people will need antibiotic prophylaxis (erythromycin, as discussed above) to prevent them from developing pertussis.

The recommended course of treatment for pertussis is 14 days. After the first 7 days of antibiotic therapy, infected people (including close contacts with symptoms after exposure to an active case) no longer pose a risk to other guests or staff. Close contacts who do not show symptoms are not considered infectious.

This 7 day period of infectivity during treatment presents a special problem for group settings. The average time from exposure to the onset of disease is only 7 to 10 days. Usually an exposed person will not have had time to complete 7 days of antibiotics before beginning to show symptoms. This person may then be able to spread infection to others, creating another group of close contacts.

One solution is the provision of separate accommodations for all identified close contacts during the first 7 days of preventive treatment. This is often impractical. Therefore, staff and guests who will spend more than one hour with any close contact during the first 7 days of prophylaxis will also need to take erythromycin.

A shelter should not discharge a close contact to another shelter or group setting until completion of at least 7 of the 14 days of prophylactic therapy.

Adult shelters

Complications are greatest in children under one year of age and include serious problems with the lungs or brain.

In larger adult shelters, prophylaxis of all guests is clearly an impractical solution. Targets for prophylaxis should include adults and children who have shared airspace with a confirmed case for 20 hours per week or more while the person was considered contagious. Caregivers should also consider treatment for close contacts who interact with children of any age. Prophylaxis is especially important for anyone who has contact with children under 12 months and those who have not had at least 3 doses of pertussis vaccine.

Summary

Pertussis or whooping cough is a serious infection that primarily affects the upper respiratory areas. It is spread by direct contact with infected secretions from the nose or throat or by breathing infected droplets in the air where an infected person has coughed.

Generally, pertussis begins with symptoms like a cold. The illness progresses with a cough that becomes dry and harsh, and occurs in bursts especially at night. The person may turn blue while coughing. The episode may end with a large intake of air that sounds like a whoop. Vomiting and exhaustion can follow these events. Older people infected with pertussis may have a less serious illness.

Complications are greatest in children under one year and include serious problems with the lungs or brain.

Treatment of pertussis requires antibiotics and supportive care. Strict respiratory isolation is necessary for the infected person until 5 days after antibiotics have been started.

Pertussis can be prevented through the routine vaccination of children.

People of any age who have been exposed to an infected person should also see a health provider for preventive therapy with antibiotics.

The local board of health or appropriate health agency must be informed of any person who has been diagnosed with pertussis as soon as possible. The agency can also provide information about the risk to the rest of the shelter guests and staff and can help with instituting control measures.

References

Bass JW, Stephenson SR. The return of pertussis. *Ped Infect Dis J* 1987; 6(2): 141-144.

Bass JW. Erythromycin for treatment and prevention of pertussis. *Ped Infect Dis J* 1986; 5(1): 154-157.

Bass JW. Pertussis: current status of prevention and treatment. *Ped Infect Dis J* 1985; 4(6): 614-619.

Cherry JD, Brunell PA, Golden GS, Karzon DT. Report of the task force on pertussis and pertussis immunization - 1988. *Pediatrics* 1988; 81(6): 945-976.

Feigin RD, Cherry JD, eds. *Textbook of Pediatric Infectious Diseases*. 2nd ed. Philadelphia: WB Saunders; 1987: 1227-1238.

Geller RJ. The pertussis syndrome: a persistent problem. *Ped Infect Dis J* 1984; 3(2): 182-186.

Georges P, Hall CB, Lepow ML, Phillips CF, eds. *The 1988 Red Book: Report of the Committee on Infectious Diseases*. 21st ed. Elk Grove Village, Illinois: American Academy of Pediatrics; 1988: 266-275.

Griffin MR, Ray WA, Mortimer EA, Fenichel GM, Schaffner W. Risk of seizures and encephalopathy after immunization with the diphtheria-tetanus-pertussis vaccine. *JAMA* 1990; 263(12): 1641-1645.

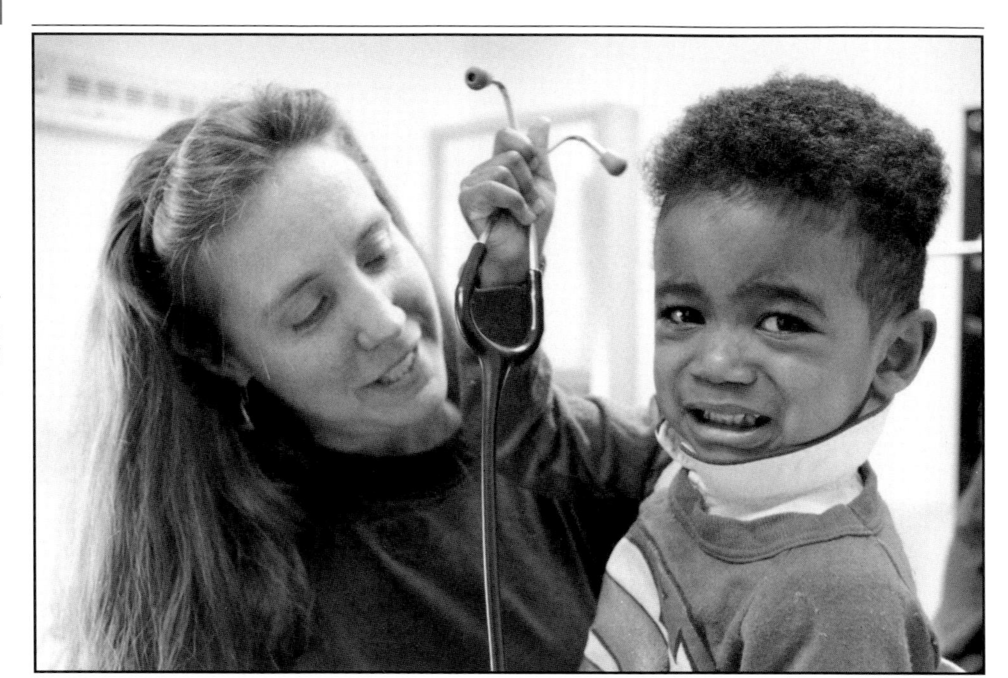

BHCHP nurse practitioner Jean Molloy attempts to win the trust of this 2 year old child with otitis media.

Streptococcal Pharyngitis (Strep Throat)

Maria Pitaro, M.D.

Streptococcal infection of the throat (strep throat or strep pharyngitis) is a very common bacterial infection in children and adults. The Group A beta-hemolytic streptococcus (GAS) is responsible for most of these infections, although other strains (specifically, Groups C and G) can also infect the throat.

Pharyngitis due to GAS varies in severity. One-third to one-half of people infected have a very slight illness or no symptoms at all. Others may experience fever (often 101°F/38°C or higher), sore throat with exudate, and occasionally headache, malaise, and anorexia.

Children commonly have nausea, vomiting, and abdominal pain along with the above symptoms. Infants can have a protracted course known as streptococcal fever. Symptoms may include persistent nasal discharge, low-grade fever, and enlarged lymph nodes. Throat inflammation with exudate is uncommon under age 3.

Certain strains of GAS may create a pharyngeal infection with a sandpaper-like rash known as scarlet fever. It is due to the body's reaction to the toxin produced by the bacteria.

Complications

Two classes of complications exist: suppurative and non-suppurative. Suppurative complications of strep throat include:

- retropharyngeal infections;
- otitis media;
- sinusitis;
- peritonsillar abscess in young adults;
- cervical lymphadenitis.

Non-suppurative complications of streptococcal pharyngitis include rheumatic fever and glomerulonephritis. Rheumatic fever is an inflammatory disease involving the heart, joints, connective tissue, and nervous system, which can occur after a streptococcal upper respiratory infection. Rheumatic fever usually arises within 18 days of the pharyngitis, but can take as long as 2 months to manifest. Rheumatic fever happens in less than 3 percent of untreated cases occurring during an epidemic and in less than one-half of 1 percent of sporadic cases. Antibiotics can prevent rheumatic fever when given within 9 days of the onset of the initial infection. Recurrence of rheumatic fever is common and can lead to progressive rheumatic heart disease. Longterm antibiotic prophylaxis in confirmed cases of rheumatic fever or rheumatic heart disease is required to prevent recurrence of the disease.

Approximately 5 percent of cases of GAS infection are followed by post-streptococcal glomerulonephritis, an acute inflammatory problem of the renal glomeruli. Glomerulonephritis usually arises within 10 days following a GAS upper respiratory infection and within 3 weeks following a GAS skin infection. Patients present with the acute onset of hematuria, proteinuria, hypertension, and edema. Unlike rheumatic fever, antimicrobial therapy does not prevent post-streptococcal glomerulonephritis. Recurrence is rare, and the disease does not usually lead to residual renal damage.

Prevalence and Distribution

GAS accounts for 20 to 30 percent of all cases of acute pharyngitis. GAS most often affects children and young adults (3 to 15 years of age). The average child will have 1 attack every 3 to 5 years. Up to 1 in 5 healthy children may have positive throat cultures for GAS while remaining asymptomatic. GAS pharyngitis is most common in late winter and spring.

Transmission

GAS pharyngitis spreads when a person coughs or sneezes infected droplets into the air that then come into contact with another person's mucous membranes. Rarely, transmission can happen with direct contact to secretions from the upper respiratory tract of an infected person (on soiled hands or tissues, for example).

Crowded settings such as schools and shelters heighten the chance of transmission among pupils and guests. Contaminated food, particularly eggs, can result in streptococcal infection of the throat on rare occasions.

The average incubation period of streptococcal pharyngitis is 2 to 4 days.

The highest risk of transmission occurs during the acute stage. After an infected person completes 24-48 hours of antibiotics, the risk of transmission diminishes significantly.

Carriers are those in whom GAS has colonized the nose, throat, or skin, and these persons rarely transmit streptococcal infection.

Diagnosis

1. Clinical diagnosis

GAS infection of the throat usually produces enlarged, erythematous tonsils. Gray-white exudate is common. The cervical lymph nodes may be enlarged and tender. Especially in infants, infection can cause excoriated nares. Unaccompanied by the previous symptoms, conjunctivitis, hoarseness and cough are not characteristic of streptococcal pharyngitis.

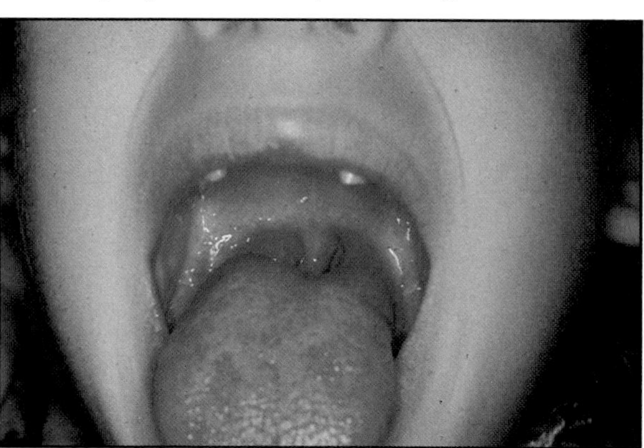

Streptococcal Pharyngitis (Strep Throat). The tonsils are swollen and reddened in this child with a fever, tender anterior cervical adenopathy, and an absence of cough.

When scarlet fever accompanies streptococcal pharyngitis, the patient has a diffuse, erythematous rash with the texture of sandpaper that blanches when pressed. The rash can cover almost the entire body, but is usually most visible on the neck and chest and in the folds of the skin. The face, palms, and soles are usually not involved. Flushing of the cheeks and pallor around the mouth is common, and the tongue becomes swollen, red, and mottled ("strawberry tongue"). Both skin and tongue may peel during recovery.

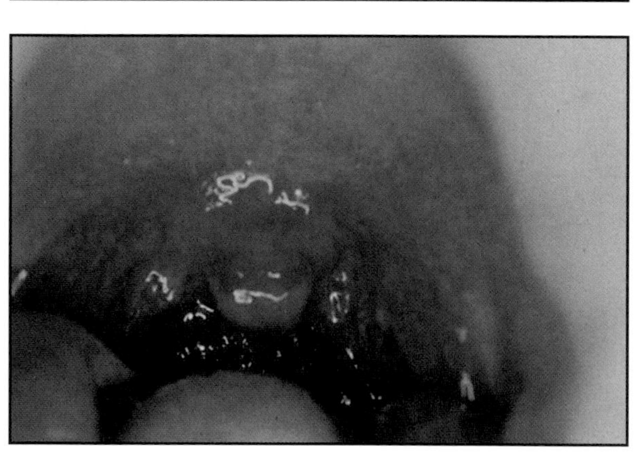

Streptococcal Pharyngitis (Strep Throat). There is moderate redness of the throat, but an early white exudate has appeared on the left tonsil. The diagnosis of strep throat was confirmed by a throat culture.

2. Laboratory diagnosis

Laboratory confirmation of GAS pharyngitis is necessary to distinguish this infection from other types of pharyngitis: viral, streptococcal group C and G, infectious mononucleosis, gonorrhea (with a history of oral sex), and diphtheria. Rapid diagnostic tests that identify GAS antigens from throat swabs (the rapid strep test) are available in some settings. False negative results can happen. Definitive diagnosis requires a throat culture. A false positive may result from a GAS carrier who has pharyngitis due to another organism. Antibody tests, such as anti-streptolysin O (ASLO), can confirm recent streptococcal infection but do not help with the diagnosis of acute disease.

Treatment

All patients who have clinical evidence of GAS should begin treatment promptly. Before initiating antibiotics, caregivers should obtain a throat culture. Therapy should be discontinued if the results are negative. Patients with milder symptoms who have not been associated with an outbreak may have GAS infection confirmed by culture before beginning treatment.

Penicillin is the treatment of choice for those with no history of allergy. An oral regimen of penicillin VK 125-250 mg, 4 times daily for 10 days, is one treatment of choice. Alternatively, intramuscular benzathine penicillin G (1,200,000 U in adults and children over 60 pounds and 600,000 U in children under 60 pounds) may be a more practical regimen for those who will have difficulty following the oral regimen. Those allergic to penicillin can receive erythromycin (250 mg 4 times daily for 10 days).

Treatment of strep throat can prevent rheumatic fever.

Antibiotics prevent local complications and can limit the spread of disease, which is an important consideration in the shelter setting. Treatment also prevents rheumatic fever, even if delayed for 9 days after infection. If oral therapy is chosen, it is essential to complete the full 10 day course to prevent rheumatic fever. Symptoms generally subside before the therapy is complete.

Prevention and Control

Prompt diagnosis and treatment of infections can prevent transmission. Caregivers should ensure that patients complete the full course of therapy even when their symptoms have resolved. Patients with a history of rheumatic fever may prevent recurrent bouts by using continuous antibiotic prophylaxis.

Caregivers should monitor close contacts to an acute case of GAS pharyngitis. Close contacts need throat cultures if they become symptomatic within 2 weeks of exposure to an infectious case. Family members and other close contacts of a person who has developed acute rheumatic fever or glomerulonephritis should receive throat cultures and, if results are positive, should proceed with treatment regardless of symptoms.

Massachusetts state law requires caregivers to report only epidemics of GAS infection (i.e. more than 10 percent of the total population of a shelter) to the local board of health or appropriate health agency.

Summary

Many different organisms cause throat infections. The bacterium streptococcus (Group A, beta-hemolytic) is responsible for strep throat. These bacteria account for less than a third of throat infections, but diagnosis and treatment of strep throat is essential to prevent complications. Throat abscesses, kidney problems, and rheumatic fever are some complications that arise from strep infections in the throat.

Strep throat is common in children and young adults. It most often spreads when a person coughs or sneezes infected droplets into the air that another person then inhales. The symptoms are sore throat, fever, and swollen, tender glands in the neck. The symptoms usually resolve in several days even without treatment.

Strep throat is diagnosed by throat culture. Infected people receive penicillin or erythromycin for 10 days. Symptoms will disappear before the completion of treatment, but those with strep throat need to take the full 10-day course to prevent complications.

Infections such as strep throat spread easily in shelters. When a guest or staff person shows symptoms of strep infection, they should see a doctor or nurse practitioner immediately. Prompt diagnosis and treatment can go a long way in preventing further infection in this population.

References

Benenson AS, ed. *Control of Communicable Diseases in Man*. 15th ed. Washington, DC: American Public Health Association; 1990: 411-417.

Bisno, A. Streptococcal infections. In: Wilson JD, Braunwald E, Isselbacher KJ, Petersdorf RG, Martin JB, Fauci AS, Root RK, eds. *Harrison's Principles of Internal Medicine*. 12th ed. New York: McGraw Hill; 1991: 563-566.

Georges P, Hall CB, Lepow ML, Phillips CF, eds. *The 1988 Red Book: Report of the Committee on Infectious Diseases*. 21st ed. Elk Grove Village, Illinois: American Academy of Pediatrics; 1988: 386-395.

Kawplan EL, Wannamaker LW. Group A streptococcal infections. In: Feigin RD, Cherry JD, eds. *Textbook of Pediatric Infectious Diseases*. 2nd ed. Philadelphia: WB Saunders; 1987: 1312-1322.

Tuberculosis (TB)

John Bernardo, M.D.

Although the prevalence of tuberculosis (TB) had declined in recent decades, this disease is once again becoming a major public health problem in the USA. The high incidence of TB among people with AIDS has contributed significantly to this resurgence and will require the allocation of more public health resources for tuberculosis.

The complexities in treatment of tuberculosis infection and disease call for close cooperation among public health officials, health care providers, and those assigned to the care of people-at-risk.

Tuberculosis is preventable and treatable. To prevent TB disease, people infected with tuberculosis need to be identified, especially those at increased risk for developing disease, including homeless people and drug abusers. Early recognition and prompt intervention for TB disease is the key to limiting the spread of TB to others.

Transmission

Tuberculosis is caused by the bacterium *Mycobacterium tuberculosis*. These bacteria usually infect people through the respiratory tract. A person with pulmonary TB can cough the organisms into the air, and others may inhale these droplet nuclei and become infected. TB can infect other parts of the body after it enters through the lungs, but these infections seldom lead to the transmission of organisms.

The infectiousness of each person varies, but tuberculosis is not highly infectious in general. People who have had prolonged contact with an infectious person are at highest risk for infection, particularly sleeping partners or those who share close airspace for several hours.

A person with active pulmonary TB is unlikely to continue transmitting the organism once proper therapy has been instituted for 14 days.

TB infection

After a susceptible person inhales the organisms responsible for TB infection, the bacteria begin to multiply in the lungs and then spread through the body via the blood and lymph systems. The body's immune system eventually controls the tuberculosis organism. This immune response, called "sensitization", takes from 4 to 12 weeks. The tuberculin (PPD) skin test measures this immune response, or sensitization, to the tuberculosis organism.

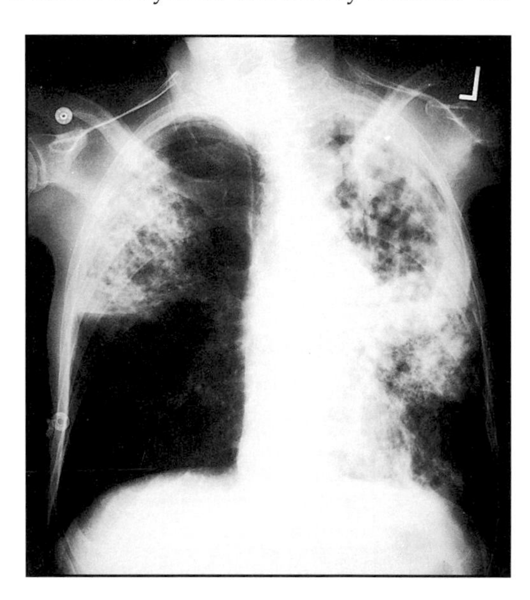

Pulmonary Tuberculosis. This man was brought to our shelter clinic with a history of weight loss and cough. He offered no complaints, and other than a low-grade fever of 99.8° F and soft scattered rhonchi in both lungs, his examination was benign. Note the small right upper lobe pneumothorax.

A positive PPD skin test shows that a TB infection has happened at some point. Infected people may carry a "latent infection". This infection may not become active until later in life. Others with a positive skin test may have active disease. Everyone with a positive skin test should have proper follow-up to determine the stage of infection.

The Centers for Disease Control and the American Thoracic Society have recently revised guidelines for reading PPD skin tests. A "positive" skin test now includes not only the measurement of induration (in millimeters), but also assesses factors in a person's risk for TB disease. These new criteria are summarized in Chart 2 on page 87.

There are occasions when a person infected with TB may not show a positive PPD skin test. Provided enough time has passed to allow for "sensitization", certain illness such as malignancies, sarcoidosis, or infection with the human immunodeficiency virus (HIV) may suppress the body's response to the PPD test. The inability to mount a response to a panel of PPD and PPD-like skin tests is known as anergy.

Tuberculosis disease

Tuberculosis disease happens when a latent infection becomes active. Symptoms of tuberculosis are not specific and may be overlooked easily. Active infection may lead to a cough, the production of sputum, fevers, weight loss, night sweats, swollen lymph glands, and general weakness and fatigue.

Caregivers should suspect TB in anyone who exhibits these symptoms and has had:

- a recent close exposure to an active case of infectious TB;
- a history of a positive PPD skin test;
- an abnormal chest x-ray that suggests the presence of TB.

The presence of any of the following should also increase suspicion of TB:

- people with poor immune systems, including those at risk for infection with the human immunodeficiency virus (HIV);
- recent PPD skin test conversion (negative to positive within the past 2 years);
- diabetes mellitus or certain malignancies such as leukemia or lymphoma;
- prolonged therapy with corticosteroids or other immuno-suppressive drugs;
- pregnancy;
- malnourishment;
- chronic alcoholism.

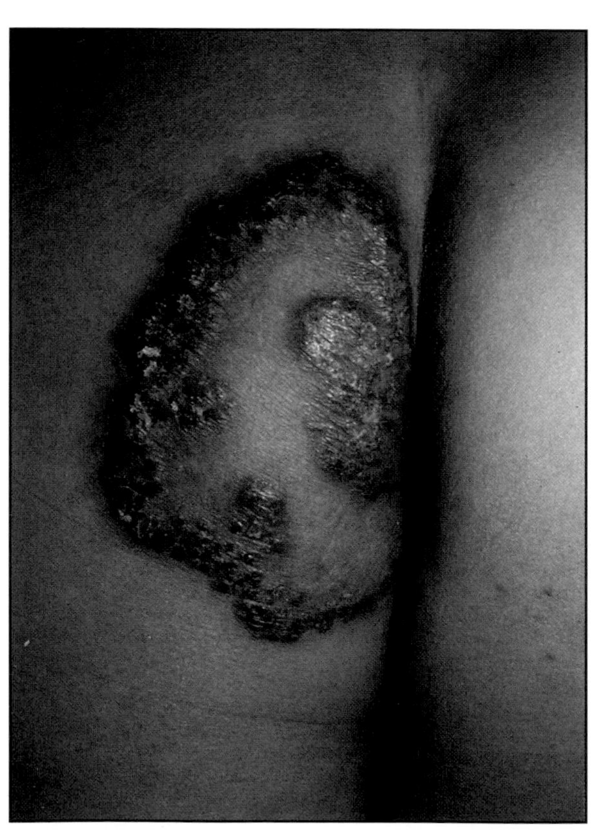

Tuberculosis of the Skin. This unusual presentation of tuberculosis was initially thought to be a fungal infection that did not respond to the usual treatment. A skin biopsy confirmed the diagnosis after a PPD was found to be positive.

Tuberculosis and HIV infection

Researchers have recently recognized that those infected with the human immunodeficiency virus (HIV) are at very high risk for tuberculosis disease. People with HIV infection or people at risk for HIV infection may reactivate a previous tuberculosis infection if they have a history of TB infection and/or a prior positive PPD skin test. These people also seem to be more likely to develop active tuberculosis when exposed to an infectious case of TB.

Rarely, TB can be fatal. Death may happen to people with poor immune systems whose initial infection can sometimes proceed unchecked and lead to overwhelming tuberculosis.

*Guidelines for Reading TB Skin Tests**

5mm or more induration is positive in persons with:

1. recent close contact to an active case of TB;
2. poor immune systems, including HIV infection;
3. chest x-rays showing previous (untreated) TB disease; and
4. high risk for HIV infection because of intravenous drug use. (Note: this must be individualized, based on local rates of HIV infection among intravenous drug users.)

10 mm or more induration is considered positive for:

1. low income people, especially those without permanent homes who must live in shelters or on the streets;
2. substance abusers;
3. foreign-born people from high prevalence countries;
4. residents in correctional institutions and nursing homes;
5. those over age 70 and children under age 15 years;
6. hospital and mycobacteriology laboratory employees;
7. persons with medical conditions known to increase the risk of TB, such as diabetes mellitus, silicosis, prolonged corticosteroid therapy, post-gastrectomy, chronic malabsorption syndromes, and people who weigh less than 90 percent of the ideal body weight;
8. service providers to the above high-risk groups.

15 mm or more is positive for:

people with none of the above risk factors.

*5 Tuberculin Units of Purified Protein Derivative - Standard.

Chart 2. Guidelines for Reading TB Skin Tests.

Source: The Centers for Disease Control and the American Thoracic Society MMWR 1990; 39: 9-12

Diagnosis

The first step in the diagnosis of tuberculosis is to identify TB organisms in clinical specimens of sputum or tissue biopsies. Because microscopic analysis may confuse other organisms with *M. tuberculosis* on stained sputum smears, a culture is necessary to confirm a diagnosis and to guide treatment.

The analysis of smears may not lead to a confirmed diagnosis by itself, but it can help to show the degree of infectiousness. When no organisms are seen in a stained sputum smear, the person is generally not very infectious. If analysis shows organisms present in a smear, caregivers should consider the person infectious.

However, a positive sputum smear without culture identification does not always mean infectious TB. For example, the *M. avium* complex, one of the so-called "atypical mycobacteria", frequently infects people with AIDS and is seen on sputum smears. These bacteria generally do not cause disease in normal humans and, for that reason, are not infectious. Cultures are essential to confirm TB in such cases.

Unfortunately, culturing tuberculosis organisms can take up to 90 days. This is an unacceptably long period to wait while a potentially infectious person is living in a shelter. If caregivers have strong reasons to suspect TB, treatment should be started before knowing the results of the culture. Sometimes, a short course of antituberculosis medications leads to noticeable improvement in a patient's condition even when the culture shows no evidence of organisms. This is known as a clinically verified case response.

Treatment

A physician familiar with antituberculosis drugs and their side effects should supervise the treatment of tuberculosis infection or tuberculosis disease. Treatment includes preventive or prophylactic therapy for people with tuberculosis infection as well as therapy for people with active tuberculosis disease.

1. Preventive therapy against tuberculosis disease

Preventive therapy is for those infected with tuberculosis (positive PPD skin test) but who do not show signs or symptoms of active disease. (Please refer to Chart 3 on page 90.) These people cannot spread tuberculosis to others. Preventive therapy destroys the residual organisms of the first infection and prevents "reactivation" of the organisms in later life.

Preventive therapy relies on a single antituberculosis drug, usually isoniazid (INH), given daily for a period of 6 to 12 months. When there is a high risk of infection with an INH-resistant tuberculosis, the prescribing physician may substitute rifampin (RIF), or use both INH and RIF.

The major side effect of both INH and RIF is toxicity to the liver. Toxicity is rare in otherwise healthy people under 35 years of age. People older than 35, those who abuse alcohol or drugs, and persons with a prior history of liver disease are at much higher risk for side effects.

Caregivers should watch for symptoms of hepatitis in people taking INH or RIF. These symptoms may include jaundice, nausea, vomiting, pain in the right upper quadrant of the abdomen, coffee or tea-colored urine, and fever. Blood tests of liver function should be monitored regularly, especially for patients with liver disease or a history of liver disease. With any indication of hepatitis, the patient should stop taking the drug and should see a physician for evaluation immediately.

INH interacts with phenytoin (Dilantin™), a common seizure medication, increasing the serum levels of both drugs. Patients taking both Dilantin™ and INH should have Dilantin™ levels monitored during concurrent therapy.

Rifampin increases metabolism of several drugs, including methadone and warfarin (Coumadin™), an anti-coagulant drug. Dosages of these drugs may have to be increased during therapy with rifampin. Also, rifampin may accelerate the clearance of hormones used in oral contraceptives. Women who take birth control pills should use an alternative form of birth control to avoid pregnancy while taking rifampin. Rifampin causes an orange discoloration of urine, sweat, tears, semen, and stool. Permanent discoloration of soft contact lenses may occur, and glasses should be worn until the completion of therapy. Please refer to Chart 1 on page 52.

Persons with a positive skin test (PPD) should have a chest x-ray and a physical examination.

2. Treatment of tuberculosis disease

Treatment of tuberculosis disease generally calls for the administration of 2 to 3 antituberculosis drugs for periods of 6 to 24 months. During the first phase of therapy, patients receive medication daily for 4 to 8 weeks. After this period, they may receive medication twice a week, generally at higher doses.

Physicians base the combination of drugs and the length of therapy on many factors, including the drug sensitivity of the *Mycobacterium tuberculosis* organism isolated from the culture and the presence of underlying disease, such as diabetes mellitus or AIDS.

Major drugs used in the therapy of tuberculosis include those discussed above, INH and RIF, as well as pyrazinimide (PZA), ethambutol (EMB), and streptomycin (SM).

PZA therapy may rarely cause major side effects, including hepatitis (see above), gastrointestinal distress, and increased levels of uric acid (which can cause gout). Ethambutol can disturb the normal function of the eye, causing decreased visual acuity and impaired red/green color discrimination. Streptomycin is only given by injection. The major side effects are toxicity to the kidneys and impaired hearing.

Compliance with therapy

Tuberculosis therapy is prolonged and often symptoms disappear shortly after starting therapy. This can create problems with compliance. Caregivers must adapt a patient's medication regimen to the lifestyle of the person as much as possible to ensure that a full course of treatment will be completed.

When compliance is not a concern, caregivers can give their patient a month's supply of medication at a time. Each person should receive detailed instructions about the symptoms of toxicity as well as instructions to discontinue therapy

Chart 3. The use of preventive therapy for tuberculous infection in the United States: recommendations of the Advisory Committee for Elimination of Tuberculosis.

Source: MMWR 1990; 39: 9-12.

Criteria for determining need for preventive therapy for persons with positive tuberculin reactions, by category and age group

	Age group (yrs)	
Category	<35	≥35
With risk factor*	Treat at all ages if reaction to 5TU purified protein derivative (PPD) ≥ 10 mm (or ≥5 mm and patient is recent contact, HIV-infected, or has radiographic evidence of old TB)	
No risk factor High-incidence group†	Treat if PPD ≥10 mm	Do not treat
No risk factor Low-incidence group	Treat if PPD ≥15 mm•	Do not treat

* Risk factors include HIV infection, recent contract with infectious person, recent skin-test conversion, abnormal chest radiograph, intravenous drug abuse, and certain medical risk factors (see text).
† High-incidence groups include foreign-born persons, medically underserved low-income populations, and residents of long-term-care facilities.
• Lower or higher cut points may be used for identifying positive reactions, depending upon the relative prevalence of *Myobacterium tuberculosis* infection and nonspecific cross-reactivity in the population.

Chart reprinted with permission from Centers for Disease Control.

and consult with the supervising physician if side effects are suspected. A physician or nurse should see the client at least once a month for follow-up.

The rigors of survival on the streets can make adherence to a rigid schedule difficult for many homeless persons. Also, there may be no safe place to store medication. Providers can enhance compliance enormously by providing therapy directly, twice a week, at a site frequented by the person. Each dose should be documented to reduce possible confusion about compliance over the long course of therapy.

Control

General control measures

One of the best measures for controlling the spread of TB is very simple: shelter staff and guests should cover their mouths and noses when they cough or sneeze. This is an important measure to reduce not only TB organisms, but any disease transmitted through the respiratory tract. Guests can comply with this measure much more easily when tissues are readily available.

Another way of reducing the incidence of airborne diseases is to provide good ventilation in all rooms. For smaller shelters, this may simply entail opening windows at least once daily. Shelters that have ventilation systems should be sure that the outflowing air is exhausted away from air intake sites.

Some shelters try to assign the same bed to their guests each night. In addition to promoting a sense of stability, this is an excellent public health principle. The fewer people exposed nightly to an undiagnosed person with active pulmonary TB, the lower the number of guests at risk for infection.

Shelter staff who have close contact with guests should receive a PPD skin test at least every 6 months. Ideally, guests should also receive a skin test every 6 months as well. Limited numbers of staff and high numbers of guests can make this a difficult goal to achieve.

Researchers have recently begun to investigate ultraviolet lights as a means of preventing the spread of TB organisms. However, the clinical usefulness of UV light has not yet been proven.

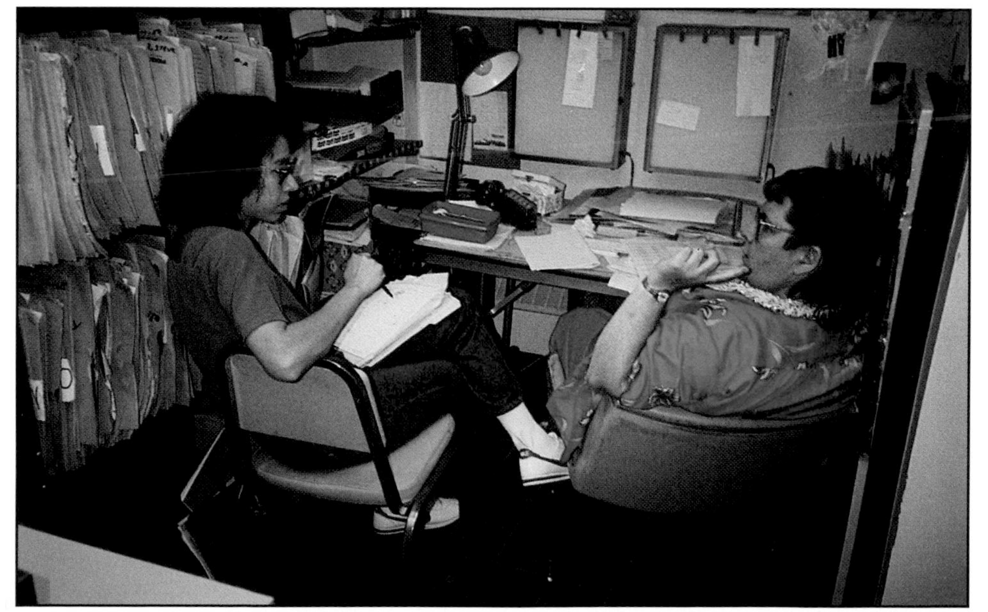

Barbara McInnis, R.N. (right), a public health nurse at Pine Street Inn, discusses surveillance strategies with BHCHP nurse practitioner Yoshiko Vann (left). Chest x-rays are offered to all guests of the shelter on Tuesday and Thursday evenings, and the results are reviewed each week by Dr. Bernardo with the nursing staff.

Contact investigation

When a guest in a shelter has been diagnosed with active tuberculosis, the local health department usually carries out an investigation into possible close contacts of the guest. This investigation enables caregivers to determine the spread of infection and identifies those who may need preventive therapy. Investigators use a chest x-ray and PPD skin test to evaluate those who have had the closest contact with the infected person.

Close contacts may include:

- friends;
- family members or coworkers who have spent several hours sharing the same airspace with the infected person;
- people who have slept next to the infected person on any night.

Shelter bedlists can help to identify those sleeping next to the infected guest. If investigators find that many close contacts have become infected, those less closely associated with the infected person may also need evaluation.

If close contacts receive skin tests very soon after their exposure and if these tests are negative, the testing can act as a baseline for a repeat test administered 12 weeks after the exposure. This will help to identify clearly those most recently infected.

Summary

Tuberculosis (TB) is a disease caused by bacteria. The TB organism infects people through the lungs. A person sick with TB can infect others by coughing or sneezing droplets filled with large numbers of living TB germs into the air. However, TB is generally not very infectious.

Once these droplets are in the lungs, the TB bacteria multiply slowly. After a few weeks, the TB organisms spread through the body. During this time, the person may or may not feel sick and cannot spread TB to anyone else. After 4 to 12 weeks, the body usually stops the spread of the bacteria by developing special immunity. Organisms that remain viable are contained in a latent, or "dormant", state by the now-sensitized immune system.

The infection may become active later in life and lead to tuberculosis disease. The PPD skin test helps to identify people who have a dormant TB infection, allowing caregivers to treat them with medicine to kill the bacteria before their infection becomes active. Because TB usually spreads when the infection becomes active, early identification and treatment of dormant infections prevents the spread of TB in the community.

A person who tests positive on the skin test should have a chest x-ray and a physical exam. If the x-ray and exam show no signs or symptoms of TB disease, medications can prevent the onset of disease. Daily doses of anti-TB drugs, usually isoniazid (INH), are taken for 6 to 12 months.

People with active TB disease can have many symptoms and signs of illness. Cough with or without phlegm, fevers, weight loss, sweats at night, swollen lymph glands, and general tiredness can be symptoms of TB. However, many other systemic illnesses show these signs and symptoms as well. If TB is suspected in a shelter staff person or guest, a prompt evaluation by a physician should be encouraged. Treatment of active TB calls for 6 to 24 months of at least 2-3 anti-TB medicines.

Treatment of active TB requires several medications which must be taken regularly for 6-24 months.

Anti-TB drugs work very well in curing TB when taken according to directions. If the patient has difficulty with adhering to a strict daily regimen, a health care worker can give the medicine directly and keep a record of the treatment for that person.

All the anti-TB medicines can have side effects, such as nausea, vomiting, fevers, or skin rashes. The most serious side effects of some of these medicines involve the liver. Signs of jaundice (yellow eyes or skin, tea-colored urine) or pain over the liver (right side of the stomach) are reasons to stop the drug immediately and refer the patient to the physician supervising the TB therapy.

Diagnosis of a case of active TB should lead to an investigation of those who have had close contact with the infected person. The local board of health usually carries out these investigations.

References

Bass JB, Farer LS, Hopewell PC, et al. Diagnostic standards and classification of tuberculosis. *American Review of Respiratory Diseases* 1990; 142: 725-735. (Joint statement of the American Thoracic Society and the Centers for Disease Control.)

Bass JB, Farer LS, Hopewell PC, Jacobs RF. Treatment of tuberculosis and tuberculosis infection in adults and children. *Am Rev Resp Dis* 1986; 134: 355-363. (Joint statement of the American Thoracic Society and the Centers for Disease Control.)

Farer LS. *Tuberculosis: what the physician should know.* American Lung Association and American Thoracic Society; 1986. (Available from local American Lung Association office.)

Upper Respiratory Infections (URI/Common Cold)

Joan Lebow, M.D.

An upper respiratory infection (URI) generally refers to the common cold. Infection involves the air passages above the lungs, including the bronchi, trachea, throat, nose, and sinuses.

Several families of viruses are associated with URIs, including:

- rhinovirus;
- parainfluenza virus;
- respiratory syncytial virus;
- adenovirus;
- coronavirus;
- coxsackievirus.

With so many possible causes, preventive therapies for URIs are difficult to develop. Each year more visits are made to physicians for the common cold than any other illness, and URIs are the leading cause of absenteeism at work and school. However, the illness is self-limiting, resolving on its own without major complications or specific treatment.

Symptoms

Typical symptoms of an upper respiratory infection include nasal discharge and congestion, sneezing, headache, sore or scratchy throat, chills, and general malaise. Nasal secretions may reach 100 times the normal quantity. Some people experience burning eyes and pressure in the ears and sinuses. Other localizing signs may appear in the respiratory tract, including bronchitis, bronchiolitis, and pneumonia.

Adults rarely have fever with URIs, and when present, fever is often less than 101° F (38° C). Children can experience fever as high as 102° F (39° C). URIs last about one week. One in 4 people will have symptoms for 2 weeks or longer.

It is important to differentiate the common cold from a streptococcal infection, or strep throat, in order to institute early treatment against strep throat. In the chapter on strep, it is noted that early treatment can prevent rheumatic fever but *not* glomerulonephritis. People with streptococcal infection may show a higher fever (to 104° F), tender cervical lymph nodes, and large, inflamed tonsils with gray-white exudate. Cough is often absent.

In contrast to URIs, most persons with influenza have an abrupt onset of illness and develop fevers.

Complications

The common cold can rarely lead to secondary bacterial infections requiring antibiotic treatment, such as infections of the sinuses (sinusitis), middle ear (otitis media), and bronchi (bronchitis).

Prevalence and Distribution

URIs are very common because of the large number of causative organisms and their ability to reinfect humans. Children have an average of 6 to 8 colds every

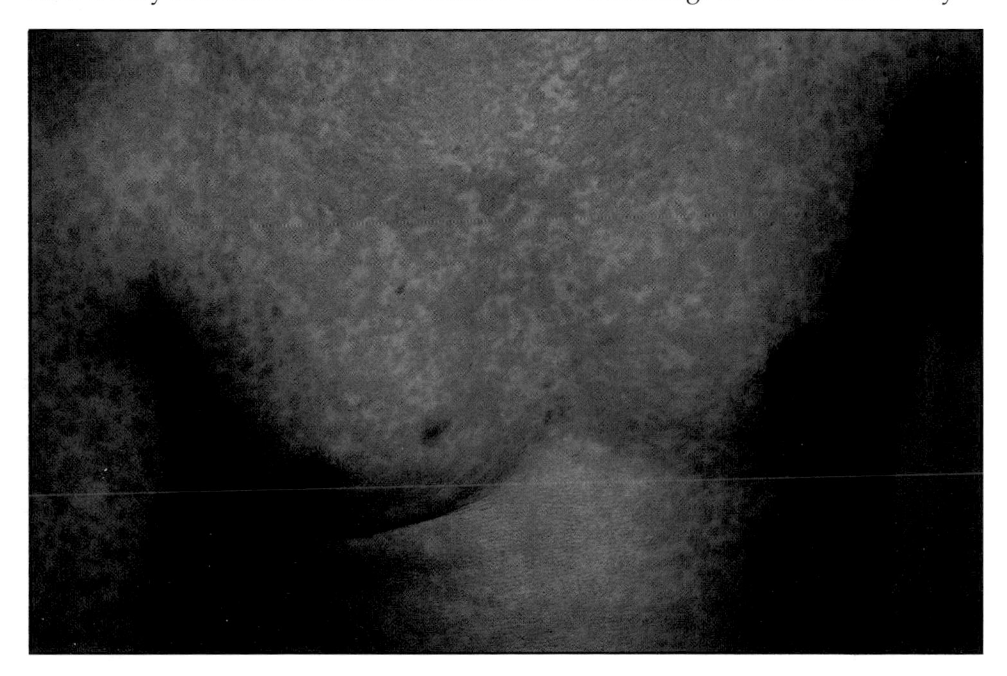

Viral Exanthem. This fine reddish macular rash is diffuse and typical of many viral illnesses. This man developed a URI several days later, which resolved within one week.

year; adults usually have 2 to 4. Adults with children in the home have more colds than those without children, presumably due to the children's exposure to a wide variety of organisms at school. Cigarette smokers have the same incidence of colds as nonsmokers, but their illness is more severe. Children of smokers have a higher incidence of URIs than children of non-smokers.

Transmission

The exact way in which URIs are spread is unclear. Young children may serve as the reservoir of these infections, passing infection to one another at school and into homes. URIs are thought to spread when infected people cough, sneeze, or rub secretions onto their hands. They then pass the disease to others who infect themselves when they rub their eyes or touch their noses or mouths.

Infected people may also sneeze or cough infected droplets into the air. The droplets can then land directly on other people's mucous membranes or on surfaces (such as toys) mouthed by others. Secretions generally lose their infectivity if allowed to dry, but they can stay infectious for hours or even days on skin, nylon, and surfaces such as stainless steel and Formica™.

Diagnosis

Patients usually recognize the typical symptoms of the common cold and diagnose themselves. Clinical examination does not help to identify the specific virus. It is important to rule out streptococcal infection by throat culture.

Direct complications of the URI, such as bacterial bronchitis, sinusitis, and otitis media, need to be identified and treated with the proper antibiotic. Clues to the occurrence of secondary bacterial infections include:

- fevers over 101° F (38° C) in adults and 102° F (39° C) in children;
- green or yellow purulent drainage from the nose accompanied by headache or facial pain;
- cough that produces green or yellow sputum;
- pain in one or both ears (more than a sensation of pressure).

These symptoms often show the need for laboratory tests to confirm the diagnosis. Useful tests include a throat or sputum culture, a sinus or chest x-ray, and a complete blood count (CBC). An elevated white blood count almost always points to something other than the common cold.

Treatment

In the USA, people with URIs spend $600 million annually on preparations that relieve symptoms of the common cold. However, no specific cure exists.

Drinking plenty of fluids will help prevent dehydration from coughing and low-grade temperatures. Bedrest, if the shelter setting permits, can help with the general fatigue that accompanies a cold, hasten recovery, and minimize transmission of the virus.

Saline gargles can reduce the pain of a sore throat. Decongestants such as pseudoephedrine (Sudafed™) are designed to decrease nasal secretions and decrease the swelling of sinus passages. Patients should not take decongestants for more than 3 to 4 days to avoid a rebound of symptoms. Cough preparations containing suppressants such as dextromethorphan, codeine, or terpin hydrate can help reduce a cough. Aspirin or Tylenol™ can help with general achiness.

Prevention and Control

The common cold evades prevention, cure, and treatment. Researchers have tried many methods such as vaccines, nasal interferon, ultraviolet light, and high dose vitamin supplements. None of these studies has yet proven conclusive for the general population.

After many centuries, the common cold still evades prevention, cure, and treament.

The best way to prevent a cold is to avoid contact with the virus. In a shelter, viruses can spread easily among a large group of people. To curtail transmission, shelters should be well-ventilated and guests and staff should have the basic tools of hygiene readily available. For the common cold, this means an adequate supply of tissues and receptacles for their disposal. Both guests and staff should be aware of how the use of tissues can limit the spread of viruses.

Parents and caregivers should discourage children (and other adults) from touching their eyes and noses. Careful handwashing with warm water and soap is also especially important before preparing, serving, or eating food.

Summary

An upper respiratory infection (URI), or the common cold, can come from many different viruses. Colds are most likely spread by coughing and sneezing infected droplets into the air. Others can then inhale these droplets. Transmission also occurs when infected people touch secretions from their noses or throats and then touch other people's hands or other objects and surfaces. Crowded shelters can promote the spread of many infections, especially when children are present.

No treatment exists for the common cold. Certain measures can relieve the symptoms, such as:

- bedrest for fatigue;
- fluids for dehydration;
- saltwater gargling for sore throats;
- medications including Tylenol™ for aching or Sudafed™ for nasal congestion.

People who have fevers over 101° F, coughs that produce sputum, or green or yellow discharge from the nose or throat, should see a health care provider immediately. These are signs of a more severe illness.

Good hygiene can help prevent the spread of cold viruses. Shelters should be well-ventilated and have an adequate supply of tissues, soap, and paper towels for guests and staff.

References

Benenson AS, ed. *Control of Communicable Diseases in Man*. 15th ed. Washington, DC: American Public Health Association; 1990: 367-372.

Dolin R. Common viral respiratory infections. In: Wilson JD, Braunwald E, Isselbacher KJ, Petersdorf RG, Martin JB, Fauci AS, Root RK, eds. *Harrison's Principles of Internal Medicine*. 12th ed. New York: McGraw Hill; 1991: 700-704.

Georges P, Hall CB, Lepow ML, Phillips CF, eds. *The 1988 Red Book: Report of the Committee on Infectious Diseases*. 21st ed. Elk Grove Village, Illinois: American Academy of Pediatrics; 1988: 61-69, 303-304.

Varicella (Chickenpox)

Janet Groth, R.N., M.S.

Varicella, or chickenpox, is caused by the varicella-zoster virus, the same virus responsible for herpes zoster (shingles). The first exposure to this virus occurs most often in childhood and results in chickenpox. A generalized rash with itchy, blister-like lesions appears along with a fever as high as 102°F (39.2° C). The rash crusts over, and the symptoms usually resolve over 4 to 6 days.

After infection with chickenpox, the virus lies dormant in nerve cells and can reactivate years later as herpes zoster. Usually herpes zoster, commonly known as shingles, appears in one limited area such as the thoracic spine or ophthalmic division of the trigeminal nerve. The rash of shingles is also blister-like and itchy, and can be very painful as well.

Although chickenpox is very contagious, it is usually a mild illness in children. Adults can have a more severe course accompanied by extreme fatigue, muscle aches, joint pain, and headaches. Adults have a higher risk of complications from chickenpox, primarily viral pneumonia. Both adults and children commonly develop bacterial infections of the skin lesions. Rarely, encephalitis can occur.

In rare cases, varicella infection early in pregnancy, particularly during the first and early second trimester, can lead to severe congenital manifestations in the child, involving the central nervous system, skin, extremities, and eyes. Children exposed to varicella in utero can develop herpes zoster at a young age without having previous varicella. If a mother is ill with varicella during the period from 5 days before until 2 days after delivery, the newborn risks developing severe generalized chickenpox, with a mortality rate as high as 30 percent. Death is most often due to pneumonia.

Varicella infection in an adult or child with a poor immune system can be a very serious event. The lesions can be extensive and healing time prolonged. The infection can become diffuse and advanced, a syndrome known as "progressive varicella", characterized by a continued eruption of vesicles and high fevers. The lungs, liver, kidneys, pancreas, brain, and meninges can be affected.

About 1 in 5 cases of Reye's syndrome, a progressive swelling of the brain along with liver complications, has been attributed to chickenpox, specifically with the concomitant use of aspirin for fever control.

Prevalence and Distribution

Almost all adults in the USA have a history of chickenpox infection. In urban settings, about 3 of 4 children under 15 years of age and 9 of 10 young adults have antibodies to chickenpox.

Chickenpox is more common in late winter and early spring.

Transmission

Immunity after varicella infection is usually lifelong. The virus can only be spread from person to person, usually when someone who has never been exposed to the virus shares breathing space with an infected person or touches the drainage from chickenpox or zoster lesions. Contact with secretions of the nose and throat can also spread chickenpox as well as contact with contaminated items such as towels, sheets, and clothing.

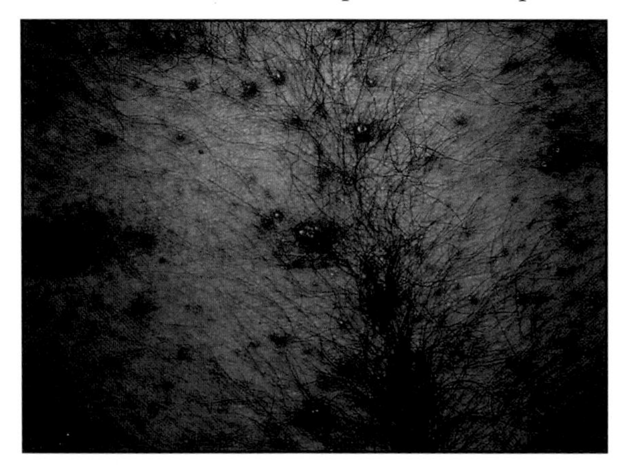

Chickenpox. An itchy rash on the abdomen of this patient shows the lesions of chickenpox in many stages, a characteristic of this virus. Note the blisters appear on a reddened base, or areola.

People with chickenpox are infectious for as many as 5 days (but more likely 2 days) before, until 6 days after, the appearance of the rash. Generally people with no prior history of exposure will show symptoms anytime from 10 days after the first day of presumed exposure until 21 days after the last day of possible exposure, or one incubation period. This latter period of 21 days can stretch to 28 days if the person has received varicella zoster immune globulin (see below). Patients with poor immune systems and generalized varicella are able to spread the virus for as long as new lesions are forming.

The drainage from zoster lesions cannot cause zoster. Contact with the blisters of zoster or shingles can spread chickenpox to those who have never had the virus.

Diagnosis

The itchy, blister-like rash characteristic of chickenpox is the easiest way to identify the disease. The vesicle is usually surrounded by a red areola. Lesions often start on the scalp or trunk and may spread to the face and proximal limbs. Lesions can appear in the mucous membranes of the conjunctiva or oropharynx, particularly in adults.

The lesions may continue to form over a period of 3 to 5 days; they will not all appear at the same stage of development. This is an important consideration when trying to distinguish chickenpox from impetigo, in which the lesions are uniform in appearance.

Chickenpox can also be confused with other forms of disseminated herpes viruses, including zoster and simplex.

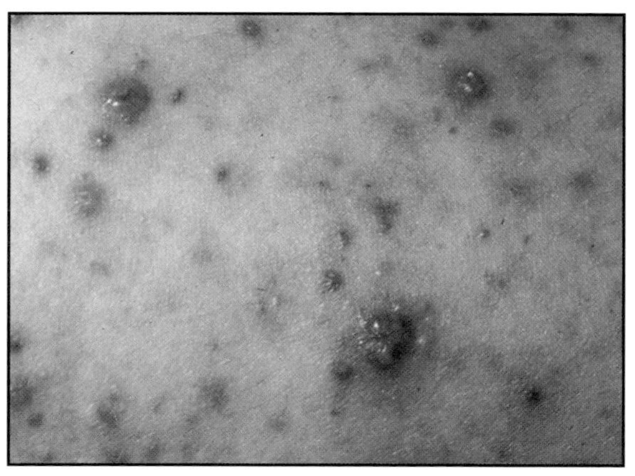

Chickenpox. Typical rash of varicella, again showing blisters in several stages. This rash usually begins on the trunk or scalp and spreads to the limbs and face. These blisters will continue to form over a period of 3-5 days. Persons can be infectious from 5 days before this rash appears until 6 days after its appearance.

During the first 3 to 4 days of the rash, microscopic examination of scrapings from the lesions can demonstrate the presence of multinucleated giant cells, a finding typical for any of the herpes virus family.

To determine a person's immunity to varicella, blood tests known as the ELISA or FAMA tests can reveal the existence of antibodies to the virus, providing proof of prior infection. If antibodies are present, the person has been infected in the past and cannot be reinfected.

Treatment

Fever and itching are common complaints of patients with uncomplicated chickenpox. Acetominophen (Tylenol™) should be used for fever. Aspirin and salicylate-containing products should be avoided due to a possible association between aspirin (salicylate) use during varicella illness and Reye's syndrome.

Daily cleansing of the lesions with soap and water is recommended to prevent infection of the lesions. Calamine lotion may provide relief from itching. Clipping of the nails should be encouraged to minimize damage to the skin from scratching.

Chickenpox infection in people with poor immune systems may require more aggressive therapy in the form of acyclovir, an antiviral drug. Acyclovir has been shown to lessen the severity of illness in immunocompromised children when started early during the disease.

Prevention and Control

In Massachusetts, as in most states, cases of varicella must be reported to the local health department which can provide information and support concerning prevention and control measures.

When a case of chickenpox occurs in a shelter, all persons should be evaluated for their risk of infection. Close contacts are those who have lived in the same house or shelter as the person with chickenpox, or those who have been indoors with the infected person for more than an hour. All close contacts should be interviewed concerning their chickenpox history and other factors that would make them candidates for varicella-zoster immune globulin, or VZIG.

VZIG is a preparation containing high levels of antibodies to the chickenpox virus. Prepared from the plasma of normal blood donors, VZIG may not prevent disease, but it can lessen the severity of illness. VZIG must be given within 96 hours of exposure to be effective. Results of blood tests for antibody titers in exposed individuals usually take longer than 3 to 4 days and therefore are not very helpful in the decision to use VZIG.

VZIG should be given to anyone exposed who has never had the disease and is at high risk for complications. VZIG can often be obtained from local chapters of the American Red Cross, or local and state health departments.

Candidates for VZIG include:

- children or adults with immune system problems;
- adults (older than 15) with no prior history of chickenpox ;
- pregnant women with a negative or unclear varicella history;
- infants born to mothers infected from 5 days before until 2 days after delivery;
- premature infants (28 weeks gestation or more) whose mothers lack a prior history of chickenpox;
- premature infants (less than 28 weeks gestation or 1,000 gms) regardless of the mother's history.

If a pregnant woman with an unclear chickenpox history becomes exposed close to term, obtaining varicella titers before administering VZIG is recommended. Titers can clarify whether the newborn will be at risk if born during the mother's incubation period.

The exact duration that VZIG recipients are protected against chickenpox is unknown. Another dose is indicated if a second exposure occurs to a susceptible person more than 3 weeks after receiving VZIG and the person has not yet shown symptoms.

Staff members and guests with a prior history of chickenpox do not risk re-infection. To reduce anxiety and confusion, each staff person should know his or her chickenpox history before cases appear in a shelter.

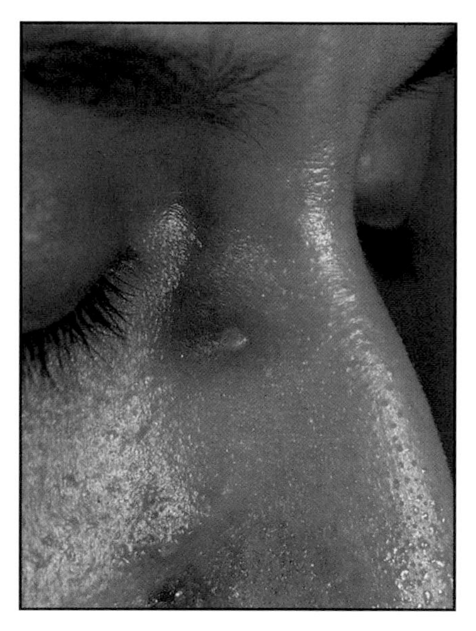

Chickenpox. A typical vesicle (blister) on a red areola. History and physical examination can usually distinguish this rash from that of other herpes viruses, including zoster or simplex.

An experimental, live varicella vaccine has proven effective in protecting children from infection, but it is not licensed in the USA at this time.

Special considerations for family shelters

When a case of chickenpox occurs in a family shelter, all new guests should be questioned about a history of chickenpox before admission to the shelter. From the first day of the rash until 21 days after the last possible exposure, no one should be admitted to the shelter who has never had chickenpox. This will protect unexposed individuals and hopefully will contain the outbreak within one incubation period.

In some situations, admissions should be screened for 2 incubation periods, such as when the staff cannot be sure that all susceptible guests and staff have been exposed from the initial case. Screening people with unknown histories by one of the blood tests for immunity is an option if time permits. If an exposed guest has received VZIG, the incubation period should be extended to 28 days after the last possible exposure to the first case.

The incubation period also serves as a reminder not to discharge a guest who has no history of chickenpox to other group settings until the time has elapsed. If someone is exposed to an active case but has no history of chickenpox, he or she may spread the virus to another setting during the incubation period.

Staff and guests should always wear gloves when handling linen and clothing of guests who have draining lesions of chickenpox or zoster. Everyone should be encouraged to wash her or his hands thoroughly following any contact with soiled items or draining lesions.

Special considerations for adult shelters

If an infected person cannot be isolated from other guests, separate accommodations should be sought. Isolation is only important until the lesions crust over and form scabs. If housing with an immune relative or friend is not available, an acute care facility may be another choice. We strongly recommend that any guest sent to alternative housing be closely followed for signs of complications of chickenpox.

Close contacts may be identified through bedlists and by interviews with the infected person. VZIG is recommended for all close contacts who have no history of chickenpox. Clearly, in the larger adult shelters it may be difficult to do a thorough investigation. Those at particularly high risk should then be the priority, such as people known to have HIV infection or other immune system problems.

Infected children or adults may have exposed others outside the shelter in day care, school, or work. Shelter staff and health care providers should work closely with the local board of health to help identify all other persons at risk.

Summary

Chickenpox, or varicella, is caused by the varicella-zoster virus, a virus that also causes shingles (herpes zoster). Chickenpox most commonly occurs in young children. Normally, the virus causes an itchy, blister-like rash that spreads over the entire body. A fever of up to 102° F (39.2° C) is also common. Both fever and rash usually disappear over 4 to 6 days. The virus then "goes to sleep" on nerve endings. It may reappear years later as shingles.

Chickenpox can spread when an infected person breathes germs into the air, or an uninfected person comes into contact with the fluid from open blisters of the rash. People who have had chickenpox as children cannot be infected again.

In most cases, the symptoms of chickenpox are easy to treat. Itching can be relieved with calamine lotion and cool baths. Fever can be controlled with acetominophen (Tylenol™). Aspirin and aspirin-containing products should be avoided because they can have dangerous side effects when used for chickenpox symptoms. Always consult a doctor or a nurse for proper diagnosis and treatment.

The illness is usually mild in young children who have no other health problems. However, adults and people with other medical problems can have very serious complications from the disease, such as infections of the lung or brain. Pregnant women and their babies are at particular risk.

Shelters and other places where many people live closely together promote the spread of chickenpox. Shelter staff should discuss the potential dangers of exposure with a health provider familiar with the shelter. The local board of health should be contacted. This agency can help to assess the risk to guests and staff in addition to instituting control measures to prevent further spread within the shelter.

References

Brunnell PA. Varicella-zoster infections. In: Feigin RD, Cherry JD, eds. *Textbook of Pediatric Infectious Diseases*. 2nd ed. Philadelphia: WB Saunders; 1987: 1602-1607.

Esmonde TF, Herdman G, Anderson G. Chickenpox pneumonia: an association with pregnancy. *Thorax* 1989; 44(10): 812-815.

Georges P, Hall CB, Lepow ML, Phillips CF, eds. *The 1988 Red Book: Report of the Committee on Infectious Diseases*. 21st ed. Elk Grove Village, Illinois: American Academy of Pediatrics; 1988: 456-461.

Hockberger RS, Rothstein RJ. Varicella pneumonia in adults: a spectrum of disease. *Ann of Emerg Med* 1986; 15(8): 931-934.

Jura E, Chadwick EG, Josephs SH. Varicella-zoster virus infection in children infected with human immunodeficiency virus. *Ped Inf Dis J* 1989; 8(9): 586-590.

Weller TH. Varicella and herpes zoster: changing concepts of the natural history, control, and importance of a not-so-benign virus. *N Engl J Med* 1983; 309: 1362-1368, 1434-1440.

Diarrhea

Joel L. Bass, M.D.

Diarrhea can be a persistent problem in any crowded setting, especially with diapered children, communal bathrooms, and shared eating facilities. Shelters are particularly prone to outbreaks of diarrhea because food management may involve many different people with varying degrees of training in safe food handling. Shelters commonly receive donations of prepared food without any information about the management of the food prior to its arrival. Part Five discusses this topic in some detail.

Fortunately, many steps to prevent and control the incidence of diarrhea can be taken if the staff understands how the illnesses are spread and all those in the shelter follow a few simple guidelines.

Causes

Dozens of infectious agents can cause diarrhea, including:

- viruses (Norwalk, Norwalk-like, and rotavirus);
- bacteria (*Campylobacter, Salmonella, Shigella, Staphylococcus, Yersinia* and *E. coli*);
- parasites (*Giardia, Cryptosporidium*).

Furthermore, any child or adult recovering from infectious diarrhea may have damaged the lining of the intestine to such a degree that chronic diarrhea results. At this point, the infection is no longer the primary concern, and focus should shift to the malabsorption of dietary carbohydrates that can lead to malnutrition.

Symptoms

Infectious agents in all three categories can cause diarrhea of varying degrees of severity and duration. Symptoms often overlap from one type of diarrhea to another. Diarrhea caused by viruses tends to be more self-limiting than that resulting from bacteria or parasites. Parasites are apt to produce subacute or chronic diarrhea, while bacterial diarrhea is often an acute illness. Needless to say, exceptions to these generalizations are common.

Gastrointestinal infection may produce a range of symptoms from mild to life-threatening. Mild symptoms include an increase in the frequency of stools, a softening or liquifying of the texture of stools, abdominal cramping, gas, nausea, vomiting, weakness, and fever. Severe diarrhea produces watery, voluminous, or explosive stools, which can lead to dehydration. Stools may contain blood or mucous depending on the specific cause of diarrhea.

Complications

Young children and infants are at the greatest risk of rapid deterioration because of the dehydration brought on by acute diarrhea. Caregivers should closely monitor any young child with diarrhea to guard against dehydration.

The signs of severe dehydration are:

- a decrease in the production of tears;
- no urine output for 8 hours;
- depressed fontanelle (in infants);
- dry mouth, tongue, and skin.

Anyone with these signs, particularly an infant or child, needs medical attention immediately.

Young children, the elderly, and those chronically ill also risk systemic infection from certain infectious diarrheas such as *Salmonella* and *E. coli*.

Prevalence

Although scant information is known about the prevalence of diarrheal illness in shelters, experience suggests that it is widespread. One study of shelters for battered women and their children found that 9 of the 73 facilities reviewed had outbreaks of diarrhea involving more than 10 people (Gross and Rosenberg, 1987).

Transmission

Infectious diarrhea spreads directly or indirectly from person to person. If staff and guests do not wash their hands carefully after using the toilet or changing a diaper, an infected person can easily contaminate food, surfaces, or objects with stool that then contacts the hands or mouths of others. The amount of stool needed to cause disease varies with different organisms.

Diarrheal germs commonly spread when people are preparing and serving food and when children, particularly those in diapers, play together.

Diarrhea germs commonly spread when people are preparing and serving food and when children, particularly those in diapers, play together.

Areas within shelters conducive to the spread of organisms include:

- communal bathrooms;
- kitchens;
- changing tables.

Some persons with bacterial or parasitic infection may remain asymptomatic. However, these carriers can still transmit the disease to others.

Food management

The primary focus of this chapter is the spread of diarrhea from an infected person to other people. Many foods, particularly dairy and meat products, are inherently prone to bacterial growth and can cause diarrheal outbreaks. If food is properly bought, stored, prepared, and served, the risk of illness is minimal. For more information concerning safe food management and handling, refer to Part Five on page 219.

Diagnosis

Different causes of diarrhea are indistinguishable by observation alone. To determine the specific cause of illness, a stool culture or smear is necessary. Diarrhea happens very frequently in crowded settings, and the decision to culture the stool is based on several factors. In adult shelters, symptoms of diarrhea that have lasted three days or more or are severe enough to risk dehydration warrant a stool culture to rule out common bacteria such as *Campylobacter* or *Salmonella.*

Family shelters are comparable to day care settings, which often experience *Shigella* and *Giardia* infections. In family shelters, health providers should collect stool specimens for both bacteria and parasites in symptomatic people. Once a child or an adult has been diagnosed with a bacterial or parasitic illness, all other symptomatic people in the shelter who share toilet facilities or have a common food source should have specimens sent for analysis.

Treatment

Specific treatment of diarrhea will vary depending on culture results. People with bacterial or parasitic diarrhea always need medical supervision. Some general observations about supportive care follow.

Infants and children

An infant with diarrhea can dehydrate rapidly and the condition may be life-threatening. Any child under 12 months of age with more than three episodes of diarrhea or unusually loose stools per day, especially if accompanied by vomiting or fever, requires a prompt medical evaluation.

Most cases of diarrhea are mild and require only temporary suspension of solid food and milk. For the first 12 to 24 hours of treatment, people with diarrhea should have clear liquids. Commercial oral solutions (e.g., Pedialyte™, Resol™) are preferable to traditional clear liquids (e.g., juice, flat ginger ale, Jell-O™), which may be deficient in electrolyte components. After the first day with clear liquids, those with diarrhea should resume regular feeding, beginning with a bland diet (rice cereal, bananas, applesauce, and toast). Lactose intolerance can commonly follow a diarrheal illness and last from 2 to 6 weeks. Soy-based, lactose-free formula may be recommended as a substitute for infants who develop this problem.

Careful handwashing with soap and warm water is the best way to prevent the spread of diarrhea.

Prevention and Control

In Massachusetts, as in many other states, the law requires that outbreaks of diarrhea illness or episodes of infectious diarrhea be reported to the local health department.

For an overview of the prevention of diarrhea, please refer to the General Guidelines on pages 33-36 and the Specific Guidelines for illnesses transmitted by the fecal-oral route on pages 38-40.

Specific prevention and control measures will depend upon the population in the shelter and the physical arrangements of the building. In the unusual situation where resources and circumstances permit, screening of all shelter residents for stool pathogens prior to entry may be helpful (Bass, Brennan, 1990). Shelter residents with poor immune systems may be at special risk during outbreaks and should see a health provider.

Summary

Diarrhea can be a common problem in crowded places such as shelters. The presence of diapered children, the use of shared bathrooms and kitchens, and inappropriate food management heighten the likelihood of diarrheal outbreaks in shelters. While an episode of diarrhea is usually short-lived, it can be very serious, particularly in young children and people with other chronic illness.

Diarrhea is spread when a person gets infected feces on the hands and then touches other hands, food, or mouthed objects. Some people can carry germs that cause diarrhea but have no symptoms themselves.

Careful handwashing with soap and warm water after using the bathroom or diapering a child is the best way to prevent the spread of diarrhea. Questions regarding episodes of diarrhea should be brought to a health provider. The local board of health and appropriate health agencies are also sources of information regarding the control of diarrhea.

Contact a health provider whenever:

- an adult has had diarrhea lasting three or more days;
- a child has diarrhea accompanied by vomiting or fever;
- a person with diarrhea appears dehydrated;
- more than 2 people from a family shelter have diarrhea simultaneously;
- the same organism has been identified in 2 different cases of diarrhea within 2 weeks in the same shelter.

References

Abramowicz M, ed. Drugs for parasitic infections. *The Medical Letter of Drugs and Therapeutics* 1988; 30: 18-22.

Bass JL, Brennan P, Mehta KA, Kodzis S. Pediatric problems in a suburban shelter for homeless families. *Pediatrics* 1990; 85(1): 33-38.

Gross TP, Rosenberg ML. Shelters for battered women and their children: an under-recognized source of communicable disease transmission. *Am J Pub Health* 1987; 77(9): 1198-1201.

Isolation and quarantine regulations. Massachusetts Department of Public Health; 1985.

Georges P, Hall CB, Lepow ML, Phillips CF, eds. *The 1988 Red Book: Report of the Committee on Infectious Diseases.* 21st ed. Elk Grove Village, Illinois: American Academy of Pediatrics; 1988.

Mandell GL, Douglas RG, Bennett JE, eds. *Principles and Practice of Infectious Diseases.* 2nd ed. New York: Churchill Livingstone; 1990.

Campylobacter

Symptoms:	Diarrhea, fever, abdominal pain, sometimes blood in stool, nausea and vomiting.
Onset:	1 to 7 days after exposure.
Infectious period:	2 to 3 weeks without treatment; 2 to 3 days with therapy.
Source:	Contact with feces of infected persons, exposure to feces of infected household pets or wild animals, including birds; improperly cooked or stored foods of animal origin.
Treatment:	Erythromycin, doxycyline, ciprofloxacin (*not* in children).
Infected person:	Special precautions for all those who are symptomatic.* No food handling until the symptoms have resolved and 2 stool cultures taken 48 hours apart are negative.**
Close Contacts:	No food handling by symptomatic persons until symptoms have resolved and 2 stool cultures taken 48 hours apart are negative.** In addition, kitchen workers who have had close contact to the infected person, regardless of symptoms, should avoid food handling until 2 stool cultures taken 48 hours apart after the last possible exposure are negative.

Cryptosporidium

Symptoms:	Frequent, watery diarrhea. Can be prolonged (up to 20 episodes per day) and lead to weight loss and malnutrition. Can become chronic and/or disseminate in persons with poor immune systems.
Onset:	1 to 12 days.
Infectious period:	Unknown.
Source:	Animals, humans (easily spread in day care centers), and water.
Treatment:	Usually supportive in otherwise healthy persons. Experimental antibiotic treatment is available for people with poor immune systems.
Infected person:	No food handling until all symptoms are gone.
Close contacts:	Evaluate stool of all who are symptomatic. Avoid food handling until asymptomatic.

Chart 4. Infectious Diarrhea: Guidelines for Public Health Nurses and Providers

Chart prepared by Janet Groth, R.N., M.S.

Sources:

Isolation and quarantine regulations. *Massachusetts Department of Public Health; 1985.*

Georges P, Hall CB, Lepow ML, Phillips CF, eds. The 1988 Red Book: Report of the Committee on Infectious Diseases. *21st ed. Elk Grove Village, Illinois: American Academy of Pediatrics; 1988.*

Mandell GL, Douglas RG, Bennett JE, eds. Principles and Practice of Infectious Diseases *2nd ed. New York: Churchill Livingstone; 1990.*

Giardia

Symptoms:	Often none. May have intermittent bouts of diarrhea, chronic diarrhea with malabsorbtion, and/or anemia. Children may show failure to thrive.
Onset:	1 to 4 weeks.
Infectious Period:	Variable; until all cysts are gone.
Source:	Infected humans, animals, contaminated water. Commonly spread in day care. May also be spread through oral-anal sexual practices.
Treatment:	*Quinicrine Hcl (Atabrine)* is 85 to 95% effective but bitter and difficult to give to children. Can cause GI upset, and occasionally jaundice. *Metronidazole (Flagyl)* is 80-95% effective but not approved for use in Giardiasis in the USA. Possibly carcinogenic. Little data available on safety in children. Causes a metallic taste as well as nausea, dizziness, and headache. Use with alcohol can cause a disulfiramlike (Antabuse) reaction. *Furazolidone (Furoxone)* is 70 to 80% effective. Liquid suspension is available. Generally the treatment of choice for young children. Can cause GI distress, headache, and dizziness. Can likewise cause a disulfiram-like reaction when taken with alcohol. *Paramomycin (Humatin)* is 50 to 70% effective. Has been used for pregnant women because the drug is not measurably absorbed from the intestines. All of the above drugs may have to be repeated in 2 weeks in the event of therapy failure.
Infected Person:	Special precautions for all those who are symptomatic.* All family members should be evaluated with stool smears for ova and parasites regardless of symptoms.**
Close contacts:	In a family shelter, an initial smear for ova and parasites should be done on persons who are symptomatic. If the problem persists, smears for ova and parasites should be done on all persons living or working in the shelter. Infected persons should not handle food until symptoms have resolved and 2 stool cultures taken 48 hours apart are negative.** Kitchen workers, regardless of symptoms, with contact to an infected person, should avoid food handling until 2 stool cultures taken 48 hours apart and after the last possible exposure are negative.

Salmonella

Symptoms:	Diarrhea, cramping, fever, headache, nausea, sometimes vomiting. May be complicated by bacteremia and/or focal infection, or a multisystem disorder called enteric fever. Asymptomatic in some, constipation in some, especially with enteric fever.
Onset:	6 to 72 hours; 3 to 60 days with enteric fever.

Infectious period:	Until the organisms are no longer excreted; can be weeks or even years in chronic carriers. Antibiotic therapy can prolong carriage.
Source:	Humans, household and farm animals, improperly prepared or stored foods, contaminated water and food.
Treatment:	Usually none for uncomplicated cases of gastroenteritis. Children less than 3 months old, people at risk for invasive disease, and persons with *Salmonella typhii* should be treated with ampicillin or TMP-SMX (if the organism shows sensitivity in cultures). Ciprofloxacin should be used for strains resistant to ampicillin and TMP-SMX, although this antibiotic should be avoided in children.
Infected Person:	Special precautions for all who are symptomatic.* No food handling until symptoms have resolved and 2 stool cultures taken 48 hours apart are negative.**
Close Contacts:	No food handling by symptomatic close contacts until symptoms have resolved and 2 cultures taken 48 hours apart are negative.** In addition, kitchen workers (regardless of symptoms) with contact to an infected persons should avoid food handling until 2 cultures taken 48 hours apart and after the last possible exposure are negative.

Shigella

Symptoms:	Mild to severe diarrhea, the latter being associated with sudden onset of fever, headache and possibly vomiting. Stools may contain blood or mucous.
Onset:	1 to 7 days.
Infectious period:	Until no longer passed in the stool, usually no longer than 4 weeks. Antibiotics can shorten this period to less than 1 week.
Source:	Humans are the only known source. Crowding, particularly in setting with few handwashing facilities, can promote spread. Eating contaminated food or water, or mouthing infected objects can also spread *shigella*. Few organisms are needed to cause infection.
Treatment:	Antibiotics are recommended in most cases. Generally TMP-SMX, ampicillin, or ciprofloxacin (not in children) are effective. However it is important to check the sensitivity pattern of the organism.
Infected Person:	Special precautions for all those who are symptomatic.* No food handling until symptoms have resolved and 2 stool cultures taken 48 hours apart are negative.**
Close Contacts:	No food handling by symptomatic close contacts until 2 cultures taken 48 hours apart are negative and symptoms have resolved.** Kitchen workers (regardless of symptoms) with close contact to an infected person should avoid food handling until 2 stool cultures taken 48 hours apart and after the last possible exposure are negative.

Staphylococcus

Symptoms:	Abrupt onset of severe cramps, vomiting and diarrhea. Fever is not usually associated with this infection.
Onset:	Very short, 30 minutes to 7 hours.
Infectious period:	Unable to be transmitted by the sick person. Can be spread to food by *Staphylococcal* carriers until organisms have cleared from site of colonization.
Source:	Usually by food handlers with staphylococci colonized in sites including normal skin, lesions (often on the face or hands), nose and throat.
Treatment:	Supportive.
Infected Person:	No control measures necessary. Review of foods eaten within 8 hours of onset should occur. If eaten in shelter, evaluate food handlers for lesions, poor hygiene.
Close contacts:	No restrictions.

Yersinia

Symptoms:	Fever, headache, watery diarrhea (blood, mucous, WBCs commonly in stool), abdominal pain. Can cause a syndrome resembling acute appendicitis in children. Arthritis, ostromyelitis, septicemia, abcesses of the liver and spleen and skin rashes have been reported in certain types (*Y. enterocolitica*).
Onset:	1 to 3 weeks.
Infectious period:	For as long as the organism is excreted (up to 6 weeks).
Source:	Household and wild animals, contaminated water and food.
Treatment:	TMP-SMX, chloramphenicol, aminoglycosides.
Infected Person:	Special precautions for all those who are symptomatic.* No food handling until symptoms have resolved and 2 stool cultures taken 48 hours apart are negative.**
Close contacts:	No food handling by symptomatic persons until 2 stool cultures taken 48 hours apart are negative and symptoms have resolved. Kitchen workers (regardless of symptoms) with contact to an infected person should avoid food handling until 2 stool cultures taken 48 hours apart and after the last possible exposure are negative.

* See Specific Guidelines in Part Two, pages 38-40.

** If antibiotics have been taken, stool cultures should be obtained at least 48 hours after discontinuing therapy.

Hepatitis A

Lori Fantry, M.D.

Hepatitis A, once called short incubation or infectious hepatitis, is a viral infection that attacks the liver. Infection with hepatitis A leads to symptoms that are very similar to other types of hepatitis. Hepatitis A is rarely fatal and has never been shown to lead to chronic liver disease. However, it is a significant cause of illness and suffering in many parts of the world, including the United States.

The clinical course of hepatitis A varies from person to person. Some people, especially infants less than two years old, never develop symptoms after infection. Older people have a higher frequency of symptoms and tend to get a more severe illness.

Hepatitis A Illness

Symptoms usually develop within 28 days after exposure. This period of incubation may be as short as 15 days or as long as 50 days. Initial symptoms usually include headache, weakness, fever, fatigue, poor appetite, nausea, vomiting, and muscle aches. Diarrhea occurs more commonly in children. Cough, sore throat, coryza (runny nose and eyes), and arthralgias (joint aches) have been reported in some outbreaks. As with other types of hepatitis, hepatitis A may alter taste and smell. Some infections can be mild (especially in children), with few if any symptoms and without jaundice.

After several days to a week, the initial symptoms usually begin to diminish. At this point, the infected person may develop yellow skin and eyes, dark urine, light stools, itching, and abdominal pain. Weight loss may continue throughout the illness.

Most people with hepatitis A recover completely within 1 to 2 months. People then cannot transmit the virus to others and are immune to further infection with hepatitis A. They can still become ill with other types of hepatitis.

Prevalence

Hepatitis A is common in all parts of the world. In the Third World, or developing countries, overcrowding and poor sanitation result in a very high incidence of the disease. Western states within the USA (Washington, Oregon, Idaho, California, and Nevada) have more reported cases than other areas of the country.

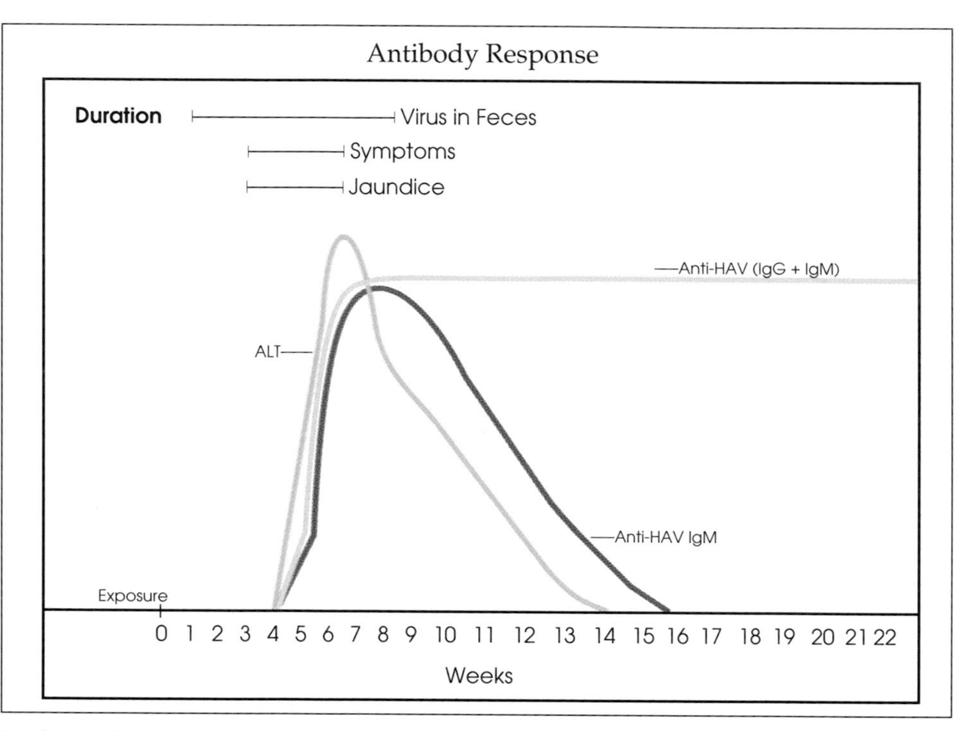

Chart 5. A Guide to the Clinical Signs and Serology of Hepatitis A Infection.

Viral shedding of HAV is present in the stool about two weeks after exposure, followed in 1-2 weeks by a rise in the liver enzyme ALT and the appearance of jaundice. One month after exposure, the IgM antibody to HAV can usually be measured in the serum. The longterm IgG antibody appears within weeks and remains for years, despite the disappearance of IgM antibody to HAV after several months.

(Chart adapted from the brochure "Serodiagnostic Assessment of Acute Viral Hepatitis" published by Abbott Diagnostics Educational Services.)

In the United States, approximately 40 percent of the adult population has been infected with hepatitis A at some time in their lives. Spread within a family or day care center is common. Certain sexual practices that involve oral-anal contact also contribute to the spread of this infection.

Transmission

Hepatitis A primarily spreads by way of infected stool. The stool can contaminate the hands of the infected person, who then transmits the virus by touching other people, food, or other objects which are then put in the mouth. Transmission is often facilitated by poor personal hygiene, lack of sanitation, and intimate sexual contact. Often, the person transmitting the virus cannot be identified. The search for the source of infection frequently leads to a young child who displays only minimal symptoms.

Stools of infected people are infectious about 2 weeks before and 1 week after the appearance of yellow skin (jaundice). The most infectious period is before jaundice appears.

Hepatitis A can also spread through contaminated food and water. The most common sources of infection are shellfish, uncooked fruits and vegetables, and milk. Each outbreak often involves many people.

Glossary

Serologic Markers

Anti-HAV IgM	**Antibody (IgM) to Hepatitis A Antigen (anti-HAV IgM).** The IgM antibody is only present during the recent acute phase of infection. This marker is useful in confirming a recent hepatitis A infection.
Anti-HAV	**Antibody (IgG and IgM) to Hepatitis A Antigen.** Detects total antibody to HAV. Indicator of recent acute as well as past infection. Useful in confirming previous exposure and immunity to hepatitis A.
ALT	**Alanine Aminotransferase.** (Also called SGPT). This enzyme increases in the bloodstream when liver cells are irritated or injured, especially by infectious agents such as viruses, drugs such as alcohol, or medications such as isoniazid (INH).

Chart 6. Serologic Markers of Hepatitis A.

(Adapted from the brochure "Serodiagnostic Assessment of Acute Viral Hepatitis" published by Abbott Diagnostics Educational Services.)

Direct infection through contact with the blood of an infected person is very rare. The virus remains in the blood stream only briefly. Injection drug users risk infection more than others, but poor hygiene rather than infected blood may be the primary cause of infection.

Unborn children are not at risk for hepatitis A unless the mother is jaundiced at the time of delivery. Breastfeeding is not contraindicated.

Urine, saliva, breast milk, and other body fluids do not transmit hepatitis A virus. Once a person has recovered from an active infection, he or she is no longer at risk for reinfection or for carrying the virus.

Diagnosis

The first sign of infection in a group setting is usually jaundice in an adult, as most infected young children do not show symptoms. A confirmed diagnosis depends on testing for the presence of hepatitis A antibody in the blood, specifically HAV IgM, the early, short-lived antibody to the hepatitis A virus (HAV). HAV IgM will remain detectable in the serum for 4-6 months after the onset of illness. This is a simple test that most medical laboratories or hospitals can perform. Blood tests for hepatitis A IgG antibody, the late, long-lived, and protective antibody to HAV, can determine whether or not a person has a history of hepatitis A.

Treatment

No specific treatment is available for hepatitis A. Certain measures help alleviate the symptoms. Most people do not require hospitalization. Bedrest may provide some comfort. If the person is having frequent vomiting, caregivers should watch for signs of dehydration.

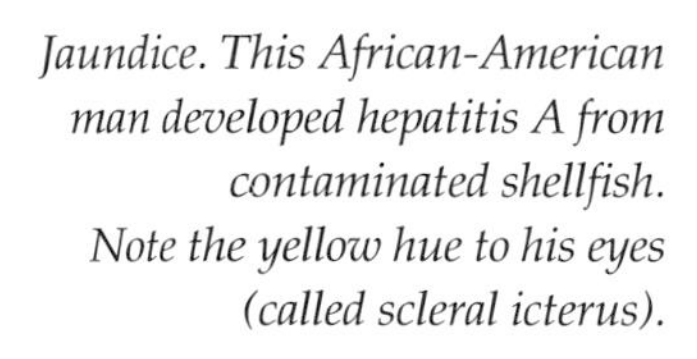

Jaundice. This African-American man developed hepatitis A from contaminated shellfish. Note the yellow hue to his eyes (called scleral icterus).

Infected people should avoid alcohol and drugs (legal and illegal) broken down by the liver. For this reason, aspirin is a safe alternative to Tylenol™ for fever and muscle aches, but should not be given to children less than 18 years of age because of a small risk of a liver-brain disorder called Reye's syndrome.

Prevention and Control

Basic Precaution Measures

Many states (including Massachusetts) require that all cases of hepatitis A be reported to the local health department or appropriate health agency.

The early symptoms of hepatitis A are similar to many other diseases and are hard to recognize until jaundice appears. As noted above, jaundice may never arise in some cases. Simple preventive measures are the best insurance against infection.

Thorough handwashing is always an essential part of preventing the spread of infection, particularly before preparing or serving food and after diapering or using the bathroom.

Those with hepatitis A do not require any special type of isolation. Infected people who regularly handle food should avoid tasks that require direct contact with food until 1 week after the appearance of jaundice.

Caregivers should wear gloves when handling the stools of infected people, and hands should be washed after removing the gloves.

Exposed Individuals

An immunization containing antibodies, called immunoglobulins or IG, against the hepatitis A virus can limit the spread of the virus. When given to close contacts within 2 weeks of exposure, the immunization will lessen the severity of illness and, in some cases, totally prevent clinical signs and symptoms.

Close contacts include:

- those who have eaten food prepared by the infected person during the week prior to and the week after the appearance of jaundice;
- kitchen workers who have worked with an infected food handler during the two weeks before jaundice;
- sexual contacts of the infected person.

Any food handler who develops symptoms of hepatitis A should be removed from food handling duties until evaluated by a health provider. The person should not return to work until hepatitis A has been ruled out and the symptoms have resolved.

Whenever there is a case of hepatitis A in a family shelter with children in diapers, all children, parents, and staff should receive IG. All new admissions to the shelter during the 6 weeks after diagnosis should also receive IG.

In most cases, when a person receives IG and also develops hepatitis A, the symptoms will be very mild. If no symptoms appear, only a blood test can determine a person's immunity to future exposures to hepatitis A. Side effects with this immunization other than pain and tenderness at the injection site are extremely rare. IG has never been reported to transmit human immunodeficiency virus (HIV), the virus responsible for the acquired immunodeficiency syndrome (AIDS).

Immunization against hepatitis A before exposure is recommended for those traveling to developing countries. The length of protection depends on the dose administered. IG is free to Massachusetts residents through the local board of health or public health department.

Summary

Hepatitis A is a viral infection of the liver that may cause a short-term sickness but generally does not cause prolonged liver disease. It affects both children and adults. Adults tend to have a more severe course of illness. In fact, many children are infected but never show signs of hepatitis. A person can only become infected once in his or her lifetime with hepatitis A.

An infected person may develop cold- or flu-like symptoms from 15-50 days after exposure to the virus. The typical signs of hepatitis appear a few days later: yellowing of the skin and eyes, dark urine, itching, and abdominal pain. The illness usually lasts 4 to 8 weeks.

Hepatitis A usually spreads through the stool of an infected person. The stool can contaminate the hands of the infected person, who then transmits the virus by touching other people or food and objects shared with others.

No treatment exists for hepatitis A, but certain measures can lessen the symptoms. Bedrest, high calorie foods, and aspirin can help muscle aches, abdominal pain, and fevers. Prescription medications can relieve itching.

Hepatitis A can spread rapidly through a shelter if certain precautions are not followed. The local board of health or public health department should be informed of any cases of hepatitis A as soon as possible. They can help initiate steps that may lessen the risk of spread to other staff and guests.

The most basic and effective preventive measure each staff member and guest can take is to practice frequent, thorough handwashing, particularly before eating or handling food and after using the bathroom or changing a diaper.

References

Centers for Disease Control. Protection against viral hepatitis. *MMWR* 1989; 39(RR-2): 2-5.

Dienstag JL, Wands JR, Isselbacher KJ. Acute hepatitis. In: Wilson JD, Braunwald E, Isselbacher KJ, Petersdorf RG, Martin JB, Fauci AS, Root RK, eds. *Harrison's Principles of Internal Medicine*. 12th ed. New York: McGraw Hill Book Company; 1991: 1322-1336.

Gerety R. *Hepatitis A*. New York: Academic Press, Inc; 1984.

Gust I. Prevention and control of hepatitis A. In: Zuckerman B, ed. *Viral Hepatitis and Liver Disease*. New York: Alan R. Liss, Inc; 1988: 77-80.

Lemon S. Type A viral hepatitis: new developments in an old disease. *N Engl J Med* 1985; 313(17): 1059-1067.

Pinworm

Maya Mundkur, R.N.,C., M.S.N.

The pinworm, or *Enterobius vermicularis*, is a parasite that commonly infects the intestines of humans. The male is 2 to 5 millimeters long and lives in the lower gastrointestinal tract. Females can be twice as long as males. Pregnant females typically migrate to the rectal area to lay eggs, often during the night. Pinworms may also deposit their eggs along the perineum and even in the vagina. The females usually die after depositing their eggs.

Clinical course

Pinworm infection can cause intense itchiness in the perianal region. Persistent scratching can produce an excoriated rash. The discomfort from pinworms usually results in restless sleep. Thankfully, the infection is self-limited, and serious complications are rare.

Prevalence

Infection with pinworms is very common, especially among pre-school and school-aged children. Pinworms infect 20 to 30 percent of all children world-wide and 90 to 100 percent of institutionalized children. While infection in adults is far less common, parents and other household members often become infected by children with pinworms.

Transmission

Pinworms can be spread in several ways, most commonly by direct contact with the eggs. People can continually reinfect themselves by scratching the perianal area and touching their mouths or touching objects that are then mouthed or eaten.

Pinworms also spread through indirect contact when someone touches clothes, underwear, or bedding that contain eggs. These eggs can then spread to food, toys or other objects that often go into children's mouths. Eggs can also be dispersed around a room when contaminated articles are shaken, causing the eggs to settle into dust. In ideal conditions, the eggs can live up to 3 weeks in bedding, clothing, and dust; however, less than 1 out of 10 will be alive after 2 days at room temperature.

A third mode of transmission is retroinfection. This happens when the pinworms reinfect the host by hatching in the perianal region and then migrating back into the rectum.

Diagnosis

Perianal and perineal itching and rash coupled with insomnia are the most common complaints of pinworm infection. However, many pinworm infections are entirely without symptoms.

The presence of pinworms can be confirmed in one of two ways. The first is to observe adult worms around the anus, perineum, or entrance to the vagina. The optimum time to see the worms is 1 to 2 hours after a child has gone to bed or on awakening in the morning. A flashlight will help with the search. The eggs, which are no bigger than the head of a pin, may also be observed under a microscope. A 2-inch strip of scotch tape can be applied to the child's perianal area in the morning. The tape may then be transferred to a glass slide for examination.

In ideal conditions, the eggs can live up to 3 weeks in bedding, clothing, and dust.

There is a 50 percent chance of identifying pinworms using either of these tests once. This test should be repeated over 3 to 5 consecutive mornings before accepting a negative result. Pinworm infection usually runs in families, which means that a diagnosis in one person calls for the examination of all family and household members.

Treatment

Most people in single family households will get rid of pinworms without treatment. Unfortunately, larger group settings such as shelters and day care centers facilitate transmission and persistent infection. Breaking the cycle of reinfection through direct and indirect contact can be very difficult. Early treatment and thorough examination of family members and close friends favors eradication. If more than one child in more than one family is diagnosed with pinworms within a short time, the entire facility may require treatment.

Mebendazole (Vermox™) is an antihelminthic that comes in chewable tablets of 100 mg, is given as a single dose, and has few side effects. It is not recommended for pregnant women or children under two years of age.

Pyrantel pamoate (Antiminth™) also effectively destroys pinworms at dosages of 11 mg/kg to a maximum dose of 1 gram. Antiminth™ can be used in people of all ages and is not contraindicated in pregnant women. Some people have headaches and stomach pain when taking the drug, but these side effects are

Enteroviruses are spread among people when infected feces come into contact with hands, food, or objects that in turn come into contact with the mouths of others. They may also be spread through infected nose and throat secretions.

If a case of viral meningitis arises in a shelter, it is important to notify both the local board of health and a health provider familiar with your shelter.

People within the shelter who develop a febrile illness and/or severe headaches should be referred for medical evaluation without delay.

Viral meningitis can be due to other viruses, such as herpes simplex or cytomegalovirus. These are discussed in other chapters of this manual.

References

Benenson AS, ed. *Control of Communicable Diseases in Man.* 15th ed. Washington, DC: American Public Health Association; 1990: 277-279.

Cherry JD. Acute aseptic meningitis. In: Behrman RE, Vaughan VC, eds. *Nelson Textbook of Pediatrics.* 13th ed. Philadelphia: WB. Saunders; 1987: 555-556.

Klein JO, Feigin RD, McCracken GH. Report of the task force on diagnosis and management of meningitis. *Pediatrics* 1986; 78: 959-982.

McGee ZA, Baringer JR. Acute meningitis. In: Mandell GL, Douglas RG, Bennett JE, eds. *Principles and Practice of Infectious Diseases.* 2nd ed. New York: Churchill Livingstone; 1988: 741-754.

Aide Marsha Adderly offers comfort and a smile to a new guest of the BHCHP Medical Respite Unit.

Conjunctivitis (Red Eye)

Thomas Bennett, M.D.

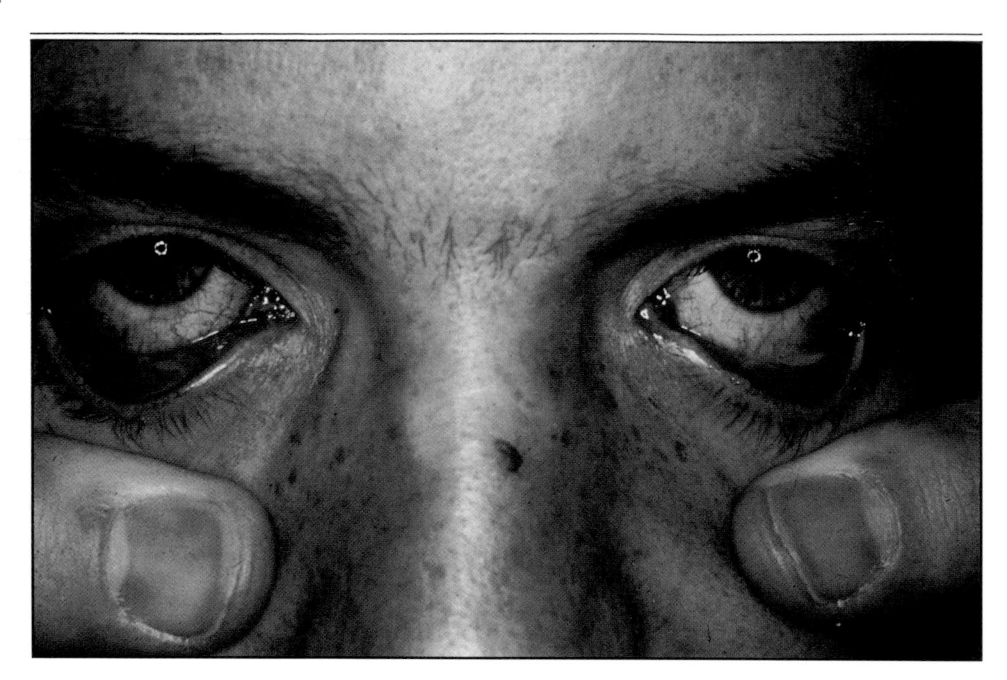

Conjunctivitis. Both eyes are reddened and teary. This man has gonococcal conjunctivitis, one of the many infectious causes of this common eye condition.

Conjunctivitis, or inflammation of the conjunctiva, is the most common eye disease in the Western Hemisphere. The conjunctiva is the thin, transparent lining covering the inner surface of the eyelids and extending over the surface of the eye to the margin of the cornea.

Conjunctivitis most commonly occurs when the eye fails to ward off infectious organisms. White blood cells contained in the many blood vessels of the eye and the tissue surrounding the eye normally enable the conjunctiva to fight infection. Tears and mucous form another defense against infection. Tears cleanse the conjunctiva of foreign objects and help fight bacteria by lowering the temperature of the conjunctival sac through evaporation. Many different organisms can broach these defenses and cause conjunctivitis. Conjunctivitis may also happen because of allergies, chemical irritants, or systemic illness.

The Causes of Conjunctivitis

Infectious

Bacterial: Almost any bacteria is capable of infecting the conjunctiva. The most common are *Staphylococcus, Streptococcus, Neisseria,* and *Haemophilus*. The same organism that causes gonorrhea in adults may cause a particularly severe conjunctivitis in newborns exposed to the organism in the birth canal during a vaginal delivery. Eye drops of silver nitrate, erythromycin, or tetracycline immediately after birth provide protection from infection for newborns. Older persons may acquire a gonococcal conjunctivitis through contamination from a urethral, genital, or anal infection.

Viral: Many mild infections of the conjunctiva are probably caused by viruses, sometimes associated with upper respiratory infections. The secretions tend to be less severe than bacterial infections. Most viral infections of the conjunctiva are self-limited but highly contagious. Redness, tearing, and itchiness are common. The infection is often bilateral. The herpesvirus family, especially herpes simplex and herpes zoster, can be associated with inflammation of the cornea. Immediate referral to an ophthalmologist is essential.

Chlamydia: Certain sub-types of chlamydia can cause trachoma, a chronic infection of the conjunctiva which is felt to be the leading cause of blindness worldwide. In the USA, this disease is largely confined to Native American populations. Other types of chlamydia are sexually transmitted and can lead to an inclusion conjunctivitis. Newborns may be infected during a vaginal delivery. This infection is usually bilateral with profuse discharge, arising 5-14 days after exposure.

Rickettsial: These organisms are less common causes of conjunctivitis and also cause Rocky Mountain Spotted Fever and typhus.

Fungal and Parasitic: Fungi and parasites rarely cause conjunctivitis in this country.

Non-infectious

Allergic: Conjunctivitis may accompany symptoms of hav fever or may be an allergic reaction to a chemical or medication. Swelling of the eyelids is common, and the discharge is thin and watery.

Chemical/Irritative: Any chemical or medication placed directly in the eye may cause a "chemical conjunctivitis". Eye make-up and mascara are commonly associated with this type of conjunctivitis.

Systemic illness: Certain generalized illnesses such as thyroid disease or gouty arthritis may be associated with conjunctivitis. Dacrocystitis (infection of the tear ducts) may spread to conjunctivitis, especially in infants.

Diagnosis

Conjunctivitis varies from tearing and hyperemia (a mild dilatation of the blood vessels) to severe tissue damage and cellular exudation. The condition begins as

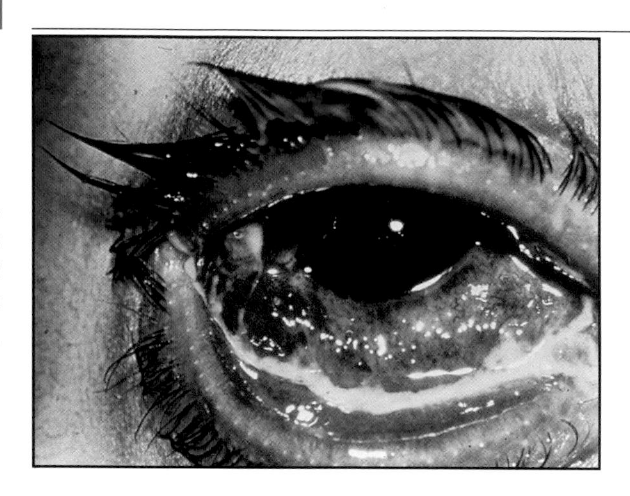

Bacterial Conjunctivitis. This severe conjunctivitis shows the engorged and reddened conjunctiva with a purulent discharge.

eye discomfort, burning, or a sensation that a foreign body has lodged in the eye. The eyes may itch, especially with allergic conditions, and vision sometimes blurs, particularly in the presence of discharge.

Severe pain is rare. Pain may indicate that the inflammation has involved either the cornea (keratitis) or the cornea and inner lining of the eye (keratoconjunctivitis). A "ciliary flush" (dilation of the vessels immediately surrounding the iris) suggests iritis or anterior uveitis. The enlargement of the pre-auricular lymph nodes (those immediately in front of the ears) accompanies several types of conjunctivitis. Persons who develop severe eye pain or visual disturbances (flashing lights, transient loss of vision, etc.) should be referred without delay to a physician.

Caregivers often assume that conjunctivitis arises from one of the common bacterial infections, such as *Streptococcus* or *Haemophilus*. A definite diagnosis of bacterial conjunctivitis is made by gram stain and culture of the drainage, although this is seldom necessary unless the symptoms do not respond to the usual treatment.

Treatment

The treatment of infectious conjunctivitis relies on the use of topical, oral, or intravenous antibiotics. Untreated, common bacterial infections may last as long as two weeks. Antibiotic therapy should begin to show results in three days. To guard against recurrence, caregivers should ensure that patients complete a full 7 to 10 day course of treatment. Chlamydial infections may require 2 to 3 weeks of therapy for maximum benefit.

Caregivers should examine and treat the sexual partners of persons with chlamydial or gonococcal eye infections. Natural parents of newborns infected with chlamydia or gonorrhea during delivery should also be examined and treated.

Prevention and Control

Guests, staff, and caregivers should not touch or rub their eyes, particularly when an active infection is present.

To prevent transmission, people caring for children or adults with conjunctivitis should wash their hands thoroughly with warm water and plenty of soap before and after contact with affected individuals.

Care must be taken to avoid sharing towels, washcloths, and personal articles, especially make-up and mascara.

Eye drops or ointments should never be shared, even among family members. Careful labeling can prevent accidental sharing.

Refer to the Specific Guidelines on pages 40-42 in Part Two for more information on prevention and control of infections transmitted by direct and indirect contact.

Conjunctivitis has many causes: infections, allergies, chemical irritants, and systemic illnesses.

Summary

Conjunctivitis is the most common eye disease in the USA. The conjunctiva is the thin, transparent lining that covers the inner surface of the eyelid and extends over the surface of the eye to the margin of the cornea.

Inflammation of the conjunctiva may be caused by infections, allergies, chemical irritants, and systemic illnesses.

Infectious conjunctivitis can be caused by bacteria (*Staphylococcus, Streptococcus, Neisseria,* and *Haemophilus*), viruses, chlamydia (which causes trachoma), rickettsia, and fungi and parasites.

The diagnosis of conjunctivitis is made by physical examination. Mild conjunctivitis can cause tearing and redness, while the most severe forms of this infection can cause tissue damage. Pain is relatively rare.

Treatment of infectious conjunctivitis relies on the use of topical, oral, or intravenous antibiotics.

Prevention of this infection requires good personal hygiene with emphasis on handwashing and the avoidance of touching and rubbing the eyes during active infection.

References

Steinert RF. The evaluation of the red eye. In: Goroll AH, May LA, Mulley AG, eds. *Primary Care Medicine.* 2nd ed. Philadelphia: Lippincott; 1987: 834-839.

Howes DS. The red eye. *Emergency Medicine Clinics of North America* 1988; 6(1): 43-56.

Reed DB. Viral and bacterial conjunctivitis: prevention of disasterous results. *Postgraduate Medicine* 1989; 86(4): 103-114.

Cytomegalovirus (CMV)

Barbara McInnis, R.N.

Cytomeglovirus (CMV) is responsible for many different infections, although CMV is very common and usually not associated with disease. In the United States, at least 4 out of every 10 adults have antibodies to CMV.

After primary infection, CMV can remain latent in the body. CMV may reactivate later in life as a result of stresses such as chronic illness or suppression of the immune system.

CMV illness

Most normal people with CMV infection are without symptoms. Occasionally CMV infection can lead to a complex illness with various manifestations. Children whose mothers became infected for the first time during pregnancy can suffer congenital complications, primarily involving the central nervous system and the liver. Antibodies passed to the child from a mother who has reactivated an earlier infection may diminish the severity of these complications but do not prevent illness in the child.

CMV causes one form of mononucleosis in adults. Fever lasting from 2 to 4 weeks is often the only symptom, although fatigue and swollen lymph nodes may also appear. Most mononucleosis cases result from primary infection. For people with poor immune systems, mononucleosis may represent reactivation of an earlier infection. Complications in this latter group can lead to pneumonia, hepatitis, retinitis, myocarditis, blood disorders, and endocrine disturbances.

Transmission

CMV can spread through repeated close contact to infected urine, saliva, mucous membranes (mouth, eyes, genital tract), and sometimes blood. CMV can pass through the placenta to a fetus in the womb. The virus may also be spread to a child during delivery by exposure to an infected genital tract, and postnatally through breast milk containing the virus.

Children under two years of age probably have the highest rate of CMV transmission. The virus spreads easily within this group because of frequent contact with saliva (through behaviors such as mouthing shared toys) and urine (diapering, toilet training). An infected child can intermittently excrete CMV virus in saliva and urine for months and even years.

Diagnosis

Most CMV infections are asymptomatic and therefore remain undiagnosed. Cultures and biopsies show the presence of the virus in body fluids and most tissues. Unfortunately, culture results may take 4 days to 4 weeks, depending on the amount of virus in the specimen. Blood tests showing a fourfold rise in antibody titers also confirm a diagnosis.

In the USA, at least 4 out of every 10 adults have antibodies to CMV....Most people with CMV infection are without symptoms.

Treatment

For most people who exhibit symptoms, treatment for CMV infection is usually palliative.

Severe complications may arise, calling for intensive medical management and the use of various antiviral therapies. Most of these therapies have shown little or no effect. However, the antiviral drug acyclovir has been shown to produce a moderate improvement in symptoms. Foscarnet and gancyclovir (DHPG) have been used for retinitis, although the latter cannot be used with AZT.

Prevention and Control

People infected with CMV do not need to follow any special precautions, nor do they need to be isolated. Every shelter probably has people shedding the virus who are asymptomatic. Preventing or minimizing the spread of CMV among shelter guests and staff requires adherence to the basic measures outlined in the General Guidelines on pages 33-36 as well as the Specific Guidelines for preventing transmission of diseases via the fecal-oral route, direct contact, and contact with blood on pages 38-46.

Pregnant women should pay particular attention to good hygiene because of the risk to the fetus when primary CMV infection is acquired during pregnancy.

Summary

Cytomegalovirus (CMV) is a very common infection, most often spread among very small children. At least 2 out of 5 adults have a history of infection with CMV.

The infection is usually without symptoms. Adults and children may show symptoms that resemble mononucleosis, such as fever, tiredness, and swollen glands. Those who get sick from CMV have never been infected before. Once infected, a person cannot become reinfected, but a previous infection can reactivate.

The unborn children of women who become infected during pregnancy are at highest risk of complications from CMV. Infection passed to these children can lead to mental retardation and hearing loss.

CMV can also cause serious complications of the lungs, liver, and eyes in people with poor immune systems.

CMV spreads when infected urine, saliva, and genital fluids come into contact with a person's mucous membranes (the mouth, eyes, or genital tract). The virus also spreads by contact with infected blood, such as transfusions or needlesticks, although transmission in these ways is less common.

Infected children do not need special isolation. Usually, the presence of CMV infection remains undetected because of the lack of symptoms. Instead of isolation, shelters should promote good general hygiene practices.

References

Benenson AS, ed. *Control of Communicable Diseases in Man.* 15th ed. Washington, DC: American Public Health Association; 1990: 115-117.

Ho M. Cytomegalovirus. In: Mandell GL, Douglas RG, Bennett JE, eds. *Principles and Practice of Infectious Diseases.* New York: Churchill Livingstone; 1988: 960-969.

Holland GN, Sidkaro Y, Kreiger AE, Hardy D, Sakamoto MJ, Frenkel LM, et al. Treatment of cytomegalovirus retinopathy with gancyclovir. *Ophthamology* 1987; 94(8): 815-823.

Meyers JD. Management of cytomegalovirus infection. *Am J Med* 1988; 85(2A): 102-106.

Pass RF, Hutto SC, Ricks R, Cloud GA. Increased rate of cytomegalovirus infection among parents of children attending day care centers. *N Engl J Med* 1986; 314(22): 1414-1418.

Georges P, Hall CB, Lepow ML, Phillips CF, eds. *The 1988 Red Book: Report of the Committee on Infectious Diseases.* 21st ed. Elk Grove Village, Illinois: American Academy of Pediatrics; 1988: 170-174.

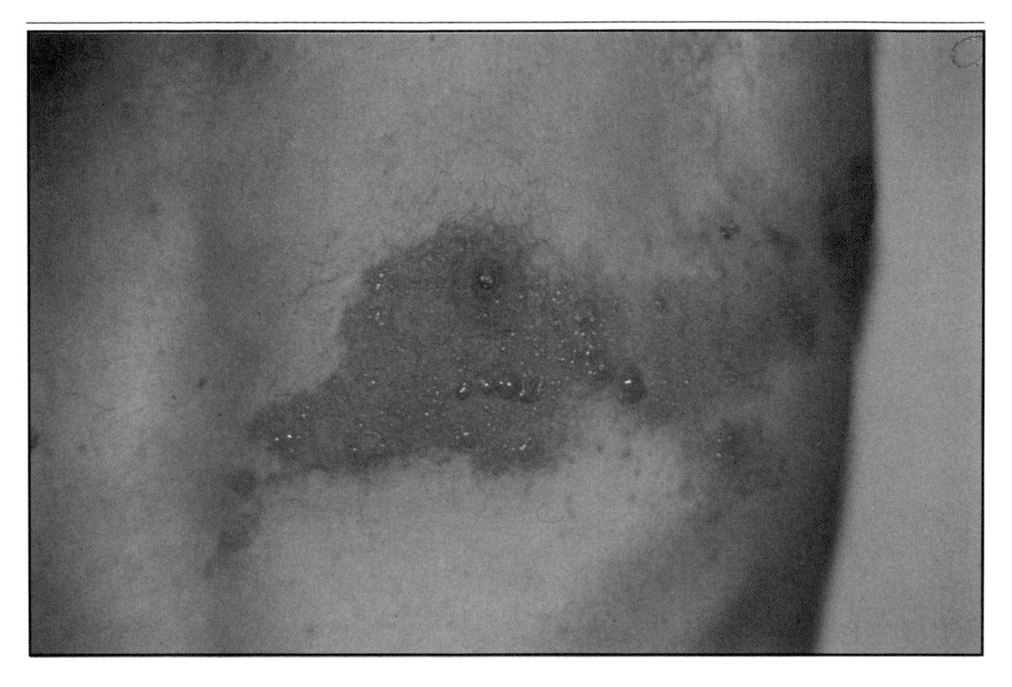

Herpes Zoster (Shingles)

Janet Groth, R.N., M.S.

Localized Herpes Zoster (Shingles) of the T5 Dermatome. The lesions are red and raised blisters, or fluid-filled vesicles, which contain varicella-zoster virus. Note that these lesions are confined to a specific area on one side of the chest.

Varicella-zoster virus (VZV) causes two distinct illnesses: varicella (chickenpox) and zoster (shingles). This chapter describes zoster. For information on varicella, see page 99. We will use zoster and shingles interchangeably, as well as varicella and chickenpox.

After someone has had chickenpox, VZV can lie dormant for decades before reappearing as the red, painful, itchy, blister-like lesions that are typical of shingles. These lesions resemble those of chickenpox but are usually confined to one area of the body. Zoster lesions erupt for several days and usually disappear within 2 to 3 weeks in children and 2 to 4 weeks in adults.

While zoster often happens in healthy people, it is more common in those who are elderly or malnourished, or those with immune systems compromised by cancer, AIDS, or chronic steroid use. Generally, the severity of infection depends upon underlying health status. A zoster infection is either localized, with lesions limited to one area of the body, or generalized, spreading over the entire body.

Localized Zoster

Localized zoster typically involves only one side of the body. Rarely do lesions erupt on both sides of the body. The dermatomes (areas of skin overlying the nerves supplying it) are most commonly involved, particularly in the thoracic and lumbar areas. Lesions can also arise in the ophthalmic branch of the trigeminal nerve which can lead to serious problems with vision.

Pain and mild fever can accompany localized zoster, but systemic symptoms are rare. Occasionally, localized zoster can appear in children with no prior history of chickenpox, most likely due to a maternal infection during pregnancy.

Generalized Zoster

Generalized or disseminated zoster (lesions on both sides of the body or including more than 3 contiguous dermatomes on the same side) is rare in healthy people, only 2 to 4 percent of all cases. Generalized zoster lesions begin in one area, as in localized zoster. After about a week, eruptions can appear over the entire body. The lesions can continue to form for up to 5 days.

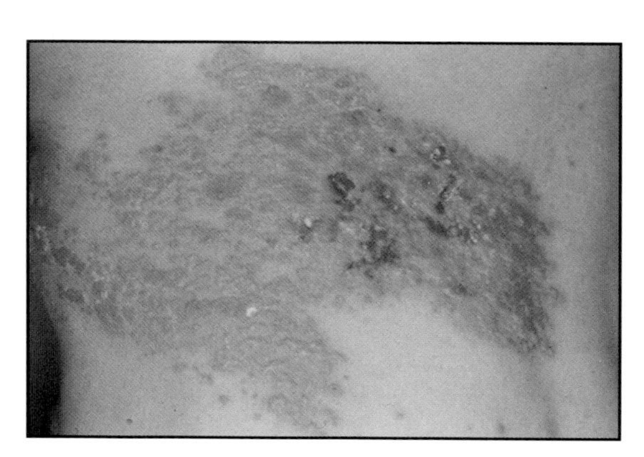

Localized Herpes Zoster (Shingles) of Dermatomes T11-12. Several of the blisters have become dried and crusted. Severe pain can accompany this infection.

Most cases of generalized zoster happen in people with poor immune systems. For those infected with the human immunodeficiency virus (HIV), the appearance of zoster may be one of the first signs of diminished cellular immunity. Generalized zoster can become prolonged but is rarely fatal. The central nervous system, lungs, liver, pancreas, and eyes may all be involved.

Complications

The most common complication of zoster is pain that lasts long after the rash is gone, known as post-herpetic neuralgia. People over the age of 50 are more likely to suffer from this complication.

Diagnosis

The appearance of classic symptoms and a knowledge of the patient's history usually allow the provider to differentiate herpes zoster from herpes simplex and chickenpox. The lesions of zoster are typically red and raised. Fluid-filled vesicles usually appear within 24 hours. These blister-like pouches become purulent, crust over, and eventually heal.

Multinucleated giant cells, indicating an infection with a herpes group virus, can be seen on microscopic examination of the fluid from the blisters. This finding identifies the lesion as herpetic; more costly blood tests are necessary to distinguish the particular viruses within the herpes group.

Treatment

Daily bathing decreases the risk of secondary infection of lesions. During the vesicular and crusted stages of the lesions, cool compresses with 1:20 Burow's solution can be applied to relieve discomfort and to aid drying. Lesions should be examined daily for signs of secondary bacterial infections.

While pain is rare in children, adults may have mild to severe pain several days before the lesions appear or even later during illness. The pain can last long after the illness ends and may call for pain management with analgesics, including narcotics. Other medications such as systemic steroids have been tried with varying degrees of success.

Uncomplicated zoster in a person with a normal immune system rarely requires antiviral medication. For those with organ involvement or underlying immunologic diseases, antivirals have proven effective, including acyclovir and vidarabine. Acyclovir works best if started early. Reports show that topical acyclovir has little effect on pain, but promotes healing of localized zoster in people with poor immune systems.

Caregivers should monitor all people who have active zoster infections. Immediate intervention is necessary for any of the following:

- confusion or change in behavior;
- lesions that appear to be spreading to the eye or other parts of the body;
- lesions that continue to appear after one week.

Prevention and Control

A person with zoster cannot transmit zoster to others. Contact to drainage from zoster lesions can cause chickenpox in people who have no history of chickenpox infection.

A person with zoster cannot transmit zoster to others. Contact to drainage from zoster lesions can cause chickenpox in people who have no history of chickenpox infection.

Every staff member of a shelter should know his or her chickenpox history. This lessens stress and confusion when an exposure to zoster happens.

Anyone who risks contact with draining skin lesions should wear gloves. This fragile virus can live for short periods on linen, clothes, and towels. The small risk posed by infection from these items warrants wearing gloves when handling the linen of infected guests. In larger adult shelters, cases of zoster may go unrecognized, and we recommend wearing gloves whenever handling used linen or laundry.

Draining zoster lesions should be covered with bandages or clothing until crusted over. With lesions properly covered and with careful handling of dressings, linen and clothing, others in the shelter are at minimal risk.

Caregivers should follow the same measures outlined for exposure to chickenpox when a person with an unknown or negative history of chickenpox has direct contact to zoster lesions. These measures are detailed in the chapter on varicella on page 99.

Summary

Herpes zoster (shingles) is a reappearance of an earlier infection with the varicella-zoster virus, the same virus that causes chickenpox. The lesions of zoster are similar to those of chickenpox, and are usually red, itchy, and blister-like. Zoster lesions can be painful and are usually confined to the nerve endings of specific areas of the body, especially the spine and the face.

Occasionally zoster can become generalized, with lesions spreading over the entire body. Complications can occur from involvement of internal organs such as the lungs or brain.

Treatment of localized zoster requires pain relievers and care to the lesions to prevent infection with bacteria. Persons with poor immune systems or those with extensive lesions may require antiviral medication and close monitoring in the hospital.

Contact to the drainage from zoster lesions cannot cause zoster infection. However, it can cause chickenpox in persons who have never had chickenpox before. If lesions are kept covered with bandages or clothing, and soiled articles are handled properly, there is minimal risk to others in the shelter.

References

Arndt KA, ed. *Manual of Dermatological Therapeutics*. 4th ed. Boston: Little, Brown & Company; 1989: 82-87.

Fox G, Stranganty JW. Varicella-zoster infections in pregnancy. *Am Fam Phys* 1989; 39(2): 89-98.

Shepp DH, Dandliker PS, Meyers JD. Treatment of varicella-zoster infection in severely immunocompromised patients: a randomized comparison of acyclovir and vidarabine. *N Engl J Med* 1986; 314(4): 208-212.

Weller TH. Varicella and herpes zoster: changing concepts of the natural history, control, and importance of a not-so-benign virus. *N Engl J Med* 1983; 309(22): 1362-1368.

Impetigo

Ben Siegel, M.D.

Impetigo is a bacterial infection of the epidermis (the outer layer of the skin). The bacteria usually infect skin that has been damaged by such things as scratching an insect bite or picking a scab. Impetigo infections commonly occur around the mouth and nose, or on the arms and legs.

Two kinds of impetigo exist: staphylococcal (usually *Staphylococcus aureus*) impetigo and streptococcal impetigo. Often lesions will have a mix of both organisms. The staphylococci are usually secondary invaders.

Streptococcal impetigo

Strep impetigo results from infection with group A, beta-hemolytic streptococci. These bacteria cause the epidermis to redden, crust, and ooze. The infection does not disappear easily with topical cleaning. The crusts are yellow and seem to be "stuck on" the skin. Satellite pustules and lesions may also appear. The lesions, which do not ulcerate or infiltrate the dermis, are painless and heal without scarring. Often, the lesions closest to the infected site swell mildly. Other systemic symptoms are rare.

In rare instances, untreated strep impetigo may cause a deeper infection of the skin known as ecthyma. The lesions can crop up on the lower extremities and extend into the dermal layers of the skin. The lesions appear "punched out" and have a greenish yellow crusting over the top.

Staphylococcal impetigo

Impetigo due to *S. aureus* accounts for less than 10 percent of all cases of impetigo and is specific to phage group II. The toxin produced by this organism makes the epidermis erupt in vesicles. These first appear as flaccid bullae (blisters) containing clear fluid, which later become cloudy. The bullae spread quickly to different areas of the skin. On rupturing, they form thin, light brown, "varnish" crusts.

Prevalence and Distribution

While people of any age can get impetigo, the disease often affects children, particularly those less than 5 years of age. Hot and humid weather, poor hygiene, and crowded settings such as day care centers and shelters, promote the development and spread of impetigo.

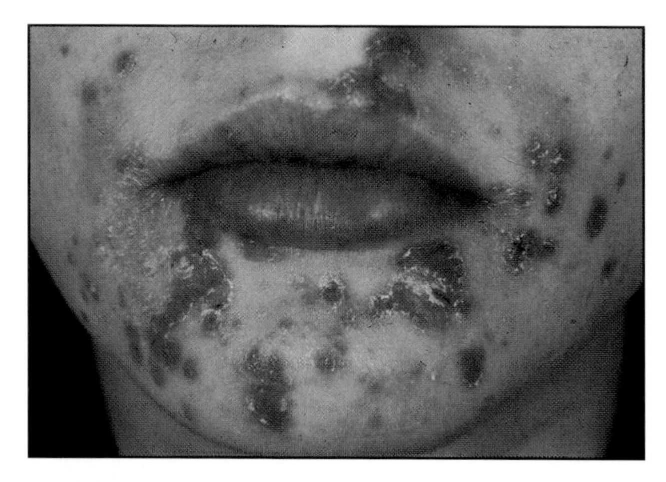

Impetigo. Round blisters and erosions with clear borders, many of which are crusted. These are scattered on the face, and some are confluent.

Impetigo. Yellow-gold crusts that glisten and have a "stuck-on" appearance. Note the oozing from many areas.

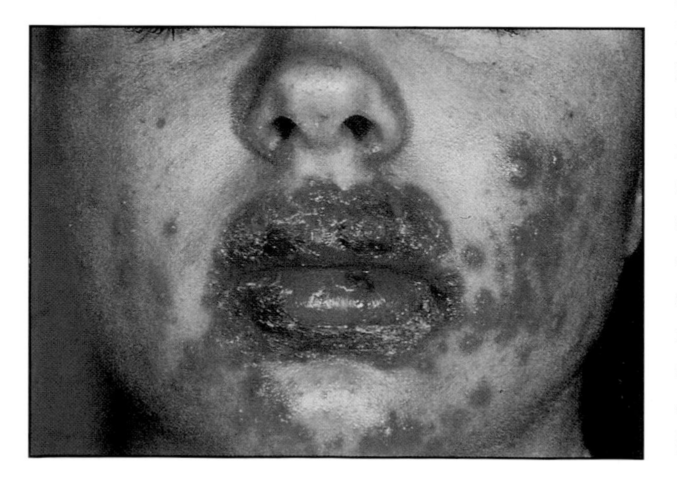

Impetigo. Dried and crusted lesions around the mouth with several satellite lesions on the face of a child with herpes simplex and impetigo.

Transmission

Impetigo usually spreads by direct contact to infected skin. People who begin treatment with oral antibiotics are no longer infectious after 24 to 48 hours.

Diagnosis

A culture from the infected area sometimes may be necessary to differentiate between streptococci and staphylococci, although both bacteria are often present.

Treatment

1. Topical

Mupirocin (Bactroban™) 2% solution is effective against both staphylococci and streptococci. The solution needs to be applied 3 times daily for up to 5 days. A sensitivity to mupirocin is the only contraindication. Stinging and burning of the skin can rarely occur. While costly, mupirocin is as effective as oral antibiotic agents and is less apt to cause resistance to develop in the organisms.

2. Systemic antibiotics

Caregivers usually employ systemic antibiotics when lesions appear to be spreading over a person's body or from one person to another. Use of systemic antibiotics accelerates healing and diminishes the period of infectivity. Since most impetigo cases result from group A streptococci, penicillin is the preferred antibiotic, either as a single intramuscular dose of benzathine penicillin or 10-day course of oral penicillin. Those allergic to penicillin may use erythromycin.

Impetigo due to *S. aureus* requires 7 to 10 days of a penicillinase-resistant penicillin such as dicloxacillin. Again, erythromycin may be substituted for those sensitive to penicillin.

Lesions that do not resolve after 1 week with conventional therapy should be cultured.

The risk of transmission of impetigo is high in shelters, and we recommend the use of systemic rather than topical antibiotics whenever possible.

Prevention and Control

Caregivers should encourage all guests and staff to seek medical care for new rashes or draining wounds.

When impetigo arises in a shelter, staff should watch for similar eruptions on other guests, especially those in close contact with the infected person(s).

If an infected person is taking oral antibiotics, all of the recommended therapy should be completed even though the rash will usually clear within 2 to 3 days.

Infected people should keep their lesions covered with bandages or clothing during the first 48 hours of antibiotic therapy.

For prevention of the spread of impetigo, see the General Guidelines on pages 33-36, and the Specific Guidelines to prevent transmission by direct and indirect contact on pages 40-42.

Summary

Impetigo is a very contagious bacterial infection of the skin, often seen around the mouth and nose or on the arms and legs. Impetigo is common in young children.

Impetigo spreads very easily during hot weather and in crowded settings. Spread can occur when a person has direct contact to the infected skin of another person.

Impetigo causes the skin to become red and blister-like. Later the affected area will ooze, causing either a yellow or varnish-colored crust to form.

Antibiotics are needed to eliminate impetigo. Left untreated, this infection can spread very quickly in a shelter. If impetigo is suspected, consult a health provider familiar with your shelter.

References

Arndt KA. *Manual of Dermatologic Therapeutics*. 4th ed. Boston: Little, Brown & Company; 1989: 21-25.

Mertz PM, Marshall DA, Eaglstein WH, Piovanetti Y, Montalvo J. Topical mupirocin treatment of impetigo is equal to oral erythromycin therapy. *Arch Derm* 1989; 125(8): 1069-1073.

Swartz MN, Weinberg AN. Infections due to gram positive bacteria. In: Fitzpatrick TB, Eisen AZ, Wolff K, Freedberg IM, Austen KF, eds. *Dermatology in General Medicine*. 3rd ed. New York: McGraw-Hill; 1987: 2100-2104.

Lice

Barry Bock, R.N.

Lice have plagued humanity for thousands of years. Today, infestations of these parasites continue to occur throughout the world, particularly in crowded settings. Lice infestations can be a common occurrence in shelters.

Lice are wingless, grayish-white insects, 1 to 4 millimeters in length. Three species of lice are found on humans:

- head lice (*pediculus capitis*);
- body lice (*pediculus humanus*);
- pubic lice or crabs (*phthirus pubis*).

The life cycle of a louse begins when the female lays eggs, known as nits. These eggs cement firmly to body hairs or clothing, which makes removal difficult. They generally hatch within 7 to 10 days and live for as long as 35 days.

Lice. Lice and eggs (nits) can cement firmly to clothing, and can usually be found along the seams, as seen in this picture. Such clothing must be washed in hot water and dried in a hot dryer for at least 30 minutes.

Transmission

Head lice spread by direct contact with an infested person's hair or through shared objects such as combs, hats, pillows, or clothing. Head lice can easily spread among children.

Body lice spread through close contact with an infested person or by sharing infested bed linen or clothing.

Pubic lice spread through close sexual contact.

Human lice do not jump or fly. Animals cannot spread human lice.

Body lice rarely appear on the skin, because they live in the seams of clothes.

Diagnosis

Lice cause the infested area to itch intensely. The individual may describe having had close contact to someone with similar symptoms. The diagnosis can usually be made by examining the affected site and direct observation of the lice.

Affected skin will usually be reddened and show signs of excoriation from scratching. Intense scratching may lead to secondary bacterial infections at the site, which makes observation of the primary lesions difficult.

Bites from head lice may appear anywhere on the scalp but are most common on the back of the head, on the neck, and behind the ears. Nits on the hair shafts resemble dandruff; unlike dandruff, however, they are very difficult to remove.

Body lice rarely appear on the skin, because they live in the seams of clothes. Caregivers should examine the clothing of a person who complains of body itching.

Pubic lice are usually found on the hair of the genital region. Pubic lice have an affinity for short hairs and may also appear on the eyebrows, eyelashes, and the scalp line of children. Since sexual contact is the primary mode of transmission, any pubic lice found on children should alert the clinician to possible child abuse.

Caregivers should evaluate anyone infested with pubic lice for other sexually transmitted diseases.

Other diseases such as scabies and cellulitis may present with similar symptoms and must be considered in the differential diagnosis.

Treatment

1. Head lice and pubic lice

Many lice-killing agents, or pediculicides, are commonly available. Most contain 1 of 3 active ingredients: lindane, pyrethrin, or permethrin.

a. Lindane

Lindane 1 percent shampoo (Kwell™) has been routinely used for the treatment of head and pubic lice. The shampoo must be thoroughly rubbed into wet hair and allowed to stand for 4 minutes before rinsing.

Lindane is potentially neurotoxic and is generally not recommended for people with seizure disorders, children under 10 years of age, pregnant women, and nursing mothers. The Pine Street Inn Nurses' Clinic in Boston has stopped using lindane for routine control of lice in their guests because of concern about these side effects.

b. Pyrethrin
Natural pyrethrin-based products such as Rid™ and A200™ are also effective for lice. They are applied as a 10-minute shampoo and are available without prescription. These products are considered to be a safer alternative for pregnant and nursing women. The Pine Street Inn Nurses' Clinic has used Rid™ with excellent results.

c. Permethrin
Permethrin 1% (Nix™) is also available for the treatment of both lice and nits. Nix™ is a synthetic pyrethroid and also has a lower potential for toxicity than lindane. A cream rinse, Nix™ is applied to the hair for 10 minutes after a normal washing. It tends to remain on the hair for a longer period; follow-up applications and removal of the nits by combing is reportedly unnecessary. Nix™ has recently become available as an OTC medication.

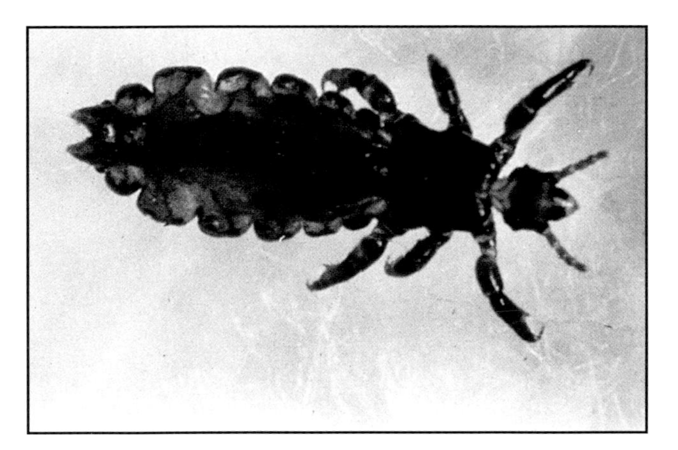

Pediculus Capitis. Under the microscope this adult head louse resembles a prehistoric creature.

Removal of nits
Excluding Nix™, most pediculicides emphasize the need to remove remaining nits with a fine-toothed comb or tweezers. An infested person should comb or pick nits after the shampoo treatment for both head and pubic lice to minimize the risk of remaining nits hatching and reinfesting the person. Depending on the extent of infestation, some people may choose to cut or shave their hair rather than remove individual nits.

Follow-up
When infested people use pediculicides, caregivers should reassess their condition after 7 to 10 days. If signs of nits or live lice are present, the patient should receive another course of treatment.

Following treatment, itchiness is not necessarily a symptom of reinfestation. Hypersensitive skin may continue to itch for as long as 2 weeks after treatment.

The use of antihistamines, topical steroid creams, and cool compresses may help reduce itching. A secondary bacterial infection requires treatment with oral or topical antibiotics.

2. Body lice

Body lice live on clothes and not on the host, so pediculicides are usually unnecessary. Generally, effective treatment entails only a shower and clean clothing. Caregivers should examine all infested clothing and manage the clothing as appropriate.

3. Lice on eyebrows and eyelashes

Pediculicides should not be used near the eyes. Infested people may treat their eyebrows and lashes with Vaseline™ twice daily for 8 to 10 days. The nits must be removed with tweezers. Do not shave the eyebrows.

Prevention and Control

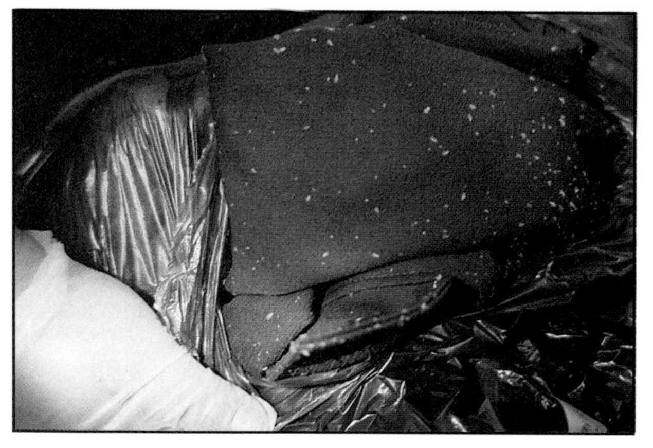

Lice. The clothes of an elderly man admitted to the hospital with pneumonia were returned to the shelter in this plastic bag. Many generations of lice can be seen.

As lice spread very easily, caregivers and shelter staff should focus on prevention. Simple prevention measures include discouraging guests from sharing hats, combs, clothing, and other personal articles.

Larger shelters that employ staff to manage beds and laundry should encourage the staff to use gloves and gowns when routinely handling soiled articles.

When infestations happen, care of clothing and the environment is generally simple. Staff and guests should wash bed linen and clothing in hot, soapy water and dry the items at 160° F (the temperature of a conventional household dryer) for 30 minutes or longer.

Combs, brushes, and hair ornaments can be disinfested by letting the articles stand in diluted pediculicide for one hour. Household cleaners or a fresh 1:10 bleach and water solution are also acceptable.

Mattresses and floors should be wiped down with standard household cleaners.

Items such as cloth furniture, rugs, or bed toys that cannot be washed may be carefully vacuumed. The contents of the vacuum should be sealed in plastic and discarded.

Chemical sprays or "bombs" are not needed to rid the environment of lice and may actually pose an unnecessary risk to the guests and staff, especially young children and pregnant women.

Close contacts

Caregivers, staff, and guests should wear washable or disposable gowns and gloves when evaluating or treating the infested person or when managing the linen of infested people.

Because symptoms may not appear immediately, some caregivers recommend treating all those who have had close contact with an infested individual. Aggressive screening programs may be another alternative.

Routine use of pediculicides in guests having no history of contact to an infested person is never indicated.

Please refer to the General Guidelines on pages 33-36, and the Specific Guidelines for the prevention of transmission of illnesses by direct and indirect contact on pages 40-42.

Summary

Lice are tiny, parasitic insects. Three different types of lice can infest humans.

Head lice live on people's hair. The eggs or nits resemble dandruff but cannot be removed easily. Head lice are very common among children. They spread through direct contact with an infested person's hair or by sharing combs, brushes, and other personal articles.

Body lice live on people's clothing, especially in the seams. They are most often found when a person develops a rash from itching. Body lice spread when an infested person has contact with other people. They can also be spread when people share articles such as linen or clothing that have body lice on them.

Pubic lice spread most often by sexual contact; they may also infest hair of the face (including eyelashes), axilla (armpits), and body surfaces. People with pubic lice should also be evaluated for other sexually transmitted diseases. Pubic lice on children should raise the suspicion of sexual abuse.

Lice are relatively easy to treat. Head lice and pubic lice can be treated with a special shampoo or cream rinse. Freshly-cleaned clothing should be worn after showering. No clothing or linen should be used until it is washed in hot water and dried in a hot dryer for 30 minutes.

To remove any remaining nits from the environment, mattresses and floors can either be wiped down with regular household cleaners or vacuumed carefully. Any articles that cannot be washed, such as stuffed animals or cloth furniture, can be carefully vacuumed.

Care of clothing, linen, grooming articles, and the environment is generally simple.

References

Buttaravoli PM, Stair TO. *Common Simple Emergencies.* Bowie, Maryland: Prentice-Hall Publishing; 1985: 271-274.

Kastrup EK, et al. *Drug Facts and Comparisons.* St. Louis: JB Lippincott Co; 1989.

Stawiski M. Insect bites and stings. *Emerg Med Clinics of North America* 1985; 3(4): 785-792.

Taplin D, Meinking TL. Scabies, lice, and fungal infections. *Primary Care Clinics in Office Practice* 1989; 16(3): 551-576.

Zissner H. *Rats, Lice and History.* Boston: Little, Brown & Co; 1963.

Acknowledgements:
The author is grateful to the National Pediculosis Association in Newton, Massachusetts, and the Pregnancy Environmental Hotline for information used in this chapter. Some of this material is controversial and does not necessarily reflect the views of these other agencies.

Thanks to Paula M. McKeever for her editorial assistance with this chapter.

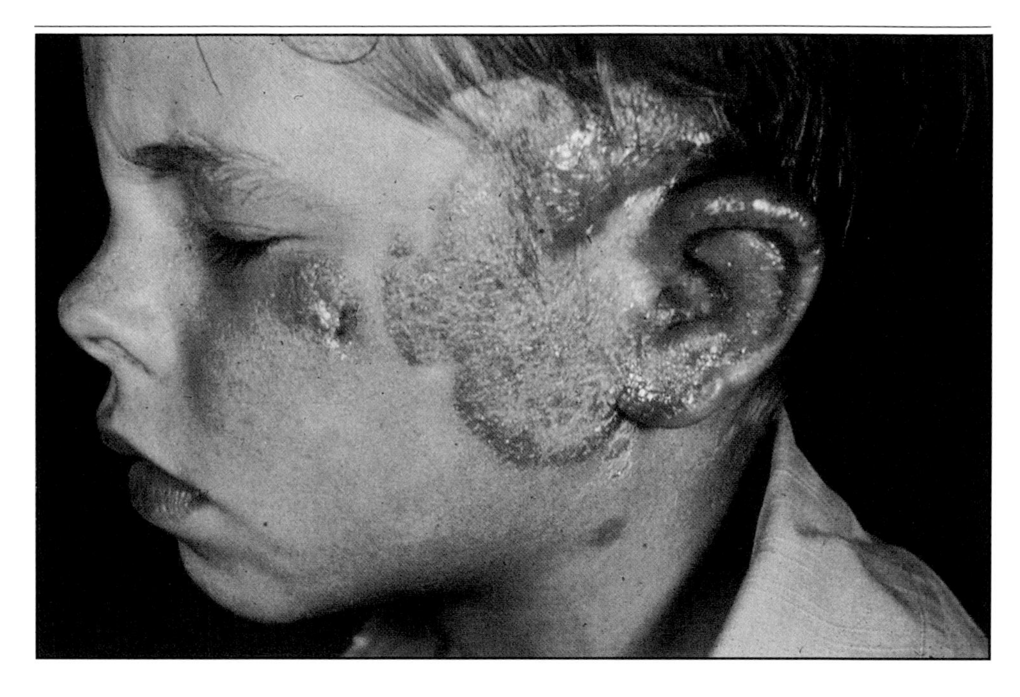

Ringworm

Ben Siegel, M.D.

Ringworm is the name given to several fungi that invade different parts of the body. The most common fungi and their sites are:

- *tinea capitis*, on the scalp and head;
- *tinea corporis*, on layers of the skin;
- *tinea pedis* (athlete's foot) and *manus*, on the feet and hands;
- *tinea unguium*, under the nails;
- *tinea cruris* ("jock itch"), on the groin area.

Infection of the scalp is especially troublesome, as it may cause permanent hair loss when untreated. Ringworm infection of the nails can be very difficult to eradicate and can cause severe damage to the fingernails and toenails. In people with poor immune systems, fungal infections promote the growth of other bacteria on the skin.

Tinea Corporis. This young boy has an itchy ring-like rash involving the face and ear. The borders are clearly marked, the central area is clear, and there is prominent scaling of the skin.

Prevalence and Distribution

Fungal infections of the scalp and skin are common in young children, while infections of the feet and toes are not. Adults frequently have fungal infections of the groin, feet, toes, and nails.

Transmission

Ringworm infection happens through direct contact with an infected person or animal, such as a cat or dog. Broken or irritated skin promotes transmission, as does warmth and humidity for some fungi.

Combs, clothing, hats, and barber's instruments can spread ringworm indirectly to the scalp. Damp floors, rugs, bathtubs, and shower stalls and benches contribute to the infection of skin, feet, and occasionally, nails.

Symptoms usually appear 10-14 days after exposure. Persons with ringworm are infectious for as long as cultures of the lesions show the presence of fungi or as long as there is scaling and redness, or as long as examination using a Wood's lamp is positive for ringworm.

Diagnosis

1. Clinical

Slightly itchy, well-demarcated, ring-like shapes accompanied by scaling characterize fungal infections of the skin (*tinea corporis, pedis,* and *manus*). The central area of these infections is usually clear. The hands and feet may show scaling, especially between the toes, and including dryness and scaling of the bottom of the feet. Ringworm infection of the feet occasionally leads to intense inflammation and swelling due to secondary bacterial infections.

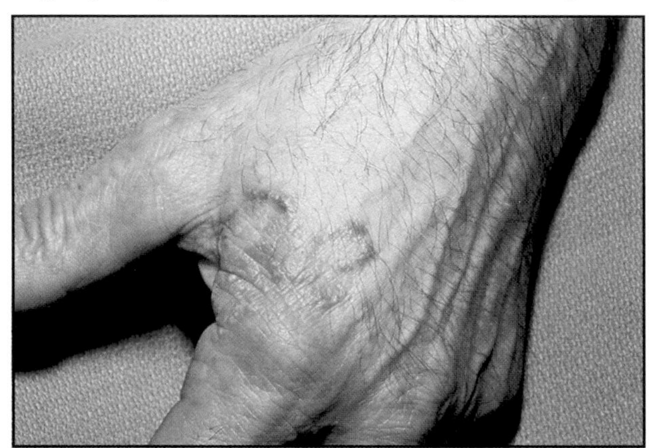

Ringworm of the Hand (Tinea Manus). Itchy, ring-like, scaling lesions on the dorsum of this patient's hand. This responded to the topical antifungal cream, clotrimazole (Lotrimin™ 1 percent cream), used twice a day for one month.

Ringworm of the scalp (*tinea capitis*) can be inflammatory or non-inflammatory. Pustules and hair loss characterize inflammatory infections. Inflammation of the hair follicles causes the hair to break off and the scalp to become scaled and red. The infection may spread locally, creating a larger circle of lost hair, or it may diffuse over the entire scalp.

Non-inflammatory *tinea capitis* produces little scaling, redness, or pustules. The hair shaft can break at the scalp causing a "black dot" appearance.

Nails infected with ringworm (*tinea unguium*) will generally thicken, become brittle, ridged, and finally split. Caseation produced by the infection causes a tan to brown discoloration of the nail plate. The infection may make the nail very difficult to cut.

2. Laboratory

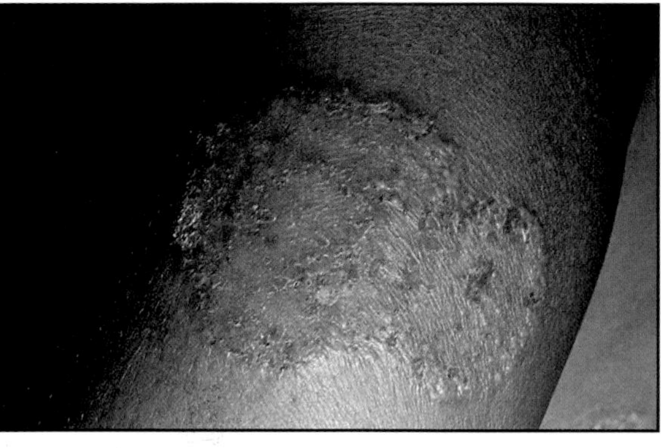

Tinea Corporis. This fungal infection involved the skin of the upper arm and back, and the appearance of these ring-like lesions with sharp borders and central clearing is very typical.

Fungal infections of the skin, scalp and nails can be confirmed by microscopic exam using potassium hydroxide preparation (KOH). As microscopic exams are often negative, a culture using a special medium (Sabouraud's agar, D.T.M.) may be necessary. A Wood's light illumination helps to identify infections of the scalp.

Treatment

Caregivers usually treat fungal infections of the skin with topical antifungal creams such as clotrimazole (Lotrimin™ 1% cream or lotion) or miconazole (Monostat™), twice daily for 2 to 4 weeks. Topical ketoconazole (Nizoral™) has proven effective as well, although it remains very expensive. These medications are also used often as the initial treatment for infections of the hands and feet.

Griseofulvin is the most common oral antifungal agent currently used for cutaneous fungal infections. Griseofulvin is indicated for:

- *tinea capitis;*
- severe *tinea corporis*, or *tinea cruris;*
- *tinea unguium;*
- severe, chronic *tinea pedis* that hasn't responded to topical therapy.

Therapy lasts 4 to 8 weeks (or until 2 weeks after clinical signs have abated) depending on the location of the infection and the response of the infection to treatment. For noninflammatory fungal infections of the scalp, a one-time dose of griseofulvin (3 grams orally) has an 80 percent cure rate. Inflammatory infections require at least 6 to 8 weeks of griseofulvin therapy.

This drug may cause headaches and gastrointestinal disturbances. Griseofulvin can also temporarily interfere with normal liver enzymes, necessitating frequent tests to monitor liver function, especially when treating refractory cases for prolonged periods, treating nail infections, or using doses of 20 mg/kg or higher.

An anti-dandruff shampoo such as Selsun™ (2.5 percent, not the 1 percent found in over-the-counter shampoos) can eliminate some of the spores in the scalp. Infected people do not need to wear a cap during their treatment.

Fungal infections of the nails may be difficult to eradicate and sometimes require up to 18 months of daily oral griseofulvin. Approximately 1 in 5 fingernail infections recur. Toenail infections are less responsive to treatment, recurring in more than half of those infected.

Burow's Solution helps relieve severe inflammation of the hands and feet.

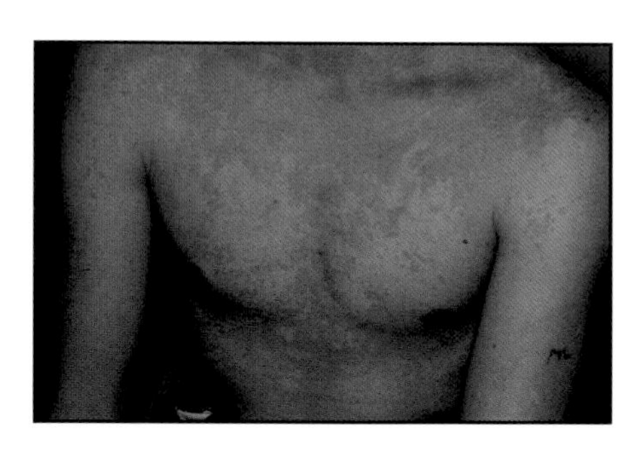

Tinea Versicolor. This chronic, asymptomatic fungal infection of the skin is marked by areas of hypopigmentation which become especially prominent during exposure to sunlight. The macules are often oval and scaling, and scrapings will reveal hyphae and spores when prepared with a KOH preparation and viewed under the microscope. The scales will show a faint yellow-green flourescence under the Wood's lamp.

Control

Persons who have had close contact to anyone with ringworm should be informed of the signs of this fungal infection and instructed to see a health care provider if any of these signs appear on their skin, scalp, feet, hands, or nails.

The prevention and control of ringworm depends on appropriate treatment and follow-up. See the General Guidelines on pages 33-36 and the Specific Guidelines to prevent transmission by direct and indirect contact on pages 40-42.

Summary

"Ringworm" refers to several diseases caused by fungi that can invade the skin, scalp, and nails. Depending on the location of the infection, mild to moderate inflammation can occur as well as a possible loss of hair or damage to nails. While seldom life-threatening, fungal infections may lead to other local infections, especially in people with poor immune systems.

Ringworm spreads by direct contact with infected areas on the skin, scalp, or nails. It can also be spread by contact with contaminated bathroom floors, shower stalls, tubs, benches, combs, and brushes. Treatment generally involves either antibiotic pills or antifungal cream, depending on the area infected and the severity of infection.

References

Georges P, Hall CB, Lepow ML, Phillips CF, eds. *The 1988 Red Book: Report of the Committee on Infectious Diseases.* 21st ed. Elk Grove Village, Illinois: American Academy of Pediatrics; 1988: 414-419.

Goslen JB, Kobayashi GS. Mycologic infections. In: Fitzpatrick TB, Eisen AZ, Wolff K, Freedberg IM, Austen KF, eds. *Dermatology in General Medicine.* 3rd ed. New York; McGraw-Hill; 1987: 2207-2229.

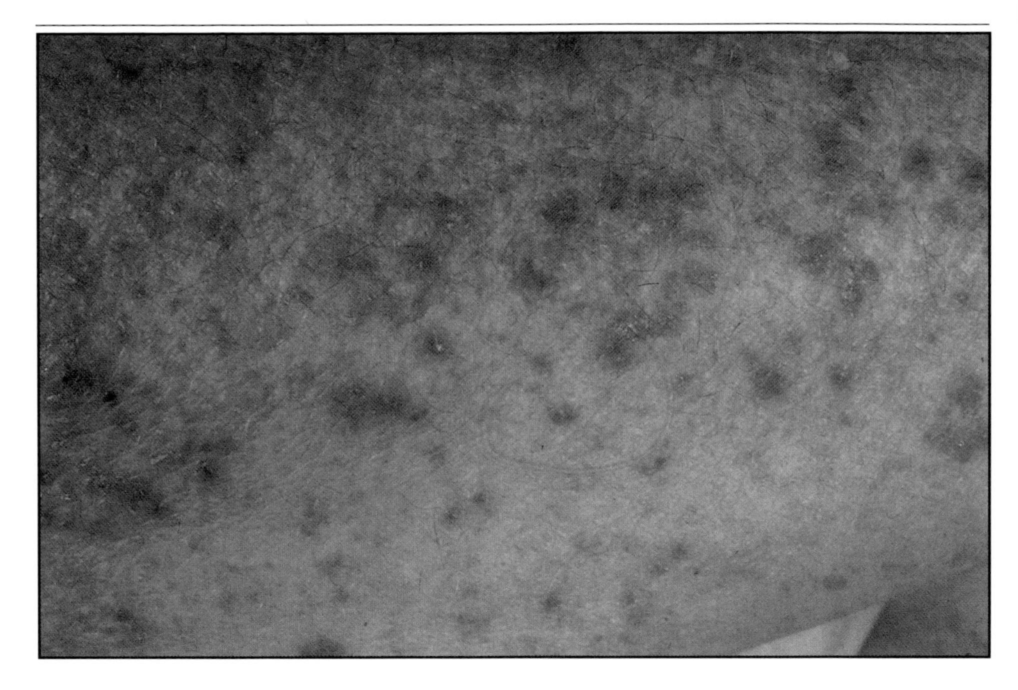

Scabies

Barry Bock, R.N.

Scabies. A papular eruption of the skin, with faint linear or wavy ridges where the mites have burrowed under the skin. This rash is intensely itchy.

Scabies (*Sarcoptes scabiei*) are microscopic mites that burrow into a human host to obtain nutrients. Similar to lice, scabies have afflicted mankind for thousands of years and continue to spread efficiently in crowded settings.

Infestation with scabies can cause intense itchiness anywhere on the body. The trunk, extremities, and folds of the skin are the most common sites. Scabies usually cause greater discomfort than lice.

Severe infestation

Severe infestation with scabies is known as "Norwegian scabies" or "crusted scabies". This extreme degree of infestation usually happens to people with compromised immune systems.

Norwegian scabies has a dramatic appearance. Scores of mites often infest large areas of the skin, causing the skin to crust over and scale. People with crusted scabies are highly contagious.

Caregivers should suspect underlying immune problems in all those who show signs of severe infestation with scabies.

Transmission

Scabies are relatively easy to transmit and do not always require close physical contact. Scabies may spread through shared clothing or bed linen that has been infested.

Symptoms generally arise 2 to 6 weeks after exposure in persons without a history of previous exposure. Persons previously infested can develop symptoms within 1 to 4 days after re-exposure.

Diagnosis

The burrowing of the mite causes a raised, red, linear lesion. Constant scratching of these lesions may give rise to secondary bacterial infections. Patient history and physical findings are usually sufficient to rule out lice, cellulitis, allergic reactions, and other causes.

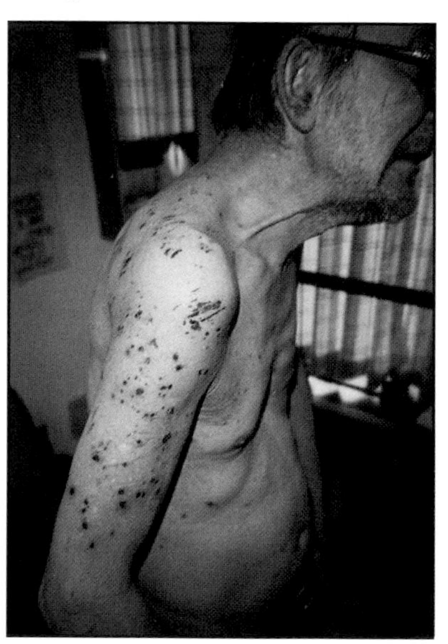

Scabies. This man came to our clinic complaining of a cough and was diagnosed with a trilobar pneumonia. He had an incidental scabies infestation, which had been excoriated (scratched) and resulted in this secondary bacterial infection of the skin.

Microscopic examination of the mite is possible by placing a small drop of mineral oil on a burrow and scraping the burrow with a #15 scalpel blade. However, the mites are extremely difficult to visualize and the diagnosis is usually made on the basis of the physical findings.

Treatment

For many years, the primary treatment for scabies has been a 1% solution of lindane (Kwell™). Scabies rarely infest adults above the neck, so the patient can apply the lotion from the neck down over the entire body. The lotion should remain on the body for 8 to 12 hours, and then the patient should rinse it off thoroughly.

Lindane is potentially neurotoxic. To diminish absorption, other creams and ointments should not be applied at the same time as lindane. Absorption through the skin can also be minimized by waiting for the skin to cool after bathing or showering before applying lindane.

Caregivers should use lindane with extreme caution for:

- young children;
- infants;
- pregnant or nursing women;
- people with seizure disorders.

Crotamiton (Eurax™) can be substituted for the groups listed above.

Unlike adults, scabies can infest young children, particularly infants, on the head and neck. Caregivers should apply crotamiton for 8 to 12 hours over the entire body of a young child including the head and neck. The young child should receive a second application one day later.

Permethrin 5% cream (Elimite™) has recently been approved for the treatment of scabies, and should be viewed as the drug of choice for persons older than 2 months of age.

In the adult and older child, scabies treatment rarely requires repetition. Caregivers should find conclusive evidence of scabies reinfestation (i.e., observation of the mite) before initiating a second treatment, particularly if using lindane.

Itching may last for several weeks after treatment and does not indicate reinfestation. To relieve itching, patients can use antihistamines, steroid creams, or cold compresses.

Secondary bacterial infections may require oral or topical antibiotics.

Control

1. Clothing and environment

The clothing and bed linen of an infested person should be discarded or washed in hot, soapy water and then dried in a dryer that attains a temperature of 160° F (the temperature of a household clothes dryer at the highest setting).

Mites may be able to live a short time on surfaces, and staff and guests should carefully vacuum objects that cannot be washed, such as rugs, mattresses, and floors.

2. Close contacts

Some clinicians recommend treatment of all close contacts, especially spouses and other family members. This may be impossible in larger shelters. For such situations, aggressive screening of close contacts can help during an outbreak of scabies.

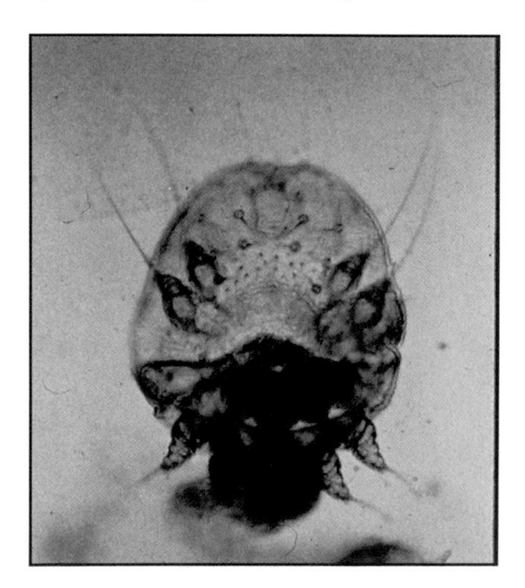

The mite which causes scabies, as seen under the microscope.

Summary

Scabies are tiny, parasitic mites that burrow under people's skin and cause intense itching. Scabies spread easily, especially in crowded places. They often appear as a rash because of scratching. Closer examination of the rash may reveal the tiny burrows of the mites under the skin.

Scabies spread when an infested person is in close contact with others.

An infestation of scabies is easy to treat, requiring only the application of a lotion for one night and care of personal articles the following day.

A caregiver should look for signs of scabies on anyone who has had close contact with the infested person.

References

Buttaravoli PM, Stair TO. *Common Simple Emergencies*. Bowie, Maryland: Prentice-Hall; 1985: 271-274.

Danish M. What is the recommended treatment for scabies in pregnant women? *US Pharmacist* 1988; 24: 24.

Taplin D, Meinking TL. Scabies, lice, and fungal infections. *Primary Care Clinics in Office Practice* 1989; 16(3): 551-576.

Van Neste DJ. Immunology of scabies. *Parasitology Today* 1986; 2(7): 194-196.

Acknowledgements:
The author is grateful to the Pregnancy Environmental Hotline for information used in this chapter.

Thanks to Paula M. McKeever for her editorial assistance with this chapter.

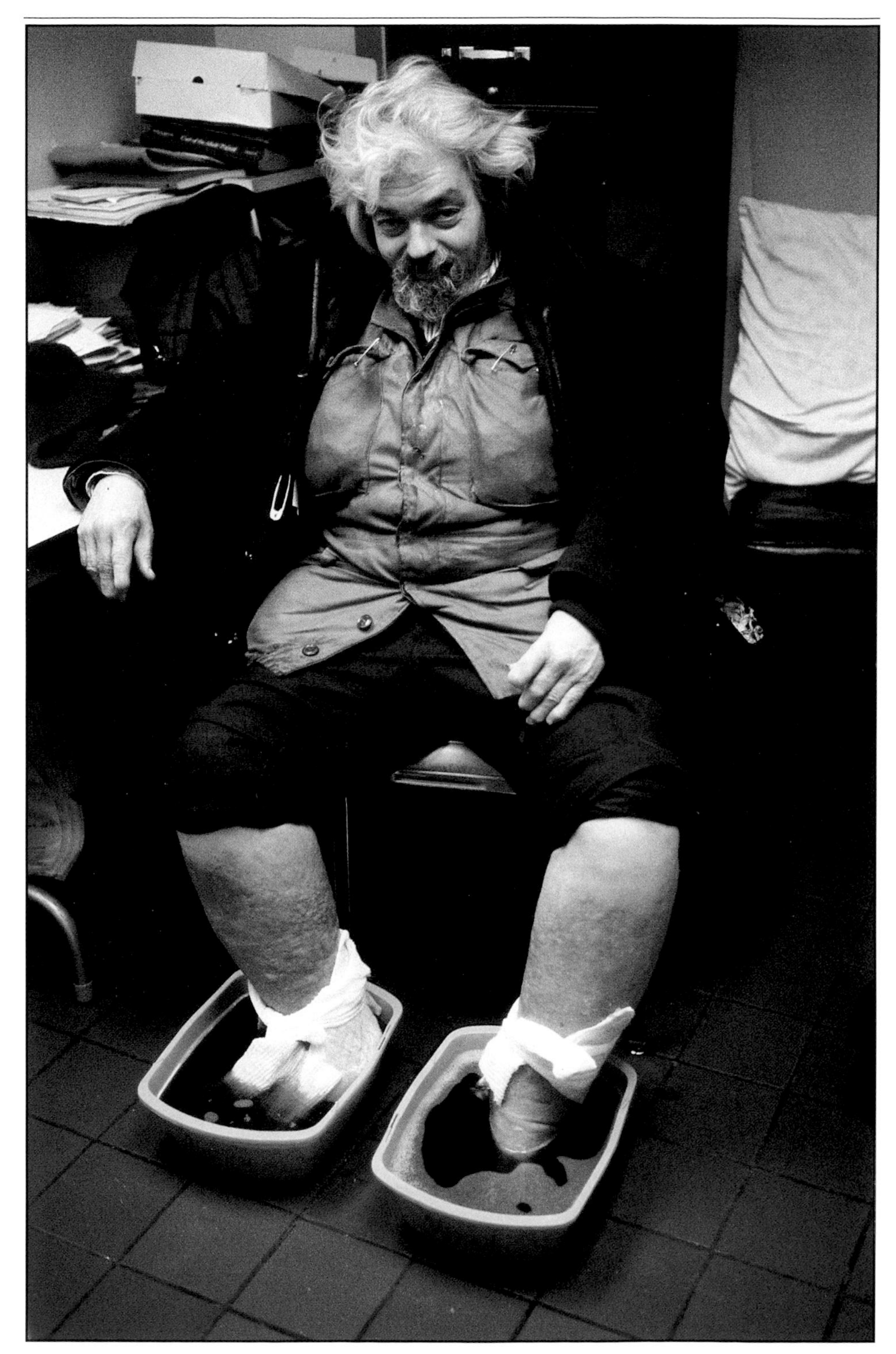

This man with chronic venous stasis and lower extremity edema receives daily footsoaks in the Pine Street Inn Nurses' Clinic. This ritual service cleanses and soothes the feet after the day's wanderings, and affirms the dignity of each individual in an anonymous world. Many of our patients have been engaged in primary health care through this wonderful gesture of the nursing staff.

AIDS and HIV Infection

Robin K. Avery, M.D.

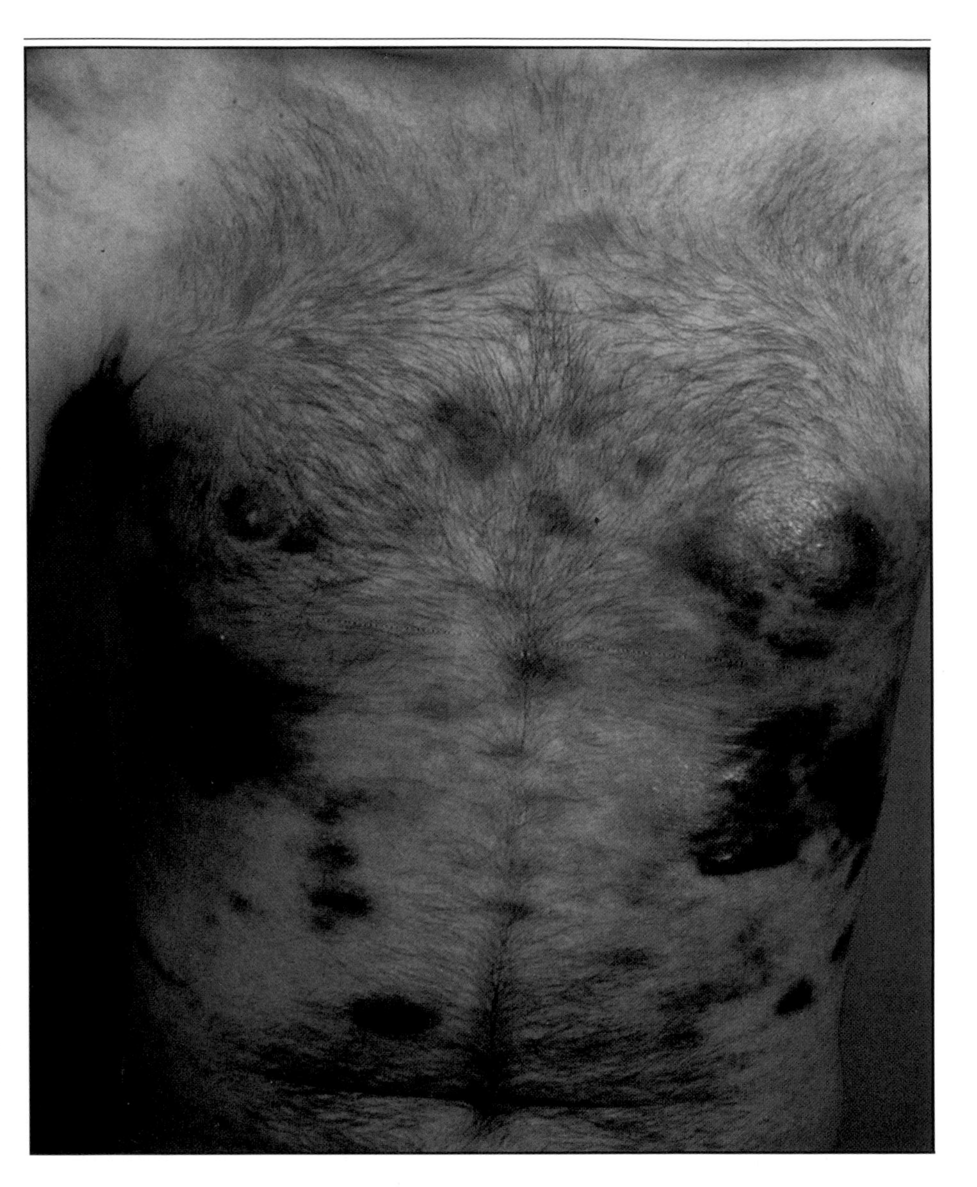

Kaposi's Sarcoma. This man presented with axillary lymphadenopathy and fatigue in addition to these raised, violaceous skin nodules. The lesions had started as flat macules that soon developed into elevated papules and later coalesced into these nodules. Kaposi's sarcoma can occur in the deeper organs as well, including the lungs and GI tract.

In increasing numbers, homeless people are being diagnosed with the acquired immunodeficiency syndrome (AIDS), AIDS-related complex (ARC), and other illnesses caused by the human immunodeficiency virus or HIV. Still more are healthy but are "HIV positive", meaning they have tested positive for HIV antibodies. Every year, more and more of those who are healthy and HIV-positive will become ill due to the virus.

HIV is part of a family of viruses known as retroviruses that have only recently been shown to cause disease in humans. The retrovirus responsible for ARC and

AIDS is technically termed HIV-1. Although HIV infection is not "curable", a number of advances have enabled some people with HIV to live longer and have fewer serious infections.

Homelessness is **NOT** a risk factor for AIDS. We strongly believe that shelters are dangerously unhealthy environments for persons with AIDS, and society must make every effort to find affordable and decent housing for these individuals and families. In addition, we believe that every person with HIV has the right to information about the latest developments in treatment. Regular medical follow-up and early recognition of signs and symptoms of infection in an HIV-positive person are crucial. All shelter personnel should be well-informed about modes of transmission, current medical understanding, and appropriate counseling strategies.

Homelessness is NOT a risk factor for AIDS.

Until affordable housing becomes available for homeless people with HIV, shelter personnel will continue to play a vital role in providing the medical and social supports that such individuals need. Each person is likely to have a unique constellation of many different needs: medical, psychosocial, financial, and spiritual.

An HIV-positive person may be battling an addiction or attending to unresolved conflicts with family members and friends, while at the same time trying to cope with the fear and pain of a life-threatening illness. Housing, employment, child custody, and other personal goals may seem unattainable. Understanding, patience, and sympathy on the part of the shelter staff are absolutely essential; efforts should be made to connect the person to the best possible support network. Confidentiality, always a difficult issue in the close quarters of a shelter, must be respected to the utmost.

Clinical Signs and Symptoms

A person who tests positive for HIV may look and feel completely healthy. The virus may take up to 10 years to produce symptoms after infection. During this phase, however, the person can transmit the virus to others. Also, the HIV antibody test may not turn positive for months after infection.

In general, those with HIV are likely to get sicker over time. The virus attacks a type of white blood cell that helps the immune system identify foreign invaders and activate an appropriate response. These cells are known as helper T-lymphocytes or T4 cells. In addition to the ability of the virus to disable the immune system, the virus tends to infect the central nervous system (brain and spinal cord), and over time may produce a condition known as "HIV dementia", in which the affected person displays progressive loss of attention span, memory, and engagement with his or her surroundings.

In addition to testing positive for antibody to HIV, a diagnosis of AIDS means that the person has had one or more conditions indicating that the immune system is severely compromised by the virus. An example is *Pneumocystis carinii* pneumonia (PCP), a major illness affecting those with advanced HIV-infection. A complete list of these conditions can be found in the revision of the CDC surveillance case definition for AIDS found in the August 14, 1987 issue of *Morbidity and Mortality Reports (MMWR).*

People who have symptoms related to HIV but who do not meet the criteria for a diagnosis of AIDS are said to have ARC, or AIDS-related complex. ARC covers a wide spectrum of illnesses; people may feel only mildly ill or may be severely debilitated by symptoms. Persons with ARC may have fevers, drenching night-sweats, adenopathy (swollen lymph nodes), oral thrush (a mouth infection with the yeast called *Candida*), severe fatigue, weight loss, and unexplained persistent diarrhea. Note that all of the above symptoms can be caused by many other conditions, and a thorough medical checkup is necessary to determine whether or not the person is suffering from ARC.

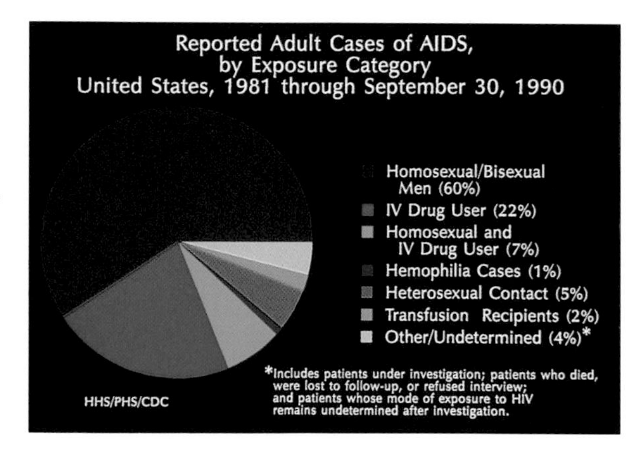

Chart 7. Reported adult cases of AIDS by exposure category.

Source: Centers for Disease Control, Atlanta, Georgia.

No way exists to determine exactly how long people have had HIV, how long they are likely to live, or what complications they will have. Naturally, these are questions people often ask. A medical evaluation can provide a rough idea of how ill a person is at the time. It is important, however, to emphasize that HIV infection is very different from one person to another. Individuals should not assume that they will have a course similar to others they have known with HIV-related illness.

In addition, new developments in treatment occur all the time, and still more advances will be made in the near future. In the meantime, close medical follow-up and access to available therapies are very important. Good nutrition and groups that offer support as well as foster positive thinking can help preserve both physical and psychological well-being.

Transmission

Despite the expansion of the AIDS epidemic, the HIV virus is actually less infectious than many of the other agents described in this manual. It is transmitted through sexual contact, blood (predominantly needle-sharing with an infected individual), or from pregnant mother to unborn child. Although sexual transmission was first noted in the male homosexual community, unsafe sexual relations with any member of a risk group may transmit the virus. Groups at risk include prostitutes and people with sexual partners who are injection drug users.

Casual or household contact has never been known to transmit HIV, an important fact to emphasize in shelters where many people share living and dining quarters.

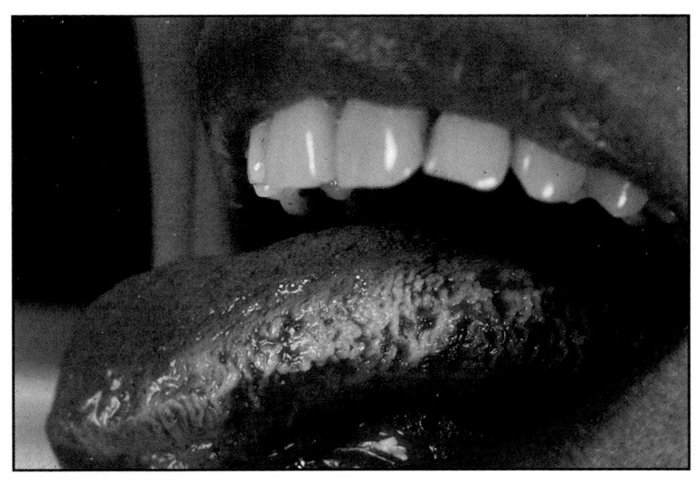

Oral Hairy Leukoplakia. This lesion of the tongue is usually asymptomatic and indicates immunocompromise and a poor prognosis. The white, irregular lesions can appear as columns on the lateral surface of the tongue, often with fine corrugations or folds resembling hairs.

Diagnosis

No blood test exists for AIDS. The available blood test indicates the presence of antibodies against HIV. The blood test is done in two parts, the ELISA and the Western Blot. A positive test for HIV antibodies means that the person has the virus in his or her system and can transmit it to others. It does not mean that the person has AIDS or ARC, which are clinical diagnoses that depend on a variety of medical conditions that the person may develop in addition to being HIV-positive.

Treatment

Regular medical follow-up and early detection and treatment of infections are crucial. Depending on the extent of illness, people may also be eligible for medications that interfere with the virus, protect the immune system, or prevent *Pneumocystis carinii* pneumonia. Experimental therapies are also available if the person wishes to enter a study and is eligible. Homeless individuals should have the same access to experimental trials as others.

1. AZT

At present, the only medication licensed for use against HIV is zidovudine (AZT). AZT is a drug that interferes with the ability of the virus to reproduce itself. AZT does not eliminate the virus from the system. When AZT was first tested in a group of people with AIDS and severe ARC, it enabled subjects to survive longer with fewer serious infections. Some evidence suggests that AZT may improve cognitive function in those with HIV dementia.

Resistance to AZT may develop in patients taking this medication for longer than 18 months, and further studies are necessary to understand the clinical implications. A recent small study from the Veterans Administration (with less than 400 participants) suggested that Latino and African-American males do less well with AZT. Clearly, we have much to learn about this medication. However, at the present time AZT remains a useful medication and should at least be offered to all those with AIDS or ARC, as well as HIV-infected individuals without symptoms but whose T4 cell counts are less than 500. The hope is that AZT will help to maintain the individual's health until more effective forms of therapy can be found.

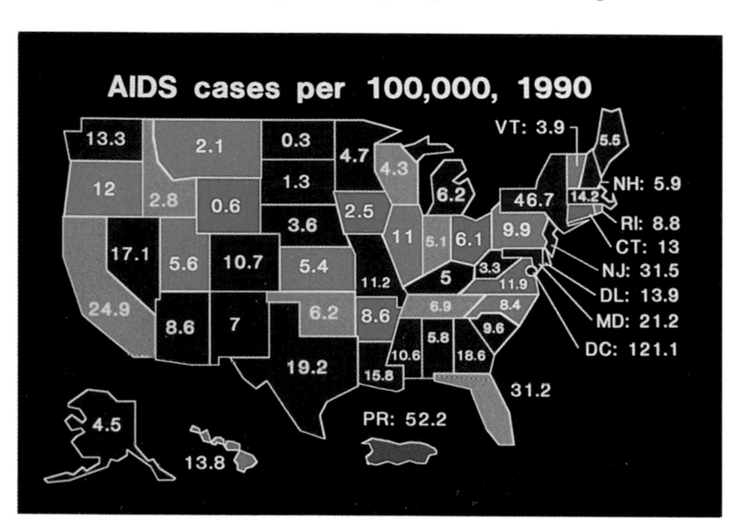

Chart 8. AIDS cases per 100,000 persons in each state as of December, 1990.

Source: Jon Fuller, S.J., M.D.

AZT therapy must be carefully monitored with frequent blood tests, because its administration can result in a drop in blood counts. In addition, AZT is generally taken every four hours, which may be difficult in a shelter setting even when the optional late night dose is skipped. Hopefully, newer drugs related to AZT will have fewer side effects and a more convenient dosing schedule.

2. PCP prophylaxis

People with AIDS, ARC, or low T4 cell counts are also eligible for therapy to prevent *Pneumocystis carinii* pneumonia (PCP). Rather than waiting for this potentially devastating infection to occur, clinicians are focusing more on prevention. This may take the form of pills such as trimethoprim-sulfamethoxazole (Bactrim™, Septra™) or dapsone. Each of these medications can cause side effects that require close monitoring by health care providers.

Aerosolized pentamidine has been shown to be effective in preventing PCP and has few if any side effects. Aerosolized pentamidine is also convenient because it requires only a brief breathing treatment every month. It can be given at home, and efforts are underway to make it more available to people in shelters.

Prevention and Control

Shelter staff can play a vital role in educating shelter guests and others about transmission of HIV. Posters and sessions on safer sex practices, the dangers of needle-sharing, and prenatal counseling may have a tremendous impact; the distribution of condoms and bleach can also help limit transmission. Information sources, such as phone numbers for the AIDS Action Committee, local AIDS hotlines, drug treatment programs, and multilingual information should be prominently posted. Brochures may be obtained from the AIDS Action Committee, the state or local health department, and other organizations. Information is also available in comic-book form for those with limited literacy. Since shelter staff may function as a major source of information for guests, they should understand the modes of transmission of HIV.

Latex condoms should be worn from the beginning to the end of sexual activity because the virus is in the seminal fluid as well as in the semen.

1. Safer sex

Because the HIV virus can be transmitted via semen, blood, or vaginal fluids, abstinence is the best prevention. Sexually active adults and adolescents should practice the safest possible methods to minimize the risk of HIV infection. Men should always wear latex condoms from the beginning to the end of sexual activity. This is vitally important because the virus is concentrated in the seminal fluid which is expressed during foreplay as well in the semen at ejaculation. Condoms should never be used more than once and should not be lubricated with oil- or pertroleum-based substances such as vegetable oil or Vaseline™ that can damage a condom. Oral sex with a man should also be done with a condom in place. A person of either sex should not allow blood or sexual fluid to enter his or her mouth. For oral sex with a woman, many have recommended a barrier such as a dental dam to decrease the chance of transmission.

Safe activities include touching, hugging, dry kissing, and masturbation. Deep (French) kissing has never been shown to transmit the virus, but may be risky as the virus has been found in saliva. Many recommend particular caution if a person has open sores on the lips or mouth. These measures to make sex safer should be encouraged whether or not the sexual partners know themselves to be infected.

Pregnant women and women considering pregnancy or who are sexually active without contraception should be informed about the possibility of transmitting the HIV virus to an unborn child.

2. Avoidance of Needle-Sharing

The HIV virus can be very effectively spread by needle-sharing in the use of intravenous drugs. The best prevention is through education and helping addicts to become drug-free. Although this is the goal, it is unrealistic to expect that all users will stop using and sharing needles. For those who continue to use, bleach can help clean the needle, syringe, and cooker, reducing transmission of the virus.

3. Casual contact

Shelter staff should be aware of things that do not transmit HIV. In particular, studies of household contacts of people with AIDS have shown no evidence of transmission by casual contact. This includes hugging, shaking hands, sneezing, sleeping in close quarters, touching, and helping a person to dress or eat. There is no need for HIV-positive people to have separate bathrooms, laundry, dishwashing, or dining facilities.

HIV Concentration	
Low	High
Tears	Blood & Bloody Fluids
Saliva	Sperm & Seminal Fluid
Urine	Cervical Secretions

Spectrum of Risk		
Safe	?	Unsafe
Hugging Dry Kissing	Oral Sex	Intercourse Insertive or Receptive, Vaginal or Rectal

Chart 9. Concentration of HIV in common body fluids / spectrum of risk for sexual behaviors.

Source: Jon Fuller, S.J., M.D.

Reasonable hygiene should be maintained, and gloves should be worn in cleaning up spills of body fluid from an infected person. Many household cleaning products kill the HIV virus; for example, a 1:10 concentration of ordinary household bleach is adequate for disinfection of items or surfaces contaminated with infected material. All potentially infectious material should be disposed in specially marked bags, and all sharp objects should be placed safely in impermeable containers designated for sharp object disposal. Individuals should not share razors, toothbrushes, or other sharp objects that may have come in contact with blood.

All people who may come into contact with infectious body fluids should wear gloves, especially if they have open skin wounds or cracks; good thorough handwashing procedures are important for sanitation in general. If called to perform CPR (cardiopulmonary resuscitation), gloves and a mouth guard or mask should be used. If these reasonably simple guidelines are followed, there should be no reason to make HIV-positive persons "stand out" from other shelter guests; the same precautions should be applied universally.

Psychological effects of HIV diagnosis

Another vitally important form of prevention is to counter the despair and potential for suicide that can accompany the positive results of an HIV antibody test. A homeless person should be tested for HIV with the maximum social supports in place and the best possible counseling. For many who are already bearing an almost impossible burden of losses, the news of a positive HIV test may be the final blow. Exacerbating fear, people frequently confuse a positive HIV test result with a diagnosis of AIDS, and often their experience of AIDS involves the terror of friends dying in the streets.

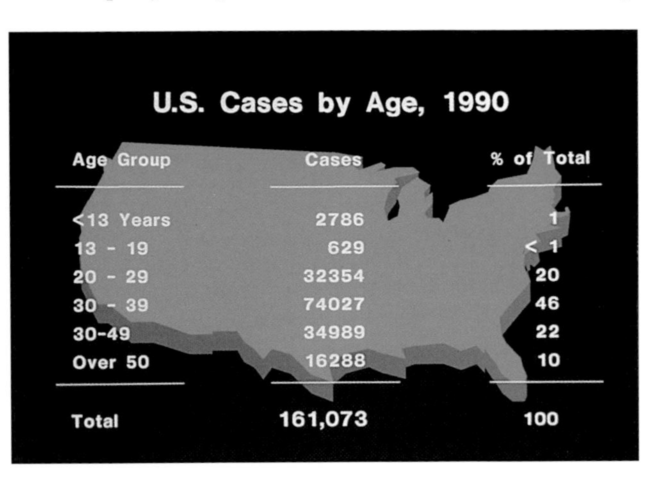

U.S. Cases by Age, 1990

Age Group	Cases	% of Total
<13 Years	2786	1
13 - 19	629	< 1
20 - 29	32354	20
30 - 39	74027	46
30-49	34989	22
Over 50	16288	10
Total	161,073	100

Chart 10. US cases by age.

Source: Jon Fuller, S.J., M.D.

As much support as possible must be provided to the newly diagnosed person, and this requires considerable effort and organization among providers and service agencies. Depending on the clinical extent of HIV infection, some who test positive may be eligible for additional economic benefits and housing assistance as well as new medical therapies. In the case of those with intravenous or injection drug use as a behavioral risk factor, an addict advocacy organization such as Project TRUST in Boston may make a vital difference. Such an organization can provide HIV testing, counseling, and referrals in a non-judgemental setting. Shelter staff should be acquainted with local resources. If nothing is available, shelters should consider starting an organization to meet the needs of shelter guests.

Summary

Human immunodeficiency virus is a retrovirus that causes AIDS and AIDS-related complex (ARC). Many people acquire the virus and remain without symptoms for many months to many years, although a blood test can measure the presence of antibodies to the virus in these persons.

HIV attacks the immune system, specifically the T4 or "helper" lymphocytes. The virus also affects many organ systems, including the central nervous system. A diagnosis of AIDS means that a person with HIV antibodies develops one or more illnesses indicating that the immune system is severely compromised (e.g. *Pneumocystis carinii* pneumonia, Kaposi's sarcoma).

This virus is transmitted through sexual contact, blood and blood products (transfusions and needle-sharing with an infected person), or from a pregnant mother to her unborn child.

The treatment of HIV is very complicated and changes often as new medicines are discovered. The basis of good health care is regular medical follow-up and early detection and treatment of infections, coupled with prophylaxis whenever indicated (e.g. AZT, aerosolized pentamidine). All persons with HIV infection, regardless of whether or not they have homes, are entitled to quality health care that includes access to appropriate experimental protocols.

The AIDS epidemic has been devastating to persons of all walks of life, and particularly tragic for those people who must suffer without homes. Providers must remember that people with this infection require a range of supportive services: medical, psychosocial, economic, and spiritual.

References

Centers for Disease Control. Revision of the CDC surveillance case definition for acquired immunodeficiency syndrome. *MMWR* 1987; 36: 1S, 3S-15S.

Centers for Disease Control. Summary: recommendations for preventing transmission of infection with human T-lymphotropic virus type III/lymphadenopathy-associated virus in the workplace. *MMWR* 1985; 34(45): 681-689.

Fischl MA, Richman DD, Grieco MH, Gottlieb MS, Volberding PA, Laskin OL, et al. The efficacy of azidothymidine (AZT) in the treatment of patients with AIDS and AIDS-related complex: a double-blind, placebo-controlled trial. *N Engl J Med* 1987; 317(4): 192.

Friedland GH, Saltzman BR, Rogers MF, Kahl PA, Lesser ML, Mayers MM, et al. Lack of transmission of HTLV III/LAV infection to household contacts of patients with AIDS or AIDS-related complex with oral candidiasis. *N Engl J Med* 1986; 314(6): 344-349.

Freidland GH, Klein RS. Transmission of the human immunodeficiency virus: an updated review. *N Engl J Med* 1987; 317(18): 1125-1135.

Libman H, Witzburg RA, eds. *Clinical Manual for Care of the Adult Patient with HIV Infection.* Department of Medicine, Boston City Hospital; 1990.

Reitmeijer CA, Krebs JW, Feorino PM, Judson FN. Condoms as physical and chemical barriers against human immunodeficiency virus. *JAMA* 1988; 259(12): 1851-1853.

Sande MA, Volberding PA, eds. *The Medical Management of AIDS.* Philadelphia: WB Saunders Co; 1988.

Volberding PA, Lagakos SW, Koch MA, Pettinelli C, Meyers MW, Booth DK, et al. Zidovudine in asymptomatic human immunodeficiency virus infection: a controlled trial in persons with fewer than 500 CD4-positive cells per cubic millimeter. *N Engl J Med* 1990; 322(14): 941-949.

Weinberg DS, Murray HW. Coping with AIDS: the special problems of New York City. *N Engl J Med* 1987; 317(23): 1469-1472.

Winkelstein W, Lyman DM, Padian N, Grant R, Samuel M, Wiley JA, et al. Sexual practices and risk of infection by the human immunodeficiency virus: The San Francisco Men's Health Study. *JAMA* 1987; 257(3): 321-325.

Chlamydia

Diane Duffy, R.N.

Chlamydia is the most common sexually transmitted disease (STD) in the United States. The bacterium *Chlamydia trachomatis* causes most chlamydial infections in this country.

Each year, at least 4.5 million adults acquire a chlamydial infection. While three times more common than gonorrhea, this disease is unknown to many. Two-thirds of those diagnosed with gonorrhea may have coexisting chlamydial infection.

Symptoms of chlamydia infection are often very subtle. Eight of 10 infected women have no noticeable symptoms. Men are more apt to have symptoms, but at least 2 of every 10 remain asymptomatic.

Symptoms usually appear 1 week to 1 month after exposure, if they appear at all. The symptoms of chlamydia are often like those of gonorrhea. Untreated, they can persist for months and even years.

Symptoms in men and women

Symptoms of chlamydia infection in men may include a discharge from the penis, burning upon urination, burning and itching around the opening of the penis, and a tingling sensation inside the penis. These symptoms may appear early in the day, disappear, and then return later in the day.

Symptoms of chlamydia infection in women often include a watery or mucous-like vaginal discharge, burning with urination, vaginal itching, spotting or bleeding between menstrual periods, lower abdominal pain, and pain during sexual intercourse.

Complications

Genital chlamydia infections can damage the reproductive organs of both men and women, making this disease a leading cause of infertility.

In men, genital chlamydia infection is responsible for up to one-half of the cases of non-gonococcal urethritis (NGU). NGU starts in the urethra and can spread to the testicles, causing pain and possibly leading to sterility.

In women, genital chlamydia infection is a major cause of cervicitis, salpingitis, (infection of the fallopian tube) and pelvic inflammatory disease (PID). PID may block the fallopian tubes with scar tissue, leading to infertility and chronic pain.

Chlamydia infection in pregnant women may lead to miscarriages and premature delivery. About half of the infants exposed to C. *trachomatis* at birth can develop conjunctivitis within 1 to 40 days. Pulmonary infection in the neonate generally arises 1 to 4 months after delivery. Half of the infants diagnosed with pulmonary involvement will have a concurrent or recent history of conjunctivitis.

Diagnosis

Smears of the urethra, cervix, rectum, and eye are necessary for detection of C. *trachomatis* antigens. It is recommended that all women suspected of chlamydial infection also be cultured due to variations in the sensitivity of the rapid antigen tests.

Chlamydial infections are the leading cause of infertility in the USA.

Serology for the presence of antibodies to C. *trachomatis* has limited use because blood samples must be taken during the acute stage of infection. To confirm a diagnosis, serology must show a fourfold rise in a chlamydia antibody titer or a positive IgM antibody (early antibody) titer.

In clinical settings where testing for chlamydia is neither routine nor available, a diagnosis may only depend upon the physical examination, the presence of polymorphonuclear cells on a wet prep, or a concurrent gonorrhea infection (due to the high rate of chlamydia coexisting with gonorrhea).

Transmission

Anyone who has ever had sexual intercourse could have a chlamydial infection. The infection is most common in teenagers, young adults, and people who have more than one sex partner. Those who use non-barrier methods of birth control (pill, IUD) or who have other STDs are also at risk.

Most chlamydia infections spread during vaginal or anal sexual contact. Chlamydia can be spread to a newborn during vaginal delivery.

Direct contact with drainage from an eye infected with the C. *trachomatis* can also spread the organism.

Treatment

In uncomplicated urethral, endocervical, or rectal chlamydial infection, almost all cases respond effectively to a 7 day course of doxycycline (100 mg orally twice daily) or tetracycline (500 mg orally four times per day). For pregnant women, caregivers should substitute either erythromycin base or erythromycin ethylsuccinate. Erythromycin estolate is contraindicated during pregnancy as drug-related hepatotoxicity can result. Amoxacillin (500 mg orally three times per day for one week) has also been used successfully for pregnant women with chlamydia.

Because of the high rate of chlamydia infections coexisting with gonorrhea, therapy for *C. trachomatis* often follows the standard treatment for gonorrhea. Please refer to the following chapter on gonorrhea on page 174.

All sexual partners during the 30 days prior to onset of symptoms or clinical evaluation should receive treatment simultaneously to prevent reinfection and complications. Infected people should avoid sexual intercourse without the use of condoms and diaphragms until completion of the week-long course of therapy.

Neonates with uncomplicated infections are usually treated with 14 days of oral erythromycin. Caregivers should also examine and treat the parents. The presence of chlamydial infection in a child not exposed during delivery points to the possibility of sexual abuse.

Chlamydia infections complicated by pelvic inflammatory diseases (PID) in women, or epididymitis in men, require more aggressive and prolonged antibiotic therapy. Treatment regimens will depend upon the severity of the symptoms and the ability of the patient to comply with the treatment.

Prevention

Abstinence is the most reliable way to prevent the spread of this and all sexually transmitted diseases. Latex condoms (rubbers) used correctly from start to finish for each sexual encounter can also provide protection. Lubricants with a petroleum base, such as Vaseline™, should never be used. These substances weaken latex.

All sexually active people should have regular medical examinations and find a reliable source of condoms.

Eyes infected with *C. trachomatis* should not be rubbed or touched. Regular, careful handwashing should continue until treatment has been completed.

For further information on prevention, refer to the Specific Guidelines for illnesses transmitted by sexual contact on pages 42-46.

Summary

Chlamydia is the most common sexually transmitted disease in the United States. Symptoms of chlamydia infection are often subtle or even absent, particularly in women. Common symptoms may include penile or vaginal discharge, burning upon urination, and itching. Women may experience abdominal pain, pain during sexual intercourse, and bleeding.

Chlamydia can cause serious damage to the reproductive organs of both men and women and is the leading cause of infertility in the USA.

Pregnant women can spread chlamydia to their children during delivery, leading to infections of the lungs and eyes in the newborn.

Treatment of uncomplicated chlamydia usually consists of one to two weeks of antibiotic pills for infected persons and their partner(s).

Education about sexually transmitted diseases is the best way to prevent the spread of this and other infections. Abstinence or the use of latex condoms are two ways of limiting chlamydial infections. Sexually active people should know where to find condoms.

Massachusetts law requires caregivers to report all cases of chlamydia to the state Department of Public Health. Except in cases where an infant has been exposed during delivery, chlamydial infection in a young child should raise the question of possible child abuse.

References

Centers for Disease Control. 1989 sexually transmitted diseases treatment guide. *MMWR* 1989; 38(S-8): 27-29.

Hoger PH. Chlamydia trachomatis infections in children. In: Simon C, Wilkinson P, eds. *Diagnosis of Infectious Diseases - New Aspects.* New York: Schattaur; 1986: 157-176.

Levin S, Benson CA, Goodman LJ, Pottage LJ, Kessler HA, Trenholme GM. *The Clinician's Guide to Sexually Transmitted Diseases.* Chicago: Year Book Medical Publisher, Inc; 1987: 18-20.

Monif G. *Infectious Diseases in Obstetrics and Gynecology.* 2nd ed. Philadelphia: Harper and Row; 1982: 238-243.

Gonorrhea

Michael Bierer, M.D., M.P.H.

Gonorrhea is the name of a wide range of diseases produced by the bacterium *Neisseria gonorrhoeae*. These gonococci, also known as GC, cause many types of infections in sexually active people, including pelvic inflammatory disease (PID) and urethritis (the "drip" or "clap"). GC can lead to serious infections in newborn babies. Some women with recurrent PID may have difficulty bearing children. If left untreated, GC infections can be fatal.

GC infection: men and women

Adult men and women acquire infection through sexual contact. In males, symptoms may arise from 1 to 30 days after infection, but usually appear within 5 days. Symptoms typically include a painful burning sensation when urinating accompanied by a yellowish discharge from the penis (the "drip"). Occasionally the tip of the penis becomes red. Acute epididymitis and prostatitis are possible complications for males.

For females, GC infection primarily involves the cervix. Cultures taken from the vagina, urethra, and rectum may also show the presence of GC. Symptoms usually arise within 10 days of infection. A genital infection can cause itching, discharge, abdominal discomfort, and burning with urination. The most common symptoms of an ascending genital infection - pelvic inflammatory disease (PID) - are lower abdominal pain and tenderness. Dysuria, vaginal discharge, bleeding, and fever may accompany the infection. Infected women usually notice these symptoms shortly after menstruating. Patients can develop salpingitis (infection in the tubes), peritonitis, and other local complications.

GC infection during pregnancy may cause spontaneous abortion, premature delivery, and perinatal mortality. Newborns exposed to GC, either in the womb or during vaginal delivery, may suffer generalized disease or local infection of the scalp, joints, or eyes.

Infection of the posterior mouth and throat (pharyngitis) often happens without symptoms but may result in a sore throat and swollen tonsils.

The anus may become infected (proctitis) through sexual contact, producing rectal itching, bleeding, or discharge, as well as painful bowel movements.

Infection in both men and women may become widespread in the bloodstream, resulting in fevers, rashes, and painful, swollen joints. Rarely, GC infection leads to meningitis or endocarditis.

Many of the symptoms and conditions caused by GC can also arise from infection with chlamydia, an unrelated organism. Simultaneous infection with both GC and chlamydia is very common.

Prevalence and Distribution

Nine of 10 cases of GC occur among teenagers and young adults. Men and women have about equal probabilities of becoming infected. However, men are more apt to show symptoms; therefore, infection in males is reported at higher rates. Both men and women may be asymptomatic for long periods.

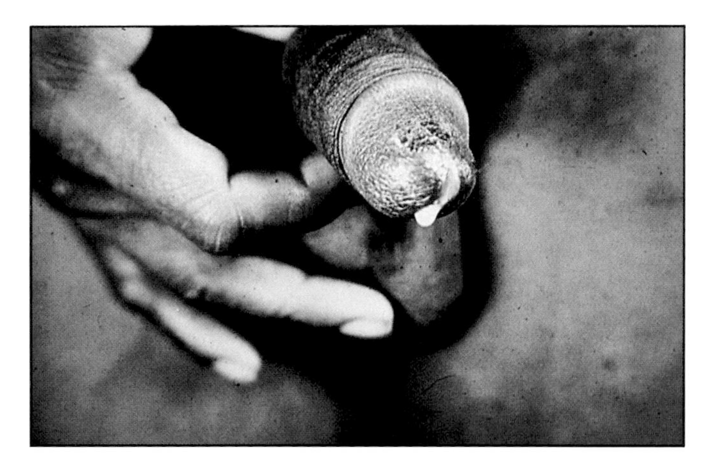

Gonococcal Urethritis. The typical symptom of gonorrhea in males is a painful burning sensation when urinating, accompanied by this purulent discharge from the penis. Gram negative intracellular diplococci were seen under the microscope.

Transmission

GC usually spreads by intimate exposure, including sexual contact and childbirth. Transmission of the bacteria only happens through direct contact with infected secretions from the mucous membranes of the anus, penis, vagina, throat, mouth, and eyes. Asymptomatic people can still spread the organism. Infected women can transmit infection to the newborn during vaginal delivery and very rarely by contaminated hands during routine care after delivery. Aside from GC infection at birth, the presence of GC in a child should raise the suspicion of possible sexual abuse.

Diagnosis

The presence of Gram negative, intracellular diplococci in secretions from eyes, urethra, skin lesions, prepubertal vagina, and joint fluid aids in diagnosing gonorrhea. However, microscopic examination of specimens from the throat or vagina is less useful than culturing because of the presence of other organisms that resemble GC. Cultures of these sites can confirm the diagnosis. This organism requires a special medium for growth in culture, called chocolate agar.

Sometimes the diagnosis depends on examining the sexual partner of the patient. Caregivers should try to examine the sexual partner(s) of a patient whenever the diagnosis cannot be made through other means.

Treatment

The treatment of GC infection requires antibiotic therapy. The type of antibiotic depends on the site of the infection. Because new, resistant strains continually arise, state and local public health officials are the best source of recommendations for treatment in a specific area. An extensive review of treatment guidelines is published each year by the Centers for Disease Control, called the *Sexually Transmitted Diseases Treatment Guidelines*.

GC is often accompanied by other infections in the same patient. In planning the course of treatment, providers should consider testing and/or treatment for other infections as well, including syphilis and HIV infection. In some populations a coexisting chlamydia infection is likely in nearly half of those with GC. Therefore, patients with GC should generally be treated with medicines effective against both organisms.

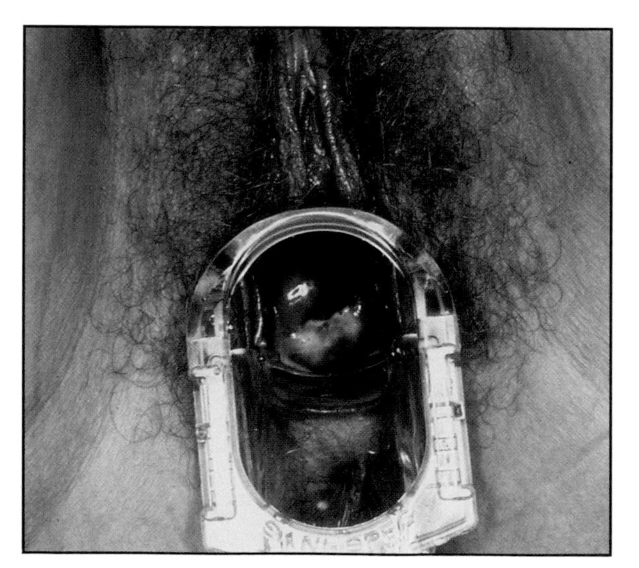

Gonorrhea of the Cervix. Gonorrhea most often involves the cervix in women, and may frequently be asymptomatic. The most typical symptoms are itching, vaginal discharge, abdominal discomfort, and burning with urination. Pelvic inflammatory disease (PID) can be a complication, accompanied by lower abdominal pain and tenderness.

Antibiotic therapy

Current recommendations for antibiotic therapy for uncomplicated GC and suspected or proven chlamydia usually consists of a one-time injection of ceftriaxone (250 mg intramuscularly) plus a 1 to 2 week course of doxycycline (100 mg orally 2 times daily) or tetracycline (500 mg 4 times per day between meals). A stat dose of amoxacillin (3 grams) or ampicillin (3.5 grams), together with 1 gram of probenecid, is an alternative to ceftriaxone in beta-lactamase negative GC.

More serious infections (e.g., PID with fever, conjunctivitis, or a widespread infection) may require a series of injections and, in some cases, admission to the hospital. Patients usually respond to treatment within 2 to 3 days.

The antibiotic used for gonorrhea in pregnant women is either ceftriaxone or spectinomycin. If the possibility of coexisting chlamydia infection exists, then erythromycin (excluding erythromycin estolate) or amoxacillin should be substituted for tetracycline. A patient should be recultured if the symptoms persist after treatment. Ideally, all cases should receive a second culture 1 to 2 months after treatment to identify nonresponsive infections or reinfections. Patients treated with regimens other than ceftriaxone with doxycycline should be recultured 4 to 7 days after completing therapy.

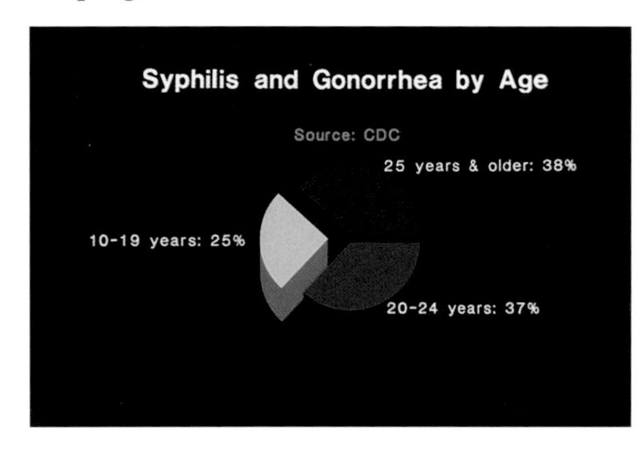

Chart 10. The Incidence of Gonorrhea and Syphilis by Age in 1990.
Over one-quarter of the cases of gonorrhea and syphilis in 1990 occurred in persons aged 10-19, indicating that current education efforts are inadequate and/or ineffective in the adolescent age group. Such unsafe sexual behavior will result in continued spread of HIV and other sexually transmitted diseases, and concerted education and prevention programs are urgently needed.

Source: Jon Fuller, S.J., M.D.

All recent sexual partners (during 30 days prior to onset of symptoms or clinical evaluation) of a person diagnosed with GC should see a caregiver for treatment immediately. Individuals found to have GC should avoid sexual contact until both they and their partner(s) have finished treatment.

Prevention and Control

The most important preventive measure against GC is either abstinence or the use of condoms with every sexual encounter, especially with partners whose histories are unknown.

Many people, especially women, have no symptoms of the infection. Therefore, sexually active people should have periodic examinations to guard against silent infection. Prostitutes, people with other sexually transmitted infections, and those whose sex partners contract gonorrhea or other STDs should regularly see a doctor or nurse practitioner.

All shelter guests should know that unprotected sexual contact puts them at risk for GC and many other infections. Ideally guests should have access to condoms. People concerned about past sexual activities and guests at high risk for acquiring or passing infection should go to a clinic for examination, cultures, and treatment. Guests who report any of the symptoms mentioned above should also seek evaluation.

All sexually active women of childbearing age who have missed a period should be tested for pregnancy. If pregnant, they should seek professional prenatal care, which usually includes examination for gonorrhea.

Newborn infants typically receive eyedrops (silver nitrate or erythromycin) to prevent conjunctival infections. While silver nitrate is quite effective against GC, it has little impact on chlamydia infection. Topical erythromycin is increasingly being used as a prophylactic agent in the delivery room.

Massachusetts law requires clinicians to report all cases of gonorrhea to the state Department of Public Health.

Summary

Gonorrhea (GC) is a bacterial infection primarily spread through sexual contact. Infection with gonorrhea, also called the "drip" or "clap", is very common. Frequently, those infected do not have any symptoms, especially women. Usual symptoms include itching, discharge, and burning while urinating.

GC can lead to inflammation of the reproductive organs, and possible infertility, particularly in women. Pregnant women infected with GC can suffer spontaneous abortions, premature delivery, and infection of the newborn.

Treatment for GC is usually simple and calls for antibiotics.

The best measure to prevent the spread of GC is either avoiding sex or using condoms with every sexual encounter. Sexually active people should receive regular examinations for GC. Also, pregnant women should seek prenatal care as soon after conception as possible. Standard prenatal care includes examination for gonorrhea.

References

Abramowicz, M. Treatment of sexually transmitted diseases. *The Medical Letter of Drugs and Therapeutics*. 1990; 32: 810.

Centers for Disease Control. 1989 sexually transmitted diseases treatment guidelines. *MMWR* 1989; 38(S-8): 21-27.

Hook EW, Holmes KK. Gonococcal infections. *Ann Int Med* 1985; 102(2): 229-243.

Karchmer AW. Sexually transmitted diseases. In: Rubenstein E, Federman DD, eds. *Scientific American Medicine* 1989; 7(XXII): 1-16.

Hepatitis B

Lori Fantry, M.D.

Hepatitis B is a viral infection that primarily affects the liver. Earlier names for this disease are "long incubation" and "serum" hepatitis. Those infected with the hepatitis B virus may show no symptoms, have a self-limited acute illness, or progress to acute liver failure or chronic liver disease.

Cold or flu-like symptoms characterize the first stages of the acute illness. These symptoms include headache, runny nose, cough, weakness, fatigue, poor appetite, nausea, vomiting, sore throat, and aches in the muscles and joints. The patient may have a mild fever. Some people lose the taste for cigarettes or coffee. Rarely, a person can develop arthritis or a rash. This early phase lasts between 1 and 28 days.

The second stage of the acute illness is the "icteric" phase. Characteristics include yellow skin (jaundice) and eyes (scleral icterus), dark urine (often Coca-Cola colored), and light or tan stools. Nausea and vomiting can continue and grow worse while other symptoms usually diminish. Some people may complain of mild right-sided abdominal pain or itching. Young children are less apt to show symptoms of illness or jaundice. However, infection without symptoms can happen at any age.

Most people recover completely within 2 to 3 months. However, some may progress to liver failure. In rare instances, the acute phase of hepatitis B can be fatal.

Some of those infected may become chronic carriers of hepatitis B. Chronic carriers may never develop signs or symptoms, but can nonetheless infect others with the virus. Chronic carriers risk chronic liver disease, cirrhosis, and carcinoma in later life.

Prevalence

The prevalence of hepatitis B varies greatly throughout the world. Africa and China have the highest number of chronic carriers while numbers in the USA are much lower. In the USA, more than 300,000 new cases of hepatitis B appear every year. Between 500,000 and 1 million people in this country chronically carry the hepatitis B virus and can infect other people.

Transmission

The spread of hepatitis B depends on the contact of blood, semen, or saliva with open skin or mucous membranes (mouth, eyes, vagina, or rectum). Blood has the highest concentration of the hepatitis B virus.

Researchers have found the hepatitis B virus in almost every other body fluid as well, including urine, feces, tears, breast milk, and menstrual fluids. However, their role in the transmission of the virus is not clearly known.

When an infected person shares a needle with others, the virus is transmitted in a very effective way. The virus can also spread by sexual intercourse, deep (French) kissing, and sharing a toothbrush or razor blade. An infant born to a mother infected with hepatitis B has a very good chance of becoming infected and carrying the virus.

The incubation period can range from 50 to 180 days. The usual incubation period is 70 to 80 days.

Diagnosis

Clinical symptoms are not sufficient for a diagnosis of hepatitis B. Blood tests must identify viral particles and serum antigens and antibodies. These tests also determine whether someone is immune to hepatitis B or a chronic carrier of the virus. Please refer to Chart 14 on page 184.

Treatment

Most cases of hepatitis B do not call for hospitalization. No specific treatments can decrease the length or severity of the illness.

Certain measures do provide symptomatic relief. Most people prefer bedrest. No set rules exist about how many days or hours in a day a person should rest. People with hepatitis B should follow a high calorie diet. The diet should supply most of the calories early in the day, because nausea and vomiting tend to be worse later. Cholestyramine, a prescription medicine, helps relieve itching. Patients should avoid drugs broken down in the liver, such as acetaminophen (Tylenol™). Alcohol and illegal drugs also burden the liver and raise the potential for severe damage.

Prevention and Control

Basic precautionary measures

The primary method of prevention relies on avoiding contact with body fluids of all people, particularly persons known to be infected with hepatitis B. Some of the most important precautions to take include:

- wear gloves when handling body fluids;
- wash hands carefully;
- cover all open, oozing wounds;
- discourage the sharing of toothbrushes and razors;
- watch children and discourage them from biting or scratching;
- use specially marked plastic bags or impermeable containers to dispose of items contaminated with blood or body fluids, such as razors;
- clean contaminated surfaces or objects such as counters or toys with a mixture of one part bleach to ten parts water (discard the solution from the previous day and mix a fresh batch every day because the bleach loses its potency over time);
- encourage all injection drug users not to share needles and to seek treatment for their addiction.

Hepatitis B vaccine may soon be part of the routine immunization schedule for all children in the USA.

People at Risk

Despite these basic precautions, some people cannot avoid being at risk. For those with no history of past exposure, the hepatitis B vaccine offers one important but costly method of prevention.

The most commonly used vaccine against hepatitis B, Recombavax™, is synthetic and derived from yeast. There are very few side effects of Recombavax™. The vaccine calls for a series of 3 shots, with the second and third given at 1 and 6 month intervals after the first. Vaccination may not provide lifelong immunity; recommendations for revaccination are not standard.

The vaccine is recommended for injection drug users, sexually active people, and others in close contact with hepatitis B carriers. Some employee health departments will provide the vaccine for workers who are at risk of exposure. Insurance may not cover this very costly vaccine for others. Local public health departments can provide specific details about the availability of the vaccine.

The CDC is currently considering hepatitis B vaccine as part of the routine immunizations for all children.

Recent Exposures

The hepatitis B immune globulin, or HBIG, is another method of prevention for individuals who have been exposed recently and have no other history of hepatitis B, including infants born to mothers with hepatitis B, sexual contacts of infected people, and those exposed directly by accidental needlestick. HBIG has passive antibodies that prevent or lessen infection if given soon enough following exposure. The hepatitis B vaccine series should begin within 7 days if the individual has never been vaccinated or has never had this virus in the past.

Chart 12. Hepatitis B virus postexposure recommendations.

Source: MMWR 1990; 39(S-2): 18

Hepatitis B virus postexposure recommendations

	HBIG		Vaccine	
Exposure	Dose	Recommended timing	Dose	Recommended timing
Perinatal	0.5 ml IM	Within 12 hours of birth	0.5 ml IM	Within 12 hours of birth•
Sexual	0.06 ml/kg IM	Single dose within 14 days of last sexual contact	1.0 ml IM	First dose at time of HBIG treatment•

• The first dose can be given the same time as the HBIG dose but in a different site; subsequent doses should be given as recommended for specific vaccine.

Chart reprinted with permission from Centers for Disease Control.

Summary

Hepatitis B is a viral infection of the liver that can cause either short- or long-term illness. Early symptoms often begin 70 to 80 days after exposure and are like those of a cold or flu. A short time after the symptoms begin the person may show yellow skin and eyes, dark urine, light colored stools, and itchy skin. Complete recovery takes 2 to 3 months.

An infected person may become a "chronic carrier". Although chronic carriers show no symptoms of the disease, they can infect others with the virus for the rest of their lives. Lifelong liver disease can also arise from hepatitis B infection.

Hepatitis B spreads most commonly by blood or semen. For example, sharing needles or having sex without using condoms transmits the virus very effectively. A person does not have to look ill to be able to spread hepatitis B. Infected persons may not even know they are hepatitis B carriers.

Once a person has symptoms, no cure exists for hepatitis B. Bedrest, high calorie food, and aspirin can help the aches and fevers. Prescription medications are available to relieve itching. Alcohol and drugs such as acetominophen (Tylenol™) or other legal and illegal substances broken down by the liver should be avoided.

Prevention of hepatitis B is possible when good general infection control principles are routinely followed.

Recommendations for hepatitis B prophylaxis following percutaneous or permucosal exposure

Status of exposed person	Status of source of exposure		
	HBsAg-positive	HBsAg-negative	Source not tested or unknown
Unvaccinated	HBIG x 1* (within 24 hours) and initiate HB vaccine within 7 days	Initiate HB vaccine	Initiate HB vaccine
Previously vaccinated known responder	Test exposed for anti-HBs 1. If adequate,• 2. If inadequate, HB vaccine booster dose	No treatment No treatment	No treatment
Known nonresponder to vaccine series	HBIG x 2 (one month apart) HBIG x 1 plus 1 dose HB vaccine	No treatment	If known high-risk source, may treat as if source were HBsAg-positive
Response to vaccine unknown	Test exposed for anti-HBs 1. If inadequate• HBIG x 1 plus HB vaccine booster dose 2. If adequate, no treatment	No treatment	Test exposed for anti-HBs 1. If inadequate•, HB vaccine booster dose 2. If adequate, no treatment

** HBIG dose 0.06 ml/kg IM.*
• Adequate anti-HBs is ≥ 10 SRU by RIA or positive by EIA.

Chart reprinted with permission from Centers for Disease Control.

Chart 13. Recommendations for hepatitis B prophylaxis following percutaneous or permucosal exposure.

Source: MMWR 1990; 39(S-2): 20

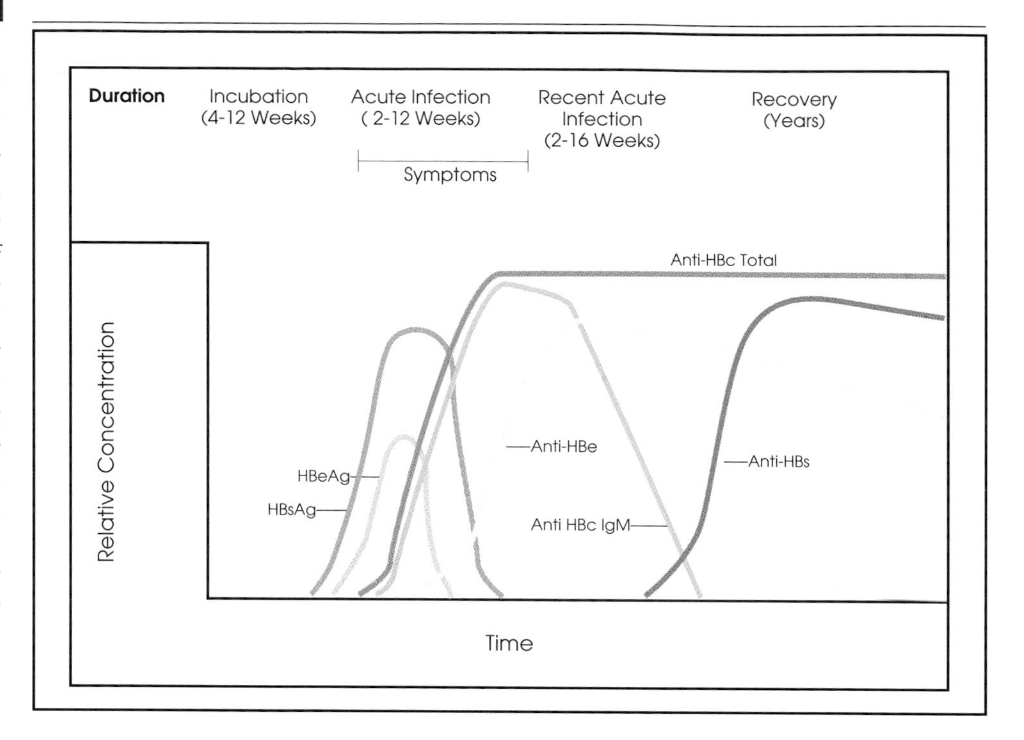

Chart 14. A Guide to the Clinical Signs and Serology of Hepatitis B Infection.

Flu-like symptoms usually appear 70-80 days after exposure to the virus, followed soon afterwards by the appearance of jaundice. A rise of HBsAg then precedes the rise in the liver enzyme ALT, and both will generally recede 4-5 months after exposure (with the exception of the chronic carriers, whose HBsAg remains elevated for life). The protective antibody HBsAb appears several months after initial infection, often after HBsAg is no longer detectable. During that "window" when neither HBsAg or HBsAb are detectable in an infected person, the anti-HBc may be the only indication of hepatitis B infection.

(Chart adapted from the brochure "Serodiagnostic Assessment of Acute Viral Hepatitis" published by Abbott Diagnostics Educational Services.)

A vaccine to protect those at high risk for hepatitis B is available. However, the vaccine is very costly, and many health insurance policies do not include it in their coverage.

References

Centers for Disease Control. Recommendations for protecting against viral hepatitis. Leads from the Morbidity and Mortality Weekly Report. *JAMA* 1985; 254(2): 197-217.

Dienstag JL, Wands JR, Isselbacher KJ. Acute hepatitis. In: Wilson JD, Braunwald E, Isselbacher KJ, Petersdorf RG, Martin JB, Fauci AS, Root RK, eds. *Harrison's Principles of Internal Medicine.* 12th ed. New York: McGraw Hill Book Company; 1991: 1322-1336.

Ockner R. Acute viral hepatitis. In: Wyngaarden JB, Smith LH, eds. *Textbook of Medicine.* 18th ed. Philadelphia: WB Saunders Company; 1988: 818-826.

Glossary

Serologic Markers

HBsAg

Hepatitis B Surface Antigen. Earliest indicator of the presence of acute infection. Also indicative of chronic infection.

Anti-HBs

Antibody to Hepatitis B Surface Antigen. Indicator of clinical recovery and subsequent immunity to hepatitis B virus. Appearance is generally 1 to 4 months following onset of symptoms, but may be delayed much longer.

Anti-HBc IgM

Antibody (IgM) to Core Antigen (anti-HBc IgM). This marker is an early indicator of acute infection. It is prominent during the acute phase of infection and is rarely detectable in chronic infection. It is also useful in distinguishing acute from chronic hepatitis B infection and hepatitis B from non-A, non-B hepatitis.

Anti-HBc

Total Antibody (IgG and IgM) to Core Antigen (anti-HBc). This is a lifelong marker that represents past infection as well as active infection in the acute/chronic period.

HBeAg

Hepatitis B e Antigen. Early indicator of acute active infection representing the most infectious period. Usually short-lived (3 to 6 weeks). Persistence to e antigen in the acute stage beyond 10 weeks is indicative of progression to chronic carrier state and probable chronic liver disease.

Anti-HBe

Antibody to Hepatitis B e Antigen. Seroconversion from HBeAg to anti-HBe during acute stage is prognostic for resolution of infection. Its presence along with anti-HBc can also confirm the convalescence stage in the absence of anti-HBs.

Chart 15. Serologic Markers of Hepatitis B.

Source: Adapted from the brochure "Serodiagnostic Assessment of Acute Viral Hepatitis" published by Abbott Diagnostics Educational Services.

BHCHP physician Rika Maeshiro examines a patient in the primary care clinic at Boston City Hospital.

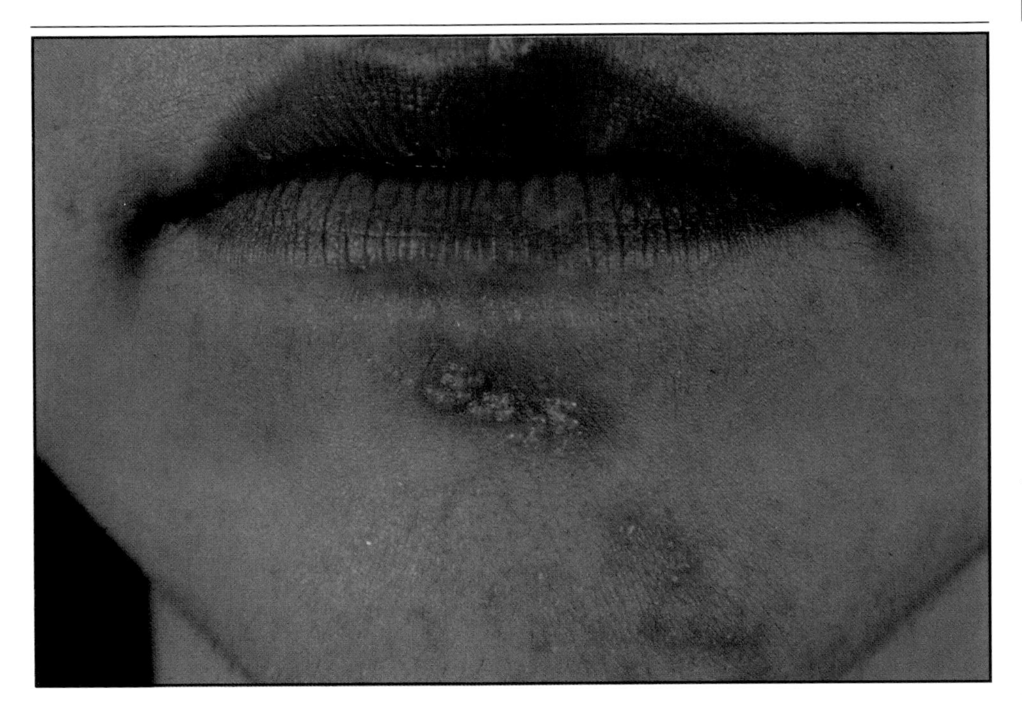

Herpes Simplex Virus (HSV)

Michael Bierer, M.D., M.P.H.

Oral Herpes Simplex. Small clear blisters are grouped on a reddish base and are frequently painful. This lesion lasts about 7-10 days, and recurred twice each year in this patient.

Herpes simplex virus (HSV) causes many common rashes, including oral herpes ("cold sores" or "fever blisters") and genital herpes. Oral herpes occurs in 20 to 40 percent of the adult population, while genital herpes affects 2 to 10 percent of adults.

For those with healthy immune systems, HSV infection is usually harmless. However, pregnant women infected with herpes simplex can pass on a severe, life-threatening disease to their newborns.

It was once believed that oral lesions arose from infection with one type of the virus (HSV-1) while another type of the virus (HSV-2) caused genital lesions. Changes in sexual practices have led to more frequent oral-genital contact, and researchers have found that both oral and genital herpes can be due to either type.

Infection with HSV is lifelong. After the first infection, the virus stays inactive in the nerves that go to the affected skin. Such factors as sunlight, fever, or other types of stress can cause the virus to become active and form the skin rash.

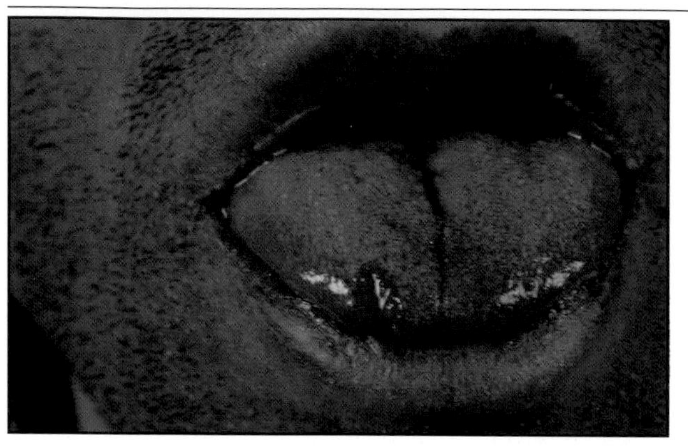

Oral Herpes Simplex.
This painful inflammation of the tongue can be accompanied by a low-grade fever and swollen neck glands. The symptoms usually resolve in about two weeks.

Oral Herpes

Most people show no symptoms following their first infection with HSV-1.

In children, a primary infection of the mouth may lead to gingivostomatitis, a painful inflammation of the roof of the mouth, cheeks, gums, and tongue. After an incubation period of several days to two weeks, lesions of HSV appear, usually accompanied by low-grade fever, swollen neck glands, and bad breath. The symptoms generally resolve within 2 weeks.

In young adults, the first HSV infection may cause a sore throat that is difficult to distinguish from other viral infections. The virus may then reactivate as the more common cold sore.

The lesions of HSV are tiny, clear blisters (vesicles) grouped on a reddish base. Tingling or itching in the affected areas often begins several hours before the lesions appear. Lesions usually occur on or around the corner of the lips where the skin meets the mucous membrane of the mouth (the vermilion border). The vesicles are painful for the first day. After 48 hours, they become ulcerated and crust over. The lesions generally heal completely within 10 days.

Lesions usually recur in the same place. The frequency of reactivation can vary from every few weeks to twice a year, or even less often.

Genital Herpes

Genital herpes is becoming more common. Infection appears in sexually active people of both sexes and all ages, although young adults have the highest incidence of the disease.

Following the first infection, the virus incubates for 2 to 7 days before the vesicles appear. The vesicles are small and painful, and they ulcerate. For women, lesions usually appear on the labia minora but can involve the vulva, perineum, buttocks, cervix, and vagina. HSV lesions in men generally arise on the glans and shaft of the penis. Infection from anal intercourse may produce lesions in the anus and rectum.

With the appearance of vesicles, the lymph nodes in the groin swell painfully. Systemic effects of primary genital herpes can include malaise, fever, and rarely, aseptic meningitis. Primary infections last for about 2 weeks.

Most primary genital infections reappear. Recurrences generally last only one week and do not make people feel sick. Symptoms generally tend to be more severe in women.

Complications

HSV encephalitis is rare but can occur in either sex at any age. The onset of this complication is unpredictable. Symptoms of encephalitis include headache, fever, confusion, seizures, and unusual behavior. If left untreated, encephalitis often results in coma and death.

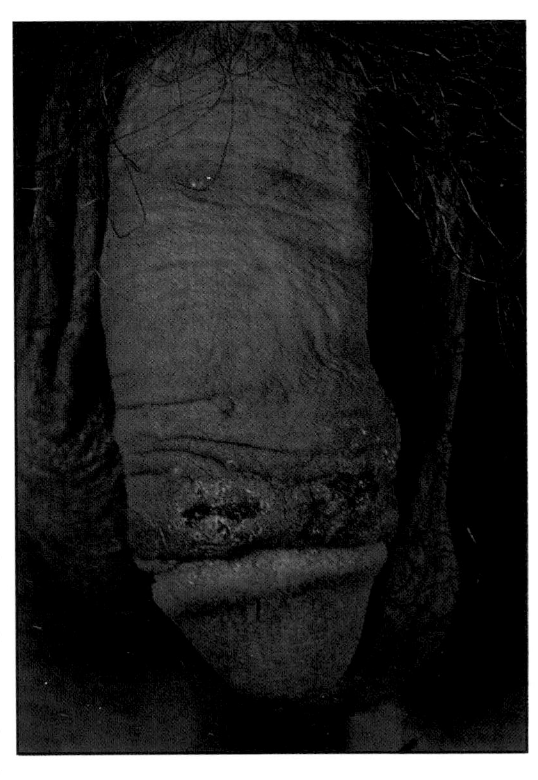

Genital Herpes. Several small blisters on the shaft of the penis in addition to areas of erosion. The differential diagnosis of these latter lesions would include chancres due to syphilis.

A mother first infected with HSV early in pregnancy runs a significant risk of losing the fetus or having a severely malformed baby. While rare, an infected woman also risks passing the infection directly to her fetus or her baby during a vaginal delivery. This can occur in the absence of lesions.

Infection of a newborn can be severe, but is preventable. Neonates exposed to the virus during a vaginal birth may develop vesicles or an eye infection. Such localized disease usually resolves with antiviral therapy. However, the disease can become diffuse in newborns, involving internal organs and the central nervous system. Death is common in untreated cases.

HSV infection of the eye usually causes it to become red, teary, and painful. The person may experience visual disturbances and damage to the cornea leading to permanent visual problems.

For people with impaired immune systems due to chronic illnesses such as AIDS or cancer, primary or recurrent HSV infections can spread rapidly. The infection may involve large areas of skin or internal organs, including the liver, lung, gastrointestinal tract, and central nervous system.

Transmission

All herpes vesicles and ulcers are highly infectious. Crusted lesions are not as infectious as vesicles. Viral particles can be spread through direct contact with lesions, saliva, and drainage from an infected eye.

Oral Herpes

Oral herpes is commonly spread through kissing. The virus can be present in saliva even when there are no symptoms. A person can also contract HSV on the fingertips by touching an infected person's saliva or lesions (herpetic whitlow).

Genital Herpes

A symptomatic person has a high chance of infecting a sexual partner after only one encounter. Two to 10 percent of asymptomatic people are also infectious.

Those with oral herpes can spread the virus to the genital area by their hands. However, caregivers should suspect the possibility of sexual abuse when HSV genital infections appear in prepubertal children.

In a pregnant woman with an active HSV genital infection, the virus may spread into the uterus, leading to fetal infection. The virus may also spread to the newborn during a vaginal delivery.

Diagnosis

Clinical diagnosis relies on the presence of the characteristic rash. A history of recurrence of the sores coupled with the specific sensations of tingling and itching may help to make the diagnosis. Caregivers may confuse the lesions with those of varicella (chickenpox). Generally, culturing to confirm the diagnosis is costly and unnecessary.

Treatment

Oral lesions are normally self-limited and do not require specific therapy. People should keep their lesions clean and dry to speed healing and prevent bacterial infection. Acyclovir, an antiviral medication, is probably not useful for oral infections.

For a primary genital infection, oral acyclovir can shorten the duration of symptoms, reduce the period of infectivity, and accelerate healing. Topical acyclovir may shorten the symptoms of genital lesions during the initial infection, but is not useful on recurrent lesions. If given early in severe recurrences, oral acyclovir may shorten the duration of lesions from 7 to 5 days. For those with severe and frequent recurrences, twice daily oral acyclovir prevents reactivation and is safe for at least as long as 3 years.

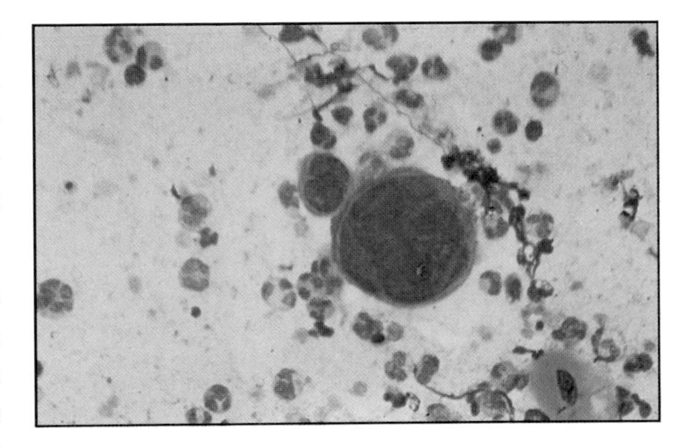

A multinucleated giant cell is seen under the microscope following a Tzanck preparation of a scraping from the base of an unroofed HSV blister. This finding indicates the presence of a virus of the herpes family. Expensive cultures are required to determine which member, but this is seldom necessary with an adequate history and physical examination.

Acyclovir is indicated for infants with both localized and generalized HSV infection. Acyclovir can be dangerous for pregnant women.

An infected person with an impaired immune system may require admission to a hospital and intravenous acyclovir whenever the herpes simplex infection becomes severe. Mild recurrences in such cases may respond to oral acyclovir.

For all types of herpes simplex infections, acyclovir does not eliminate the virus.

HSV ocular infections can be treated with topical solutions and ointments. An ophthalmologist should manage the treatment of all cases of ocular infections. Recurrence is possible, and the severity of each event is unpredictable.

Prevention and Control

No vaccine for HSV exists. The key to prevention and control lies not in the medicine chest but in knowledge, attitudes, and behavior.

People with active herpes lesions should wash their hands often with warm water and soap, especially before touching other people and after applying medication.

Infected people should avoid kissing, nuzzling, or other behaviors that would put their partners at risk of coming into contact with vesicles and early ulcers. Symptomatic people can help reduce accidental contact with their lesions by covering them with clothing or bandages. People with active infections should try to avoid touching newborns or people with poor immune systems.

Latex condoms can reduce the chance of genital herpes, but they do not completely eliminate it. The best way to reduce spread is to abstain from sex when lesions are active.

More detailed information available in the Specific Guidelines to prevent the transmission of infections through sexual contact and direct contact on pages 40-46.

Pregnant women and their partners should seek professional prenatal care to prevent the spread of HSV to their unborn children. If the mother has active genital herpes late in gestation, the baby may need to be delivered by Caesarean section to avoid exposure to the virus in the birth canal.

Education

Individual counseling for people with HSV should focus on how to change behavior during symptomatic recurrences. Counselors should provide information about transmission, including the possibilities of spread when symptoms are not present. Society attaches an unjustified stigma to those with herpes simplex, heightening anxiety in infected individuals. People with the infection should realize that HSV seldom entails severe complications, except for neonates and those with weakened immune systems.

Summary

Herpes simplex virus (HSV) is responsible for many infections from common cold sores or fever blisters to genital herpes. Herpes lesions usually appear as groups of blisters on a red base. The infection is lifelong and can recur with varying frequency.

While herpes can be uncomfortable and even painful, complications seldom occur in healthy people. People with weakened immune systems run the risk of severe infection that can spread to internal organs. Complications in newborns of infected women depend on the time of the mother's first infection. Symptoms in newborns can range from mild and localized to severe and life-threatening.

HSV spreads when uninfected people contact infected secretions through such activities as touching, kissing, or sex. Treatment may call for an antiviral medication that unfortunately does not prevent recurrences forever. People with open lesions should wash their hands often, cover their lesions, and avoid intimate contact with others while the lesions are present. Condoms can help limit the spread of herpes simplex during sexual activity.

Pregnant women and their partners should seek professional prenatal care to prevent the spread of HSV to their unborn children.

References

Baker DA, Blythe JG, Kaufman R, Hale R, Portnoy J. One year suppression of frequent recurrence of genital herpes with oral acyclovir. *Obstetrics & Gynecology* 1989; 73(1): 84-87.

Corey L, Spear PG. Infections with herpes simplex viruses (2). *N Engl J Med* 1986; 314(12): 686-691, 749-756.

Guinan ME. Oral acyclovir for treatment and suppression of genital herpes simplex virus infection. *JAMA* 1986; 255(13): 1747-1749.

Hirsh MS. Herpes simplex virus. In: Mandell GL, Douglas RG, Bennett JE, eds. *Principles and Practice of Infectious Diseases*. 3rd ed. New York: Churchill Livingstone; 1990: 1144-1153.

Kaplowitz LG, Baker M, Gelb L, Blythe J, Hale R, et al. Prolonged continuous acyclovir treatment of normal adults with frequently recurring genital herpes simplex virus infection. *JAMA* 1991; 265(6): 747-751.

Mertz GJ, Jones CC, Mills J, Fife KH, Lemon SM, Stapleton JT, et al. Long-term acyclovir suppression of frequently recurring genital herpes simplex virus infection. *JAMA* 1988; 260(2): 201-206.

Straus SE, Rooney JF, Sever JL, Seidlin M, Nusinoff-Lehrman S, et al. NIH conference: herpes simplex virus infection: biology, treatment, and prevention. *Ann Int Med* 1985; 103(3): 404-419.

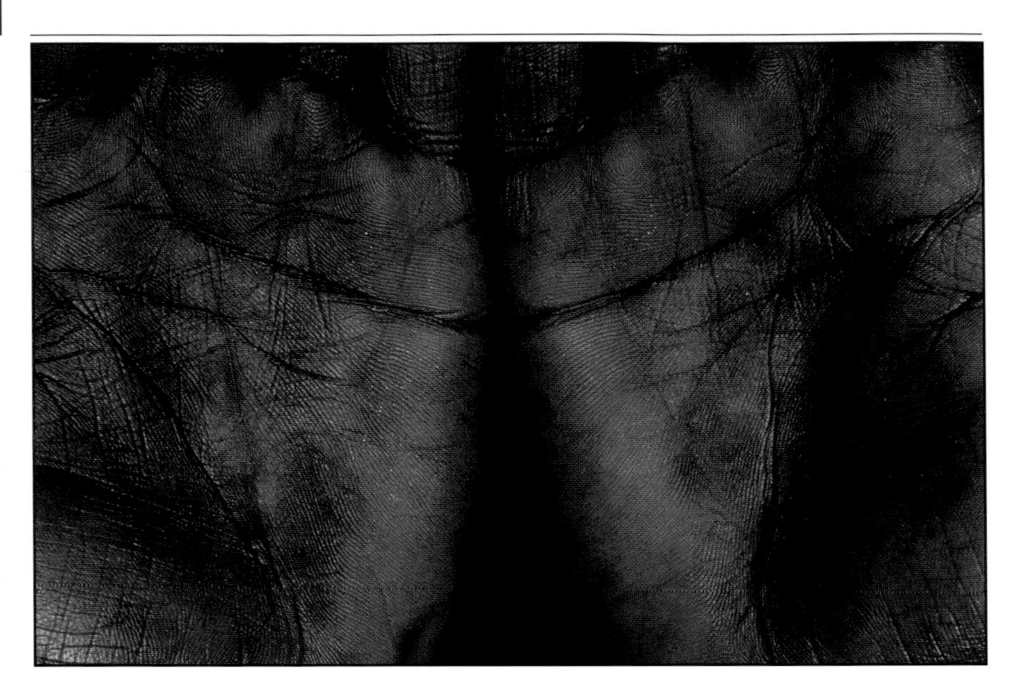

Syphilis

James J. O'Connell, M.D.

Syphilis is a very serious sexually transmitted disease (STD) found throughout the world. When penicillin was discovered in the 1940s, public health authorities hoped that this antibiotic would eliminate the disease. While the number of cases did decline dramatically in the USA during the 1950s, the incidence of syphilis has risen sharply over the past decade.

Secondary Syphilis. This man presented to the BHCHP Clinic at Boston City Hospital with a rash of the palms of his hands, the soles of his feet, and the roof of his mouth. He complained of fatigue and a loss of appetite, and did not recall a chancre or other symptoms in the past. His VDRL and FTA-ABS were positive.

Syphilis in history

Syphilis has played a prominent role in shaping Western civilization. Julius Caesar, Cleopatra and her soldiers, and Herod the King of Judea are among the many historical figures who showed signs and symptoms of this disease. King Henry VIII of England was so disabled by advanced syphilis that a pulley was needed to hoist him onto his horse. Congenital syphilis probably contributed to the cruelty his daughter Mary Tudor ("Bloody Mary") displayed toward her subjects. She had a prematurely old face, sparse hair, "pushed-in nose", a square head with a prominent forehead — all consequences of congenital syphilis.

Christopher Columbus heard voices and thought himself an "ambassador of God" during his later voyages to America. He had to be carried ashore during his last voyage in 1504 because of paralysis below the waist. Van Gogh's insanity has often been attributed to syphilis. Syphilis emerges as a central theme of James Joyce's masterpiece *Ulysses*, a metaphor for the moral and spiritual decay of Ireland. Joyce suffered a lifelong eye infection (iritis), due to congenital syphilis.

Clinical course

Syphilis is a very complicated bacterial infection caused by a spirochete called *Treponema pallidum*. This organism enters the body during sexual activity, multiplies at a very rapid rate, and spreads through the lymph and blood streams to virtually every organ and tissue in the body. The four stages characteristic of untreated syphilis are: primary, secondary, latent, and tertiary. In addition, congenital syphilis occurs when babies are born already infected with the spirochete from an infected mother.

1. Primary syphilis

The spirochete enters the body at a point of contact during sexual relations. Ten to 60 days later, a sore or chancre (pronounced "shanker") develops at that site, usually the penis, cervix, vagina, mouth, rectal area, or any place where the skin might have been cut or abraded. This chancre is painless and often goes unnoticed, especially when it occurs in hard-to-see places such as the rectum or vaginal area. Sometimes the lymph nodes will be swollen in the groin or neck. The chancre disappears within a few weeks even without treatment, but the disease continues to progress.

2. Secondary syphilis

One to 6 months after the chancre disappears, a rash may appear over the entire body, especially the soles of the feet, palms of the hands, mouth, buttocks, and genitals. Moist, wart-like lesions called condylomata lata can appear in the genital or anal area; these are highly infectious. Most people will feel sick at this time and complain of fevers, muscle aches, swollen glands, sore throat, loss of appetite, and fatigue. Body hair may become thin and fall out in patchy areas of the scalp, eyebrows, and eyelids. Similar to the first stage, these signs and symptoms will disappear completely even without treatment.

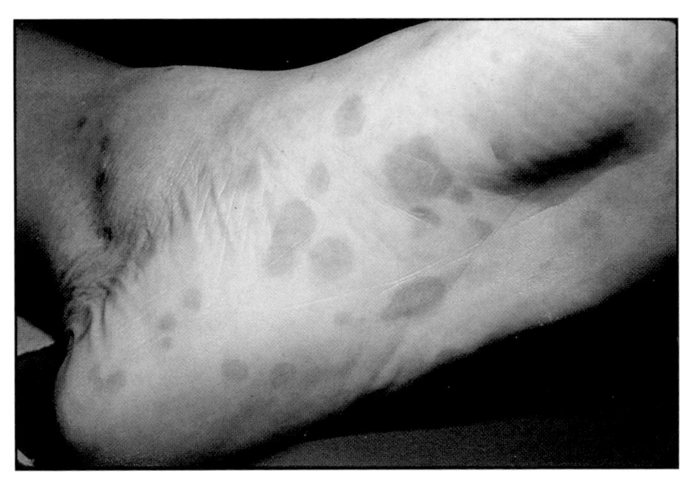

Secondary Syphilis. This itchy rash of the soles of the feet was accompanied by muscle aches and generalized lymphadenopathy. The VDRL and FTA-ABS were positive and the lumbar puncture was negative, and this pregnant woman with a history of injection drug use was treated with IM penicillin on two successive weeks.

3. Latent syphilis

Syphilis is highly infectious during the primary and secondary stages, but a latent stage then follows during which the infected person cannot transmit the spirochete to a sexual partner. The person feels fine and has no evidence of disease on physical examination. Only a blood test can help diagnose syphilis at this time.

The early form of this stage lasts for about a year. Relapses may occur as spirochetes spill into the bloodstream and cause the person to once again become infectious. The late latent stage may extend for life or may be followed by tertiary syphilis. While the spirochete cannot be passed to sexual partners at this stage, an infected pregnant woman can pass the disease on to her fetus.

4. Tertiary syphilis

The most dangerous effects of the disease are seen in tertiary syphilis, which can occur from 2 to more than 40 years after an initial, untreated infection. Large blood vessels, particularly the aorta, can become involved and lead to life-threatening aneurysms (ballooning of the blood vessels) as well as heart failure due to aortic insufficiency. Blindness and insanity can occur. Tertiary syphilis can affect virtually every organ of the body. Surprisingly, the disease is not infectious or contagious at this devastating stage.

During the past two years the number of cases of syphilis has more than doubled in large cities such as New York and Los Angeles.

Neurosyphilis is a common complication of tertiary syphilis, which occurs when the spirochete invades the brain and the spinal cord. While this usually appears during tertiary syphilis, many people infected with both HIV and syphilis have progressed rapidly to this stage. Symptoms of neurosyphilis range from no observable impairments to a wide array of devastating manifestations, such as:

- meningovascular syphilis, resulting in seizures and strokes;
- general paresis, characterized by dementia with slurred speech and difficulty walking;
- tabes dorsalis, seen only rarely, characterized by urinary incontinence, pains in the legs, constipation, and a broad-based gait;
- optic atrophy with blindness, which occurs rarely with neurosyphilis.

Other complications of tertiary syphilis include gummas or gummata. These raised, nodular skin lesions with a violet color may appear from 3 to 7 years after untreated infection. Gummas can also occur in the bone, liver, stomach, brain, heart, and lungs. The lesions can be fatal, but they generally respond dramatically to penicillin.

5. Congenital syphilis

A pregnant woman can transmit syphilis to her unborn baby during any of these stages. The spirochete passes through the umbilical cord and may cause some babies to die in the womb and may cause others to be born prematurely with a poor chance of survival. Babies born with the disease may develop a rash, runny nose, large liver and spleen, jaundice, anemia, and neurological difficulties. Because of the devastating effects of this disease on unborn children, every pregnant woman should have a blood test for syphilis during the first and third trimesters.

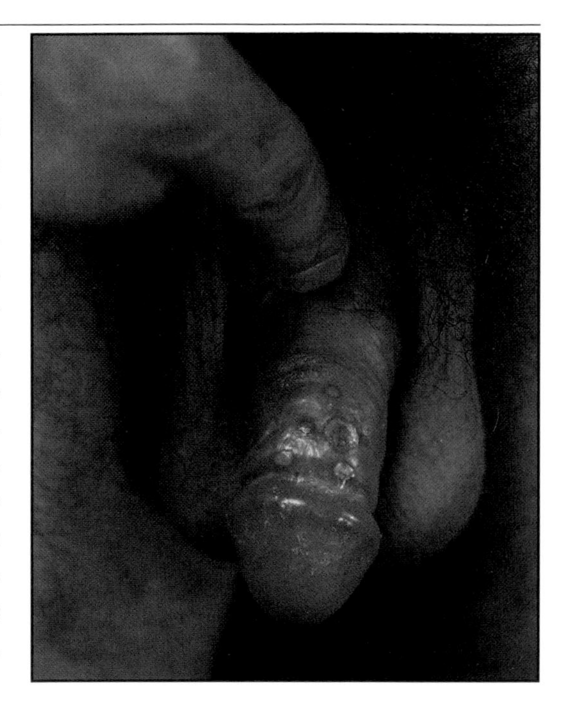

Primary Syphilis. This chancre of primary syphilis is often unnoticed because it is painless, and will disappear within a few weeks even without treatment.

Prevalence

With the discovery of penicillin in the 1940s, and major campaigns to treat all sexual contacts of those with syphilis, the number of cases in the United States declined from 106,539 in 1947 to just 6,392 in 1956. In 1988, new cases of primary and secondary syphilis jumped to 40,117, with the number of cases in large cities such as New York and Los Angeles more than doubling in 2 years. Many public health doctors and nurses view the syphilis epidemic as a precursor to a rise in the number of AIDS cases in the inner cities of our country.

The incidence of congenital syphilis has been rising since 1982 and reflects higher rates of primary and secondary syphilis among women of childbearing age. From 1986 to 1988, New York City experienced a six-fold increase of infection in newborns, prompting the state to mandate testing for syphilis at birth.

Transmission

The disease spreads through sexual or intimate contact with infectious sores or lesions. The spirochetes from these infected areas enter the partner's body through the penis, vagina and surrounding area, cervix, mouth, rectum, and any areas where the skin has broken down. About half of those having sexual contact with an infected person will develop the disease.

Because the early signs of syphilis can go undetected, infected people may not notice the disease and may then easily and unknowingly transmit it to another person. Even with use of a condom, infection is still possible from chancres at the base of the penis, an area not covered by the condom. Diaphragms and spermicides do not protect against syphilis. Anal intercourse is very dangerous because chancres in the rectal area are often difficult to see. Lesions on the lips and tongue can transmit infection as well.

Diagnosis

The transmission of syphilis is NOT prevented by condoms, diaphragms, or spermicides.

Syphilis can be diagnosed when the secretion from the chancre (primary stage) or from a moist mucosal lesion (secondary stage or congenital syphilis) shows *Treponema pallidum* under a special dark field of the microscope. If a patient has used soap or antiseptics on the affected areas, this exam will be negative. Lesions from the mouth will give false positive results because the oral cavity normally contains several other species of spirochetes.

Blood tests

The two basic tests are the VDRL (or RPR) and FTA-ABS.

1. VDRL (Venereal Disease Research Laboratory)
VDRL is inexpensive and very effective as a screening tool. Within 4 to 6 weeks, the body produces antibodies that can be quantitated by the VDRL. This test is positive in 70 percent of primary, 99 percent of secondary, 95 percent of latent, and 70 percent of tertiary syphilis. Unfortunately, many other conditions can lead to false positives for the VDRL, including some chronic infections, pregnancy, recent immunizations, febrile illnesses, and heroin addiction.

2. FTA-ABS (Flourescent Treponemal Antibody ABSorption Test)
Because of the possibility of false positives, caregivers normally order a second test to verify any positive VDRL result. This test, called the FTA-ABS , is more costly and more difficult to perform. The test is very sensitive because it directly interacts with the antigens on the spirochete. The FTA-ABS is positive for 85 percent of those with primary syphilis and virtually all of those with secondary, latent, and tertiary syphilis. Once a person receives a positive result on the FTA-ABS, he or she will continue to be positive throughout life because antibodies to syphilis will always be present. To measure the course of the disease and the response to treatment, caregivers must then use the VDRL or a similar test, the RPR.

Treatment

Penicillin is the treatment of choice for all stages of syphilis. The earlier the therapy is begun, the better the results. Early treatment cures syphilis. If treatment begins later, a cure is possible, but damage to the vital organs may be permanent.

The Centers for Disease Control (CDC) establishes guidelines for the treatment of the various stages of syphilis. All people exposed to syphilis or who have contracted the disease should immediately see a physician or seek help from the local public health department.

1. Less than one year's duration

For syphilis of less than one year's duration, the CDC currently recommends benzathine penicillin G, 2.4 million units in a single intramuscular dose. Some public health providers suggest a second dose a week later for women of childbearing age to prevent congenital syphilis.

For those allergic to penicillin, oral tetracycline (500 mg 4 times a day for 15 days) is recommended. Pregnant women should not take tetracycline. Erythromycin is commonly recommended for pregnant women who are allergic to penicillin and not candidates for desensitization to that antibiotic.

2. Untreated for more than one year

When an infected person has gone for more than a year without treatment, additional penicillin treatments are necessary. Neurosyphilis and congenital syphilis require intravenous penicillin.

3. Concurrent HIV infection

The appropriate treatment for people infected with HIV and syphilis is controversial. Evidence suggests that concurrent HIV infection accelerates the development of the later stages of syphilis, especially neurosyphilis. Caregivers should routinely screen all people with HIV infection for syphilis and refer suspected cases for immediate evaluation. Early examination of the CSF may be prudent. For patients with impaired immune systems, the VDRL can be nonreactive. They may require the FTA-ABS or other treponemal tests.

Follow-up

To assure a cure, all people treated for syphilis or exposure to syphilis should have VDRLs drawn at 1, 3, 6, and 12 months after treatment.

Caregivers should treat patients according to the guidelines for syphilis of greater than one year's duration whenever:

- the signs and symptoms of syphilis return;
- the titer of the VDRL shows a fourfold increase;
- the initially elevated VDRL fails to decrease fourfold during the course of the year.

Patients with untreated syphilis of more than one year's duration should have a VDRL drawn at 3, 6, 12, and 24 months after treatment.

Neurosyphilis requires careful follow-up with serologic tests, clinical evaluation, and repeated lumbar punctures every 6 months for 3 years.

Jarisch-Herxheimer Reaction

Over one-half of those with primary or secondary syphilis will develop a Jarisch-Herxheimer reaction about 6 to 8 hours after initiating treatment with penicillin or other antibiotics. This reaction lasts about 12 to 24 hours and consists of fever, chills, low blood pressure, fast heart rate, muscle aches, headache, sore throat, and worsening of the skin lesions of secondary syphilis.

Prevention and Control

Syphilis spreads only by sexual contact and can be prevented only by abstaining or limiting one's partners. Use of condoms and diaphragms does not guard against syphilis. Unlike HIV and hepatitis B, syphilis is not spread by intravenous or injection drug use. It cannot spread by contact with urine, stool, or sputum.

All sexually active people, especially women of childbearing age, should receive tests for syphilis every 2 to 3 years as part of routine primary care. For prenatal patients, a VDRL should be drawn at the time of the first visit and repeated early in the third trimester (28 weeks).

Each case of syphilis must be reported to the local health department within 48 hours. All sexual contacts must be notified. They need and deserve immediate treatment even if they have no signs or symptoms of the disease. People with syphilis should avoid all sexual contact until they and their partner(s) complete treatments and follow-up serologic tests confirm their cures.

People with syphilis should be encouraged to seek HIV testing, because concurrent infection with HIV appears to accelerate the course of syphilis. Likewise, all

HIV seropositive patients should receive tests for syphilis, especially those with behavioral or neurological symptoms.

Summary

Syphilis is a very dangerous sexually transmitted disease (STD) caused by the bacterium, *Treponema pallidum*. The incidence of this disease has been rising dramatically in major cities throughout the United States during the past several years.

Syphilis can involve every organ and tissue of the body. When left untreated, syphilis goes through 4 stages of development, the full course of which may take as long as 40 years. A condition known as congenital syphilis in infants can occur when pregnant women infected with syphilis transmit the disease to their unborn babies.

Blood tests and microscopic examination of secretions from the lesions of syphilis can confirm a diagnosis. Penicillin is the drug of choice for all stages of syphilis, with tetracycline or erythromycin as alternatives for those allergic to penicillin.

To help control the disease, caregivers must report all cases to the local health department. Sexual partners of an infected person should also receive treatment.

References

Centers for Disease Control. Recommendations for diagnosing and treating syphilis in HIV-infected patients. *MMWR* 1988; 37(39): 600-602, 607-608.

Holmes KK, Mardh PA, Sparling PF, Wiesner PJ, eds. *Sexually Transmitted Diseases*. 2nd ed. New York: McGraw-Hill; 1990: 3-16, 213-262.

Johns DR, Tierney M, Felsenstein D. Alteration in the natural history of neurosyphilis by concurrent infection with the human immunodeficiency virus. *N Engl J Med* 1987; 316(25): 1569-1572.

Relman DA, Schoolnik GK, Swartz MN. Syphilis and nonvenereal treponematoses. In: Rubenstein E, Federman DD, eds. *Scientific American Medicine* 1988; 7(VI): 1-10.

Siegel D, Washington AE. Syphilis: updated approach to an old disease. *Postgraduate Medicine* 1987; 81(1): 83-91.

b. Shelter Guests. The vaccine history of a shelter guest is often unknown or unclear. In addition, environmental and logistical problems such as crowding, the presence of children too young for vaccination, and the rapid turnover of guests make the prevention and control of communicable diseases extremely complicated. Our Family Program has collaborated with the neighborhood health centers to assist families with the completion of immunization "passports" that document all vaccinations. These passports are most helpful to parents when enrolling children in the Boston school system, which requires up-to-date immunizations.

c. Establishing Immunity. Accepted ways of establishing immunity for the vaccine-preventable diseases are outlined below. Detailed information about the vaccines DTP (diphtheria, tetanus and polio) and MMR (measles, mumps and rubella) can be found in the next section of Part Four.

Diphtheria and tetanus

- documentation of completion of primary series within the past 10 years, or
- documentation of primary series with booster doses every ten years since.

Measles

- born before 1/1/57*, or
- documentation of 2 doses of measles-containing vaccine on or after the first birthday and after 1/1/68, or
- laboratory evidence of measles immunity, or
- physician documentation of measles disease.

* Although the risk of not already having measles is small in those born before 1/1/57, shelter staff may wish to receive a dose of vaccine.

Mumps

- born before 1/1/57**, or
- laboratory evidence of mumps immunity, or
- physician documentation of mumps disease, or
- documentation of mumps vaccine on or after first birthday.

** Approximately 90 percent of adults born prior to 1/1/57 have had actual mumps infection, and therefore have natural immunity with minimal risk for recurrent infection.

Rubella

- documentation of vaccination on or after first birthday, or
- laboratory evidence of a past infection with rubella.

Anyone without proof of immunity to any of the above diseases is a candidate for vaccination.

Chickenpox
Immunity is likely if:

- your parent or primary caregiver can confirm a history of chickenpox, or
- you lived in the same house with siblings or other persons that were infected with chickenpox (diagnosed by a doctor), or
- you cared for someone who was ill with physician-diagnosed chickenpox.

III. The "Uncommon" Vaccine-Preventable Diseases

These illnesses, once epidemic in this country, are now relatively rare because of widespread immunization programs. For example, the CDC reported 3 cases of diphtheria, no cases of polio, and 396 cases of rubella with 1 child born with congenital rubella syndrome nationwide in 1989. However, aggressive immunization programs will continue to be necessary to prevent recurrences of these diseases.

Diphtheria

Diphtheria, a bacterial infection that most often involves the upper respiratory passages, causes swollen tonsils, enlarged cervical lymph glands, fever, and an exudate that adheres to the mucous membranes of the throat. This exudate, which varies in color from gray to black, can impair breathing if it encroaches on the upper airway. The bacteria also produce a toxin that can result in neurological and cardiac problems.

Widespread immunization has made this disease very rare in the United States. In 1989, the Centers for Disease Control received reports of only 3 cases of diphtheria nationwide. However, several cases of diphtheria were reported among adult homeless individuals in Seattle in 1990.

Diphtheria toxoid, the vaccine that prevents diphtheria, is made from inactivated toxins and cannot cause disease. The toxins retain their antigenic properties and allow the recipient to develop immunity. Children under 7 years of age normally receive 5 doses of diphtheria toxoid in early childhood. Doses begin as early as 6 weeks of age. This schedule may be adjusted for those with delayed or inadequate immunity.

Diphtheria toxoid comes in several forms:

- **DTP** (the toxoids of diphtheria and tetanus coupled with pertussis vaccine) is the standard immunization for children up to age 7;
- **DT** (diphtheria and tetanus toxoids) is for children under the age of 7 for whom pertussis immunization is deferred or contraindicated;
- **Td** (tetanus and diphtheria toxoids) is for children over 7 years of age and older adults. Td contains a lower dose of diphtheria toxoid, diminishing the risk of adverse reaction in this older age group.

To assure continued immunity, booster injections of diphtheria toxoid are recommended every 10 years following the primary series. Because people routinely receive tetanus toxoid for preventive therapy of wounds, Td includes diphtheria toxoid to provide the needed booster.

Side effects of diphtheria toxoid may include a reaction at the site of injection (redness, induration, pain) and a moderately-elevated temperature for up to 24 hours.

Adults working in shelters should show evidence of immunity to diphtheria. To prove immunity, they should have one of the following:

- documentation of a primary series with Td within the past 10 years, or
- documentation of a primary series in childhood and a booster within the preceding 10 years.

Those without proof of immunity are candidates for immunization with the appropriate diphtheria vaccine preparation (usually Td).

Persons recovering from diphtheria illness should be evaluated for immunization with diphtheria toxoid. Disease caused by toxin-producing bacteria does not always render a person immune.

In Massachusetts, as in most states, the law requires that cases of diphtheria be reported to the local board of health or the appropriate health agency.

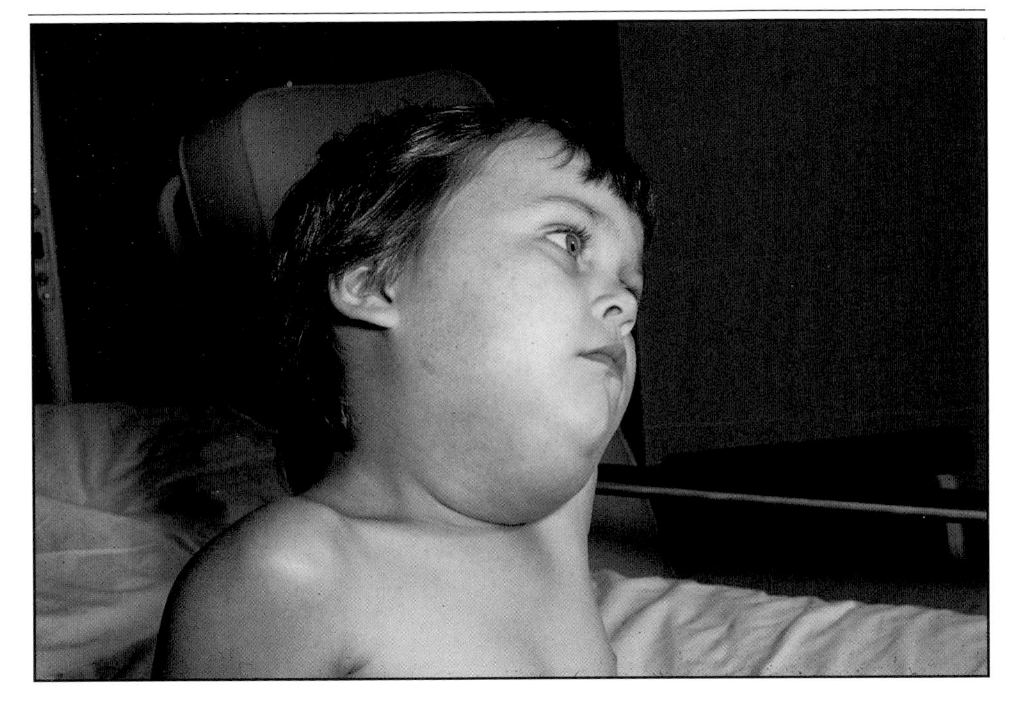

Mumps. This child has the swollen cheeks which are typical of mumps. This virus infects the parotid gland in children, as well as the testicles in teenage and adult males. Symptoms can include fever, headache, and stiff neck.

Mumps

Mumps is a paramyxoviral infection that causes the salivary glands to swell, resulting in swollen cheeks, the classic symptom of this disease. Other symptoms may also include fever, headache, stiff neck, and loss of appetite.

Mumps is easily confused with other upper respiratory infections.

Complications can include:

- swelling of the brain (encephalitis) and swelling of the lining around the brain (meningitis);
- inflammation of the testicles in teenage or adult males;
- in rare cases, the involvement of the ears, joints, kidney, pancreas, thyroid, and heart.

Complications seem to occur more often in older age groups. Mumps during the first trimester of pregnancy can lead to spontaneous abortion.

Mumps is most common in late winter and spring. In 1990, the Centers for Disease Control received reports of over 5,000 cases of mumps in the United States, similar to the number reported in 1989. While late or inadequate vaccination appears to be the primary reason for the appearance of mumps, infection can nevertheless occur among young adults with documented histories of mumps immunization.

Transmission

Mumps spreads through direct contact with infected respiratory secretions (sneezing, coughing, contact with mucous or saliva). A person is infectious from 6 days before until 9 days after the onset of swelling. The most infectious period is 48 hours before the onset of symptoms. Exposed people will usually develop symptoms within 12 to 25 days.

Diagnosis and Treatment

Nasopharyngeal secretions, urine, and spinal fluid will show the presence of mumps virus when cultured. Acute and convalescent antibody titers can also confirm a diagnosis of mumps.

Supportive care is the only treatment for mumps infection.

Prevention

Live mumps vaccine is routinely administered to children in a combined vaccine also containing measles and rubella vaccines (MMR). Normally given to infants at 15 months, the vaccine can also be safely administered to most adults. A single dose of mumps vaccine provides long-lasting immunity in more than 95 percent of recipients. Recent revisions in the recommendations for measles vaccination means that children receive a booster dose of MMR vaccine at grade school (age 4-6), or junior high school, or college entrance.

Shelter staff can help assure their own safety and diminish confusion should an outbreak occur if they have proof of immunity to mumps at the time of employment. Proof of immunity requires *one* of the following:

- a birth date before 1957 (about 90 percent of adults born prior to 1957 have had actual mumps infection, posing minimal risk for recurrent infection), or
- documentation of vaccination with mumps-containing vaccine on or after the first birthday, or
- physician documentation of mumps infection, or
- laboratory evidence of past infection with mumps.

Immunity after vaccination or infection is usually lifelong. Vaccination will not prevent infection in susceptible people who receive mumps vaccine after a recent exposure. However, the vaccine should still be offered for the purpose of future protection.

Side effects to the vaccine are uncommon.

Contraindications

Caregivers should exercise caution when administering the vaccine to those with a history of allergic reactions to eggs, including hives, swelling of the mouth and throat, dyspnea, hypotension, or shock. People who exhibit these responses to eggs may develop an allergic reaction to the vaccine.

Mumps vaccine is contraindicated in children less than 12 months of age, people with moderate to severe febrile illnesses, and women who are pregnant or planning to conceive within 3 months following the vaccine.

Certain people with compromised immune systems, including anyone receiving immunosuppressive therapy, should not receive live mumps virus vaccine.

The Immunization Practices Advisory Committee (ACIP) presently does not recommend MMR vaccine for unimmunized adults with HIV infection. According to the American Academy of Pediatrics, children with asymptomatic HIV infection should receive MMR vaccine following the usual immunization schedules.

Mumps vaccine should not be given during the 3 months following the administration of any blood products containing antibodies, including immune globulin and whole blood.

Control

In Massachusetts, as in most states, cases of mumps must be reported to the local or state health department.

All those having close contact to a person infected with mumps should have an immunization history evaluated according to the guidelines in Section II of this chapter. If proof of immunity is not available, reimmunization is warranted. Close contacts may be defined as those having direct contact to infected droplets or articles that are contaminated with infected droplets (such as cups, utensils, or mouthed toys) anytime from 2 days before until 9 days after the onset of swelling.

Family shelters

Often the crowded conditions in a family shelter lead caregivers to consider all guests and staff close contacts. If the infected person remains in the shelter, staff should allow only families with proof of immunity to be admitted for one full incubation period (25 days) following the last day of possible exposure.

Adult shelters

Follow-up of contacts in larger shelters may be prioritized through interviews with the infected person regarding recent contact with friends, and a review of bedlists.

To minimize the number of secondary cases, staff in an adult shelter should find alternative housing for those diagnosed with mumps. If safe housing is not available with an immune (naturally or by vaccination) friend or relative, admission to an acute care setting may be an option.

All shelters

Alternative housing for infected persons and their families should be arranged with extreme caution. Transferring an infected person to a hotel or to the home of a relative may only introduce new difficulties in the containment of this disease.

Shelter staff and guests should know the signs and symptoms of mumps in order to report any suspected secondary cases as soon as they arise.

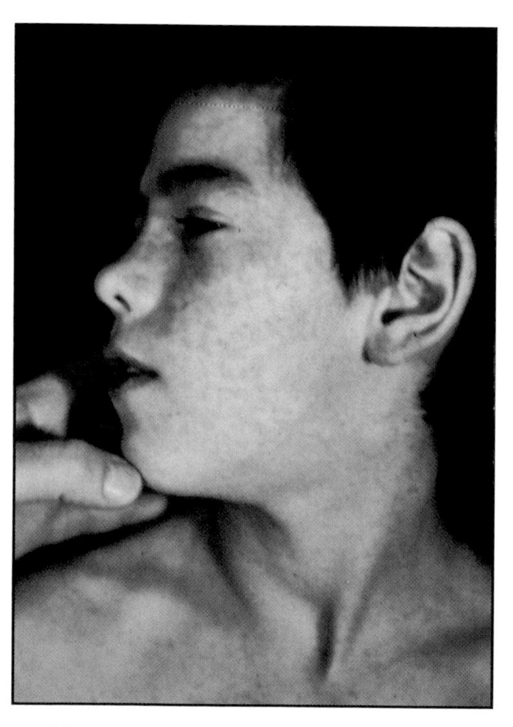

Rubella. German measles can cause swelling of the lymph nodes, particularly the posterior cervical nodes behind the neck, as seen in this boy with a rash of his face.

Rubella

Rubella, commonly known as "German measles", is a viral illness that first appears as a low-grade fever and swelling of the lymph glands, particularly those behind the ears and at the back of the neck. A flat, pink rash often begins on the face, spreading over the entire body within 24 hours. The symptoms last about 3 days, although adult women may experience joint pain for up to 4 weeks following infection.

Complications of rubella are rare but can include encephalitis or thrombocytopenia. Infection during the first and second trimesters of pregnancy can lead to very severe problems in the fetus, including defects of the eyes, ears, heart, brain, and bones. Miscarriages and stillbirths are believed to be frequent occurrences following rubella infection during pregnancy.

Prevalence

Rubella is often a mild illness that escapes specific diagnosis. Widespread immunization with rubella vaccine has also diminished the prevalence of the disease. Nationally, the Centers for Disease Control received reports of only 396 cases in 1989 with only one child born with congenital rubella syndrome. This number climbed to 1093 cases in 1990, with 11 children born with congential rubella syndrome, indicating that this disease may be increasing once again.

Rubella primarily occurs in unvaccinated adults 20 years of age and older, and children under 5 years of age.

Prevention

Rubella vaccine is a live virus vaccine that is usually included with the measles and mumps vaccines (MMR). Children routinely receive MMR at 15 months of age or older. The vaccine induces lifelong immunity to rubella in more than 98 percent of recipients. Side effects of the vaccine can include rash, fever, and swollen lymph nodes which arise 5-12 days after vaccination. Joint pain has been reported, particularly in postpubertal females. This latter symptom occurs within 7 to 21 days after vaccination.

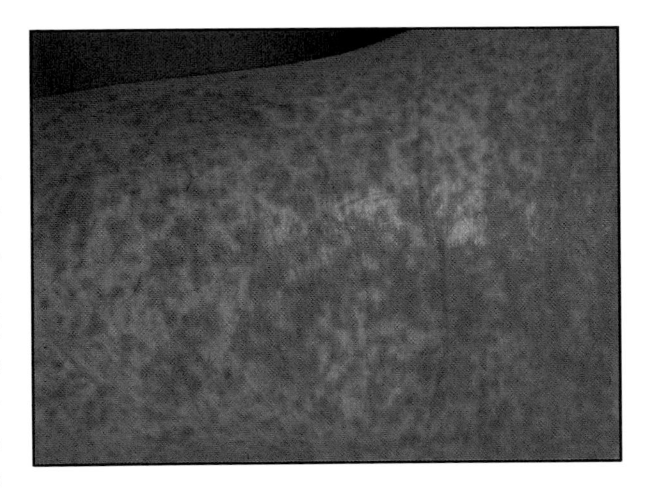

Rubella. This flat, pink rash often begins on the face and spreads to the rest of the body within 24 hours.

Evidence of immunity may be shown by:

- documentation of vaccination on or after the first birthday, or
- a positive rubella titer.

Anyone not able to meet one of these criteria should be revaccinated.

Contraindications

Rubella vaccine is contraindicated in people less than 12 months of age, those with poor immune systems, people with moderate to severe febrile illnesses, and women who are pregnant or are considering becoming pregnant during the 3 months following vaccination. The vaccine should not be given for at least 3 months following the administration of antibody-containing blood products, including immune globulin and whole blood.

Massachusetts, as most states, requires all cases of rubella to be reported to the local board of health or appropriate health agency.

Polio

Polio infections are extremely rare diseases caused by three types of enteroviruses. Polio may appear in one of three forms: a mild flu-like syndrome, aseptic meningitis, or a paralytic disease.

Prevalence

Due to widespread vaccination, very few cases of polio appear each year, with most resulting from oral polio vaccine. In 1989, no cases of polio were reported in the United States.

Prevention

Normally, 3 doses of polio vaccine are given in early childhood at 2, 4, and 15-18 months of age. A fourth dose is recommended before school entry at 4 to 6 years of age. Caregivers may adjust the schedule for those with a delayed or inadequate immunization history.

Two types of vaccines are available. Trivalent oral polio vaccine (OPV), the form most commonly given to children in the United States, is a combination of 3 live polio viruses. In rare cases, the administration of OPV has been associated with paralysis in those vaccinated and their contacts.

The second type of vaccine is called the inactivated polio virus (IPV) and consists of 3 different inactivated polio viruses. IPV is indicated for those at increased risk of polio disease from a live vaccine due to poor immune systems, including people infected with the human immunodeficiency virus (HIV). Presently there are no known serious side effects from IPV.

People receiving OPV can excrete virus after vaccination for 2 weeks in the throat and as long as 2 months in feces. Therefore, people in households with immunodeficient individuals should also receive IPV instead of OPV to prevent transmission of the disease.

Routine primary polio immunization is generally not recommended in the USA for those 18 years or older unless they are at increased risk for exposure (e.g., travel to countries where polio is epidemic or employment in a laboratory working with polio viruses).

Massachusetts, as most states, requires that all cases of polio be reported to the local board of health or appropriate health agency.

Tetanus

Tetanus is a disease caused by *Clostridium tetani*, a bacterium found in soil containing the feces of humans and animals. Illness from tetanus happens when the bacteria infect the skin, generally through severe injury or contaminated wounds, including punctures, bites, crushing, burns, and frostbite. Drug users are at particular risk for tetanus, especially those who inject drugs subcutaneously ("skin pop"). The elderly are also more susceptible because of declining immunity, or because they never received a primary series of immunizations as children and/or booster doses every 10 years as adults.

Once inside the skin, the bacteria release a toxin that leads to localized or progressive neuromuscular disease with muscle spasms. This may involve:

- the masseter, the large muscle of the jaw, resulting in "lockjaw";
- the respiratory muscles, leading to respiratory failure.

Fortunately, tetanus is rare in the USA because of widespread immunization with tetanus toxoid. Toxoids come from the toxins produced by the bacteria and are inactivated so they cannot cause disease. As with diphtheria toxoid, the antigenic properties of the toxin remain, allowing the recipient to develop immunity to the disease.

Booster doses of tetanus should be given every 10 years after the primary series has been completed.

For children under 7, tetanus immunization normally begins with a primary series of 4 doses, with the first 3 doses given no less than 4 weeks apart and the fourth following about 1 year after the last dose. A booster dose is given between ages 4 to 6, before school entry. Those older than 7 years who do not have documented prior immunization require a primary series of 3 doses of tetanus toxoid.

Completion of the primary series generally confers immunity for at least 10 years in 95 percent or more of those vaccinated. Booster doses following the primary series are recommended every 10 years. Booster doses of tetanus given more frequently than every 10 years may increase the incidence and severity of local reactions.

Pregnancy is not a contraindication for booster doses of tetanus toxoid.

Tetanus toxoid comes in 3 different forms, DTP, DT, and Td. These are fully described on page 206.

Side effects of tetanus toxoid may include minor reactions such as redness, induration, and pain at the injection site, and a moderately elevated temperature.

Prevention of tetanus in the event of injury

All wounds should be thoroughly cleaned as soon as possible to prevent multiplication of *Clostridium tetani* organisms. The decision to administer toxoid is dependent upon the person's vaccine history and extent of injury.

For minor injuries

- People with a history of receiving 3 or more immunizations with the last dose being given within the preceding 5 years do not require a booster dose for any type of wound;
- Those who received 3 or more immunizations with the last dose given more than 10 years ago should be given a booster vaccination with any type of wound;
- Persons with uncertain histories require a dose of tetanus toxoid. Arrangements should be made for completion of the primary series of immunization.

Those with severe and/or contaminated wounds should follow these guidelines:

- Those with a history of 3 or more doses of tetanus toxoid need a booster dose if the last dose was more than 5 years ago;
- Those with an uncertain immunization history or those who have received less than 3 doses of tetanus toxoid require a booster dose of tetanus toxoid and tetanus immune globulin (**TIG**). **TIG** is a preparation of human plasma containing antibodies to tetanus. A single intramuscular dose of 250 to 500 units of TIG is normally recommended. Arrangements should be made as appropriate for completion of the primary series.

Caregivers should always evaluate those recovering from tetanus disease for immunization against tetanus. Diseases caused by exotoxins do not always render a person immune.

In Massachusetts, as in most states, cases of tetanus must be reported to the local board of health or appropriate health agency.

References

Diphtheria

Centers for Disease Control. Notifiable diseases of low frequency - United States. *MMWR* 1990; 38(51-52): 886.

Feigin RD, Stechenberg BW. Diphtheria. In: Feigin RD, Cherry JD, eds. *Textbook of Pediatric Infectious Diseases*. Philadelphia: WB Saunders Company; 1987: 1134-1135.

Mumps

Benenson AS, ed. *Control of Communicable Diseases in Man.* 15th ed. Washington, DC: American Public Health Association; 1990: 293-296.

Centers for Disease Control. Mumps prevention. *MMWR* 1989; 38(22): 388-392, 397-400.

Centers for Disease Control. Cases of specified notifiable diseases - United States. *MMWR* 1991; 39(51, 52): 941.

Rubella

Centers for Disease Control. Rubella and congenital rubella - United States, 1984-1986. *MMWR* 1987; 36(40): 672-675.

Gellis SE, Gellis SS. Rubella. In: Fitzpatrick TB, Eisen AZ, Wolff K, Freedberg IM, Austen KF, eds. *Dermatology in General Medicine.* 3rd ed. New York; McGraw-Hill; 1987: 2289-2291.

Gershon AA. Rubella virus. In: Mandell GL, Douglas RG, Bennett JE, eds. *Principles and Practice of Infectious Diseases*. 3rd ed. New York: Churchill-Livingston; 1990; 1242-1247.

Robertson SE, Cochi SL, Bunn GA, Morse DL, Preblud SR. Preventing rubella: assessing missed opportunities for immunization. *Am J Pub Health* 1987; 77(10): 1347-1349.

Polio

Benenson AS, ed. *Control of Communicable Diseases in Man.* 15th ed. Washington, DC: American Public Health Association; 1990: 340-347.

Ray CG. Enteroviruses and reoviruses. In: Wilson JD, Braunwald E, Isselbacher KJ, Petersdorf RG, Martin JB, Fauci AS, Root RK, eds. *Harrison's Principles of Internal Medicine.* 12th ed. New York: McGraw-Hill, Inc; 1991: 713-714.

Tetanus

Cate TR. *Clostridium tetani.* In: Mandell GL, Douglas RG, Bennett JE, eds. *Principles and Practice of Infectious Diseases*. 3rd ed. New York: Churchill-Livingston; 1990; 1842-1846.

Centers for Disease Control. Diphtheria, tetanus, and pertussis: guidelines for vaccine prophylaxis and other preventive measures. *MMWR* 1985; 34(27): 405-414, 419-426.

Weinstein L. Tetanus. In: Feigin RD, Cherry JD, eds. *Textbook of Pediatric Infectious Diseases*. 2nd ed. Philadelphia: WB Saunders; 1987: 1126-1134.

Chart 16: Routine Childhood Immunization Schedule

Recommended Age	Vaccine(s)
2 months	DTP–1 Polio–1 HibTITER™ -1**
4 months	DTP–2 Polio–2 HibTITER™ -2
6 months	DTP–3 HibTITER™ -3
15 months	MMR–1 HibTITER™ -4
18 months	DTP–4 Polio–3
4–6 years	DTP–5 Polio–4 *MMR–2
14–16 years and every 10 years thereafter	Td

**Simultaneous administration of all vaccines (including DTP, Polio, Hib and MMR) according to age and previous vaccination status is indicated if return of the recipient for further immunizations is doubtful.*
***HibTITER™ is a product of Lederle-Praxis. An alternative, PedvaxHIB™ (Merck, Sharp & Dohme), is administered only 3 times, at 2, 4, and 12 months.*

Timing	Under 7 years old	7 years and older
First visit	DTP–1 Polio–1 *Hib MMR–1 (If 15 months or older)	Td–1 Polio–1 (if less than 18 years old) MMR-1
2 months later	DTP-2 Polio-2	Td–2 Polio–2 MMR–2
2 months later	DTP–3	
6—12 months later	DTP–4 Polio–3	Td–3 Polio–3
4—6 years	DTP–5 Polio–4 MMR–2	
Every 10 years thereafter	Td	Td

Chart 17: Delayed Immunization Schedule

* *For delayed immunization against H. Influenzae, refer to Chart 18.*

Chart 18: *H. Influenzae Vaccines: Routine and Delayed Immunization Schedules*

HibTITER (Lederle-Praxis)

Routine	2, 4, 6, and 15 months
Delayed	
age 2 - 6 months	3 doses no less than 2 months apart booster dose at 15 months
age 7 - 11 months	2 doses no less than 2 months apart booster dose at 15 months
age 12 - 14 months	1 dose booster dose at 15 months but no less than 2 months after primary dose
age 15 months - 5 years	1 dose

or

PedvaxHIB (Merck)

Routine	2, 4, and 12 months
Delayed	
age 3 - 10 months	2 doses no less than 2 months apart booster at 12 months
age 11 - 14 months	2 doses no less than 2 months apart
age 15 months - 5 years	1 dose

Part Five: Suggestions for Food Management

M. Kathleen Hennessy

The best way to prevent food contamination and food-borne illness is to handle food properly in the kitchen. Managing food involves three basic functions: reception, preparation, and storage. Certain foods require particular vigilance to prevent the growth and spread of bacteria. These are called *potentially hazardous foods* and include dairy products (such as cheese, eggs and milk), meats, poultry, seafood, cooked rice, and cooked beans.

I. Reception of Donated Food

Do not accept potentially hazardous food that has not been held at the proper temperatures during storage or preparation:

- cold foods should always be refrigerated at 45° F;
- hot foods should always be kept hot (140° F or higher) until served.

Use a food thermometer to check the temperature of donated food when possible. Reject any item in the danger zone.

Always check frozen foods for large ice crystals. Ice crystals may indicate that food has partially thawed and then refrozen, a sign of improper handling.

Make sure food has been properly wrapped and has not been exposed to air during transportation.

II. Preparation

a. Basic precautions

All persons involved in food preparation must thoroughly wash their hands with soap and warm water:

- before beginning to prepare food;
- between different procedures;
- after using the restroom or changing a diaper.

Anyone working in a kitchen should use a baseball cap, scarf, hair net, or other hair restraint. This prevents hair from touching or falling into food.

b. Thawing
Thaw foods overnight in a refrigerator.

If thawing overnight is impossible, place the food in a plastic bag and immerse the bag in a pan of running cold water (but no less than 70° F). Immersion allows the middle to thaw without exposing the edges to room temperatures.

Microwave thawing is also acceptable. Follow the directions provided by the microwave manufacturer.

c. Cutting Materials
Cutting boards used for meat or poultry must be washed and sanitized before cutting other foods, such as vegetables. Using a spray bottle containing a solution of one tablespoon of bleach to one quart of water followed by scrubbing is sufficient. Ideally, two boards should be available in the kitchen: one for meat and the other for vegetables.

Knives used for meat or poultry should be washed and sanitized before use with vegetables or other foods.

d. Cooking
Heat all potentially hazardous hot foods to an internal temperature of at least 165° F.

While guests are being served, maintain the internal temperature at 140° F. (The internal temperature is the temperature of the food as determined by a food thermometer, not the temperature of the oven.)

Cook meat thoroughly at one time. Do not cook meat in steps.

With frozen meat, lengthen the cooking time by half again as much as that allotted for meat at room or refrigerator temperature.

Before cooking meat in the microwave, remove large bones. Bones prevent thorough cooking.

e. Preparation of Baby's Milk
Breast feeding is the safest form of nutrition for any infant.

When infant formulas are used, fully-prepared formulas in individual bottles offer the least chance of contamination. Bottles with plastic inserts are a good alternative.

Plastic or glass bottles can easily be cleaned with hot soapy water and then sanitized with a mild bleach and water solution.

Contamination can happen not only when the bottle is prepared but also when open bottles of milk or cans of formula are handled by others in communal refrigerators.

The ideal rule calls for a new bottle with each feeding. This is often impractical, and when a bottle is to be used for more than one feeding, refrigerate it immediately after use.

Discard unused formula or use the leftover within a few hours .

III. Storage

a. Care and Use of Leftovers

Cover food immediately after use with plastic or foil, or store in containers with tight-fitting lids.

Refrigerate food immediately after use. Cooked food does not need to cool before storage.

Discard leftover hot food that was not held at a temperature of 140° F or above while being served.

Freeze food at 0° F or less. Articles to be frozen should be placed in freezer bags or wrapped in freezer paper or aluminum foil in order to avoid freezer burns. Freezer burns on food destroy taste and texture.

b. Storage of Staples

Store items such as pasta, rice, and flour in air-tight containers and place them in cool, dry areas that are at least six inches off the floor.

Close all boxes after use.

To avoid chemical or physical contamination, never store food near items such as soap, detergent, insect spray, abrasives, steel wool pads, or cleaners.

c. Dishwashing

Dishes, pots, pans, and utensils should ideally be washed in a dishwasher with a rinse cycle set at 180° F.

If this is not possible, soiled dishware and utensils should be washed and rinsed, and then sanitized in a dilute bleach solution to prevent the growth of bacteria. Bleach (Clorox™) in a mixture 1/4 cup bleach to one gallon of water is sufficient for this purpose.

IV. Food Donation: A Note to the Donor

Shelter staff often get calls regarding food donations. Individuals and community groups that wish to provide such gifts are welcomed and valued. However, the growing number of people residing in shelters has made the provision of safe, healthy, and wholesome food a very complicated process. Certain foods are at particular risk for causing illness, because they require excessive handling and are difficult to keep at proper temperature during transportation and serving. By following a few simple guidelines, you can assure that your food gift does not pose a health hazard for its recipients.

a. Call Ahead

Before bringing food to a shelter or soup kitchen, call and let the staff know what you plan to bring, or ask the staff for advice on specific needs.

b. Suggested Foods

1. Some *excellent* foods for donation include:
    - canned foods such as beef stews, sauces, vegetables, or fruit;
    - fresh or frozen vegetables or fruits that have been purchased within 24 hours prior to donation;
    - rice and pasta;
    - coffee and tea;
    - other dry staples.
2. Foods you should donate with *extreme caution* include:
    - uncooked meats and poultry*;
    - fish and shellfish*;
    - milk and eggs, including products made from milk and eggs, such as cheese and sauces;
    - cooked beans and rice.
3. Foods that should *never* be donated include:
    - cooked or raw meats or poultry that have not been kept frozen or refrigerated;
    - poultry, raw or cooked, containing stuffing;
    - leftover food, particularly food that has been part of a buffet (weddings, public gatherings, etc.);
    - any potentially hazardous food that has been cooked**.

* Uncooked meat, poultry, or fish should only be donated if they are frozen or refrigerated and have been kept at constant temperatures while in storage.
** Potentially hazardous foods include: dairy products (cheese, eggs, and milk), meats, poultry, seafood, cooked rice, and cooked beans.

c. Bringing Food to the Shelter

All foods should be securely wrapped or enclosed in containers with air-tight lids.

Hot foods should be kept hot, and cold foods should be kept cold.

Cans should be free of dents and damage to the seam.

Do not donate toxic items such as soap powders, cleaners, detergents, or abrasives without calling to confirm that the shelter can use such materials.

Shelters may need paper items such as towels and toilet paper. Call the shelter first to inquire about current supplies and needs before donating these products.

Certain foods are at particular risk for causing illness, because they require excessive handling and are difficult to keep at proper temperature during transportation and serving.

V. Food Management: A Note to the Volunteer

The work of volunteers is the foundation of every successful shelter or feeding program. Volunteers often make it possible to feed hundreds of people each day.

Food handling for large groups of people demands an awareness of public health and a sensitivity to issues that you wouldn't normally consider within your own family. To safeguard your own health as well as the health of shelter staff and guests, you should follow the recommendations below.

a. When *NOT* to Volunteer

Do not volunteer in a kitchen if you are coughing or have a cold. Bacteria and viruses are easily spread through coughing and sneezing.

Do not volunteer to prepare food if you have a sore, open wound, or infected cut on your hands or face. Cover or treat these sores or infections. Skin infections can contaminate food with bacteria (especially *Staphylococcus*), which can result in serious food-borne illnesses.

Do not volunteer in the kitchen whenever you or a family member has been ill with diarrhea or vomiting. Such illnesses spread easily within a family, and some family members may carry and spread the germs even though they are without symptoms.

b. Hair Care

Always wear a hair restraint when working in a kitchen or any other area where food is prepared. Suitable hair coverings include a baseball cap, scarf, or hair net. These help keep your hands out of your hair as well as your hair out of the food.

c. Cleaning Hands

Wash your hands carefully before beginning to work with food.

Wash your hands whenever you change activities. This prevents bacteria from spreading from one food to another.

Wash your hands after going to the bathroom.

If plastic gloves are used for one procedure such as cutting meat or poultry, discard them or wash them as you would your hands before beginning another procedure. Plastic gloves will spread bacteria if not used properly.

Use proper utensils for mixing, stirring, or tasting food. When you taste food, do not put the utensil back into the food.

Never use fingers or hands for food preparation.

d. Cleaning Utensils and Accessories

Sanitize towels or sponges in a mixture of bleach and water (1/4 cup bleach to one gallon of water) after you use them to wipe counters and cutting boards and before you use them for any other procedure. Outbreaks of food-borne illnesses have often been traced to contaminated towels or cutting boards.

Your volunteer effort helps ensure that the shelter runs smoothly and effectively. The above guidelines are meant to help every individual in the shelter community — guests, staff, and volunteers alike. By following these simple guidelines, your gift of help will also be a gift of health.

Part Six: Fact Sheets

This final section of the manual includes Fact Sheets on each of the illnesses discussed previously, arranged alphabetically.

Many shelter staff and families have requested basic information from our health care teams during outbreaks of infectious illnesses in the past six years. Such outbreaks, or threats of outbreaks, can be frightening times for parents and for those responsible for running the shelters.

These Fact Sheets are designed to answer basic questions, including how to recognize the early signs and symptoms of an illness and which steps can be taken to limit its spread. Our intention is that these will be photocopied and given to each guest in shelters facing real or potential outbreaks of any of these communicable diseases.

We are thankful to the many shelter guests and staff who conceived the concept of these Fact Sheets, and we hope that you find them as useful and practical as we have.

What is AIDS?

AIDS stands for "acquired immune deficiency syndrome". AIDS is not one disease; AIDS involves many different diseases. AIDS can be prevented!

What is HIV?

AIDS is caused by the human immunodeficiency virus or HIV. HIV is a virus that spreads through sexual contact and blood contact. The virus can also pass from a pregnant woman to her unborn baby.

Blood contact usually occurs when people who use intravenous drugs share needles.

Sexual contact can spread the virus between men and women as well as between partners of the same sex. HIV can spread when a boyfriend or girlfriend who shoots drugs has sexual contact with a partner who may not use drugs.

If you are pregnant or planning to become pregnant, consult your doctor or nurse about the risks of HIV infection.

How do you know if you've been infected with HIV?

People with HIV may not know it. They may feel and look very healthy. They can still spread the virus.

The only way to know if you are infected with HIV is to have a blood test. When the test is positive, it means you have been exposed to HIV.

What do you do if you're HIV positive?

A positive test for HIV does not mean you have AIDS. It means the virus is present, and you can spread the virus to other people.

Early treatment and regular follow-up are essential to staying healthy when infected with the HIV virus. New treatments are available to help people infected with HIV live longer and have fewer serious infections. You have a right to know about these treatments! Ask your doctor or seek out a support group.

What do you do if someone you know is HIV positive?

Friends or family who are HIV positive or have AIDS need lots of love and support.

How can you keep from getting HIV?

You cannot get the virus by being stung by insects, sitting on toilet seats, washing dishes, or being around someone with AIDS. Sharing bathrooms, dishes and laundry cannot spread the virus. A person infected with HIV cannot transmit the virus when he or she hugs and touches you or sneezes towards you.

You can become infected if you do not practice safer sex. Men should always wear a condom (rubber). Lubricate the condom with water-based substances such as K-Y Jelly™, For-Play™, PrePair™, or Probe™. Don't put any oil or Vaseline™ on the condom because it may break. Never use a condom more than once. Don't take chances. Use a condom from start to finish every time you have sex.

Oral sex on a man should also be done with a condom in place. For oral sex on a woman, use a dental dam to decrease the chance of transmission. Don't let blood or sexual fluids enter your mouth or your partner's.

Dry kissing, masturbation, hugging, touching are safe. Deep (French) kissing has not been shown to pass on the virus but may be risky, especially if there are sores or blood in someone's mouth.

DON'T SHOOT DRUGS! The best protection from AIDS is to get help through a drug program. When using drugs, NEVER SHARE NEEDLES. Always clean your works with bleach before and after use.

Because HIV spreads through blood, don't share sharp objects like razors and toothbrushes that may have blood on them.

Where do you get information about AIDS and HIV infection?

All people have a right to information about AIDS and HIV. Counselors or nurses at the shelter can be a good resource for information.

What is chlamydia?
Chlamydia is a sexually transmitted disease (STD or VD). Although it is very common, many people have never heard of it.

What does chlamydia look like?
Many people who have chlamydia don't know it. You may not know that you have the disease, but it can still cause many problems with your reproductive organs.

Many people who have chlamydia also have gonorrhea. The symptoms are often the same.

What happens when you get chlamydia?
If you have chlamydia, you may feel burning when you urinate. A watery or mucous-like fluid may come out of your penis or vagina, and your sex organs may itch.

If you are a woman and you have chlamydia, you may feel pain below your stomach. It may hurt when you have sex, and sometimes you may bleed between your periods.

If you are pregnant and you have chlamydia, you can pass the disease to your newborn at birth. Your baby may get infected eyes and lungs.

What do you do if you have chlamydia?
Usually, it's easy to treat chlamydia. You and your partner will have to take antibiotic pills for one or two weeks.

How do you keep from getting chlamydia?
There are two ways to keep away from chlamydia:

1) Don't have sex;

2) If you do have sex, use a condom.

Make sure you and/or your partner use condoms from start to finish every time you have sex.

You cannot get chlamydia from toilet seats, doorknobs, towels, or from lifting heavy objects and straining muscles.

What is conjunctivitis?

Conjunctivitis is sometimes called "red eye", and is a very common eye problem.

What does it look like?

If you have conjunctivitis, one or both of your eyes are red. Your eyes and eyelids burn or itch. Your eyes may water and leave a crust which can make your eyelashes stick together, especially when you wake up in the morning.

How do you get conjunctivitis?

Germs get into your eyes all the time. Some germs can grow under your eyelids. When you rub or touch your eyes, the germs can infect the eyes very easily.

Sometimes, conjunctivitis isn't caused by germs. Chemicals, allergies, or other illnesses can also give you red eye.

What do you do if you have conjunctivitis caused by an infection?

A doctor or nurse will probably give you eye drops, an ointment, or pills. These are antibiotics.

Your eye will look better after 2 or 3 days of medicine. But the germs will still be alive. You need to take all the medicine (usually it lasts for 7 to 10 days) to get rid of all the germs. Otherwise, you can get conjunctivitis again.

You don't need an eye patch if you have conjunctivitis.

If your eye stays red after treatment or you feel pain or your vision is fuzzy, see your doctor or nurse again.

How do you keep from getting eye infections?

Never share eyedrops or eye ointments, even with your family.

Do not share towels, washcloths, or makeup — especially never share these things with someone who has conjunctivitis.

If your child or your partner has an infected eye, wash your hands with lots of warm water and soap both before and after putting medicine in her or his infected eye.

If your partner, a friend, or someone in your family has conjunctivitis, you may also need to take medicine to keep from getting the disease.

CMV

What is CMV?

CMV is a very common virus. Most people have the virus without knowing it. Most people do not get sick from CMV.

What does infection with CMV look like?

If you get sick from CMV, you may have a fever and swollen glands. You may feel very tired. A doctor may say you have a type of "mono".

CMV can cause problems for newborn babies and people with poor immune systems.

How do you get CMV?

You can get CMV from having contact with other people's body fluids. The most common fluids are saliva (spit), urine, blood, semen, and vaginal fluid.

How do you keep from getting CMV?

Always wash your hands and your child's hands whenever either of you touch body fluids, especially after going to the bathroom or changing a diaper.

Throw dirty diapers into trash cans with covers. Don't let children near dirty diapers.

Keep dirty laundry with urine or body fluids away from children.

Discourage children from sharing toys, glasses, or other objects that are mouthed or chewed.

What is diarrhea?

Diarrhea is usually a change in a normal bowel pattern, with abnormal amounts of stool or liquid stool. You can get diarrhea from viruses, bacteria, or parasites. You can also get diarrhea from other medical problems.

What happens when you have diarrhea?

If you have diarrhea, you have to go to the bathroom a lot. Your bowel movements are loose and mixed with liquid. Sometimes, you get cramps, you throw up, or you have a fever. You may see blood or mucous in your bowel movements.

When diarrhea lasts for more than three days, see a doctor or a nurse. They can take a sample of your bowel movement to see what kind of diarrhea you have.

If your baby has unusually loose stools or an increase in the usual number of bowel movements, contact your health provider. Diarrhea can quickly make babies very sick.

What do you do if you or your child has diarrhea?

Whenever you have diarrhea, drink a lot of clear liquids to replace the fluids you have lost.

If your child has diarrhea, do not use solid foods or milk for the first day. Special liquids, such as Pedialyte™ or Resol™, which can be obtained from a drug store, can prevent your child from becoming dehydrated.

After the first day of liquids, give your child bananas, rice, applesauce, or toast. These foods help the intestines make solid bowel movements.

If your child still has diarrhea, contact a doctor or nurse.

Take your child to a hospital or clinic if you see any of these signs:

- your child can't make tears;
- the mouth of your child is dry;
- the eyes of your child look sunken or have dark circles around them;
- your child is very sleepy;
- your child is less than 12 months of age and is having very large or very frequent stools;
- your child has not wet a diaper in 8 hours.

If your child has diarrhea, vomits, or has a fever over 101° F (38.4° C), see a doctor or nurse.

How do you keep from getting diarrhea?

Always wash your hands:
- before fixing any food or formula;
- before eating or feeding a child;
- after changing diapers or going to the bathroom.

Toilet-trained children should always wash their hands after they go to the bathroom. You or another adult should remind children to wash their hands and watch them in the bathroom.

(Continued on next page)

If children are putting toys in their mouths, try to keep them from sharing these toys with other children. This is especially important if one of the children is sick.

If you have diarrhea, do not fix or serve food to anyone outside of your family. You can serve and fix food when your symptoms go away or your doctor or nurse tells you it's OK.

What is gonorrhea?

Most people know gonorrhea as "the clap" or "the drip". Gonorrhea can infect your eyes, mouth, vagina, rectum, joints, skin, penis, or urethra. Gonorrhea is very common.

How do you get gonorrhea?

It's an infection you can get by having sex. If you're pregnant and you have gonorrhea, the germs can be passed to your baby at birth.

If you have sex with different people, you have a good chance of getting gonorrhea. If you have sex with someone who has sex with different people, you have a good chance of getting gonorrhea.

If you are sexually active, go to a clinic for a gonorrhea exam regularly. Your health care provider can recommend how often you should visit.

What does gonorrhea do to you?

If you're a man and you have gonorrhea, your penis may burn or itch when you urinate. Also, a yellow fluid may drip from your penis ("the drip").

If you're a woman and you have gonorrhea, you may feel pain, burning and itching. You may also have a discharge. Sometimes the infection can spread to your tubes, ovaries, and pelvis. It is very important to get treatment as soon as possible to avoid longterm problems.

Some people with gonorrhea don't have any symptoms, especially women. People without symptoms can still spread the disease.

What do you do if you get gonorrhea?

Treatment for gonorrhea is usually simple. Often, you get a single shot of antibiotics followed by a week or two of pills. Sometimes, an infection needs stronger antibiotics or an overnight stay in the hospital.

How do you prevent gonorrhea?

If you don't have sex, you won't get gonorrhea.

Condoms are the next best way to prevent gonorrhea.

USE CONDOMS FROM START TO FINISH EVERY TIME you have sex . It's the best way to prevent gonorrhea and other STDs (sexually transmitted diseases).

Haemophilus Influenzae Type b

What is Hib?

Hib is a germ. It can make people very sick, especially children.

Children under five years old can get Hib infections in their brains, lungs, joints, and blood.

Most adults don't get very sick if they have Hib. If you are sick because of other things, like cancer, diabetes, alcohol problems and AIDS, Hib can make you very sick.

How do you get Hib?

Hib spreads easily in day care centers and crowded places.

When someone with Hib disease coughs or sneezes, the germ gets in the air. People can breathe the germ in the air and get sick.

You can get Hib if you kiss an infected person, share a drink or a cigarette, or use the same toothbrush. You can get Hib if you touch mucous from the nose of an infected person and then put your hands in your own mouth, nose, or eyes. This can happen when you touch a dirty tissue, and you forget to wash your hands.

How do you keep from getting Hib?

You can prevent Hib infection in your children. If your child is between the ages of 2 months and 5 years old, there is a vaccine available. Ask a doctor or nurse about the Hib vaccine.

If you or your children spend a lot of time with someone who gets Hib disease, you can take the antibiotic rifampin to make sure you don't get the disease. It needs to be taken for only four days.

You should not take rifampin if you are pregnant or have severe liver disease.

What happens if you take rifampin?

Rifampin can stain your urine, sweat, saliva, tears, semen, and stool an orange-red. This goes away once the medicine is finished.

Rifampin can stain contact lenses so you should wear glasses until the medicine is finished.

If you have to take rifampin, birth control pills can become less effective. You should use an additional method like a condom or a diaphragm until the end of the pill cycle.

If you have to take rifampin and you're in a methadone program, tell your counselor. Your methadone dose may have to be changed while you're on rifampin.

See the shelter staff if you or your children get sick with a fever after being around a person who was sick with Hib.

What is hepatitis A?

Hepatitis A is a virus that irritates your liver.

People with hepatitis A can feel very tired and have a fever, poor appetite, nausea, yellow eyes and skin, dark urine, and white bowel movements. Some people, especially children, don't have yellow skin or eyes. You usually feel sick from hepatitis A for about 2 weeks, although some people can get sick for several months and others never get sick at all.

How do you get hepatitis A?

Hepatitis A is spread through the stool of infected people. This can happen when an infected person goes to the bathroom, doesn't wash his hands, and then touches objects which others might put into their mouths. Hepatitis A can spread when you change diapers or when children put their hands into their diapers and then touch objects that go into the mouth.

You can't get hepatitis A when you talk to, touch, or sleep in the same room with a sick person.

How do you treat hepatitis A?

There is no treatment for hepatitis A. If you get sick, lots of rest and high calorie foods can make you feel better.

How can I keep from getting hepatitis A?

The best way not to get hepatitis A is to wash your hands.

- Always wash your hands before you touch food, eat, or feed your baby;
- Always wash your hands after going to the bathroom or changing a diaper;
- Always put soiled diapers in a waste basket that children can't get into.

If your children get hepatitis A or the person you live with has hepatitis A, you can get a shot called immune globulin (IG) to make sure you don't get very sick. The shot has to be given within 2 weeks of exposure, so see a caregiver as soon as possible.

Can you get hepatitis A more than once?

After you get sick from hepatitis A, you can't get it again. But remember, you can still get other types of hepatitis.

What is hepatitis B?

Hepatitis B is a virus that affects your liver. The early symptoms are like the cold or flu. After about a month, your skin may turn yellow and begin to itch. Your urine looks like Coca-Cola, but the color of your bowel movements is light. You may not see any of these symptoms for a month-and-a-half to 6 months after you first get the disease.

These symptoms can last for 1 to 2 months. Usually, you are healthy again after the symptoms go away. Some people die from hepatitis B, and others have lifelong liver problems.

What do you do if you have hepatitis B?

Rest and high calorie foods may help your fever and itching. Usually, food goes down better in the early part of the day.

Avoid drugs such as Tylenol™ that are broken down by the liver. Alcohol and illegal drugs can also damage the liver.

How do you get hepatitis B?

The virus doesn't spread when you talk to, touch, or sleep in the same room with an infected person.

Having sex without a condom or sharing needles with an infected person can spread the virus very easily.

Some people can be infected and never feel or look sick, however, they can still spread the virus.

How do you keep from getting hepatitis B?

The best way not to get hepatitis B from sharing needles is not to shoot drugs! If you share needles, use a watered down bleach solution to clean your works before and after you shoot to kill the hepatitis B on the needle. Ask shelter staff about where to find bleach.

Use a condom every time you have sex. Often, shelter staff know where you can get condoms.

Don't share toothbrushes and razors.

Cover any cuts or sores with a bandage.

If you touch any of the fluids that come out of another person's body, especially blood and urine, you need to wash your hands very well.

Be careful when throwing away razors and other sharp things! The shelter staff can tell you where to put them.

Watch children to make sure they don't bite or scratch one another.

If you get exposed to hepatitis B, ask your doctor or nurse about vaccines.

What is herpes simplex?

Herpes simplex is a virus. It is not very dangerous for most people. It can be very painful.

Once you get herpes, you have the germs for life. Most of the time, you don't notice you have herpes. Now and then, you get a rash. Stress, sunlight, and sometimes getting sick with other things can bring the rash out again.

What does herpes look like?

If you have herpes, you get groups of little blisters on a red base.

You can get the rash on your lips or the corners of your mouth. People call these cold sores or fever blisters. Doctors call them oral herpes.

You can get the rash on your penis or on the inner lips of your vagina or around your anus. The rash can also spread to your buttocks, the small of your back and your thighs. This is called genital herpes.

The blisters of both genital and oral herpes break open and then crust over. Cold sores on the lips take about a week to go away. Sores of genital herpes can take two weeks to go away.

If you have a rash that looks like herpes, see a doctor or nurse. They can show you how to take care of your rash.

How do you get herpes?

You get herpes by touching the sores of people with herpes.

You get oral herpes by kissing or nuzzling someone who has sores.

You get genital herpes by having sex with someone who has sores.

Newborn babies can get herpes from their mothers, if their mothers have sores.

What do you do if you have herpes?

Wash your hands often with warm water and soap. Wash your hands every time you touch your sores.

Cover your sores with a cloth or a bandage until they crust over.

Keep the rash clean and dry. When it's clean, the rash can't get infected.

No medicine gets rid of the virus completely. Some medicines can help heal the sores. There is no vaccine to prevent herpes.

If you have genital herpes, a nurse or a doctor can give you some medicine which may help.

See a doctor or nurse if you have herpes and:

- your rash spreads;
- you feel ill (headache, fever, strange behavior);
- your rash spreads to your eye;
- you think you might be pregnant.

How do you keep from getting herpes?

Don't touch the sores or saliva of someone who has herpes.

Don't have sex or kiss your partner when he or she has sores. If you or your partner has sores on the penis or vaginal area, wait for them to heal before having sex, or use a condom from start to finish.

Shingles

What is herpes zoster?

Herpes zoster is a rash known as shingles. Shingles come from the same germs that cause chickenpox. After you have chickenpox, the virus "sleeps" for many years and can "wake up" at any time to cause painful blisters on your skin at the nerve endings.

What do shingles look like?

The rash looks like chickenpox and can sometimes hurt. You get many little red bumps that can itch and ooze.

You can get shingles more than once, but you can't get chickenpox more than once.

How do you get shingles?

You have to get chickenpox before you can get shingles. If you touch the blisters of someone with shingles, you don't get shingles. But you can get chickenpox if you have not had chickenpox before.

The drainage from the blisters of shingles can spread germs to other people who have not had chickenpox. You should cover open or wet blisters with a bandage or clean clothes.

If you have not had chickenpox and you have contact with someone with a shingles rash, see a doctor or a nurse.

What do you do if you have shingles?

Keep the shingles lesions clean with soap and water to prevent them from getting infected. Ask your health care provider about soaking the lesions in Burow's solution. You may also need to take pain relievers.

See a nurse or a doctor often. They can help you with the pain. Also, they can make sure that your rash doesn't get worse.

See a caregiver immediately if any of the these signs or symptoms appear:

- blisters spread to your eyes or other parts of your body;
- blisters are still appearing after one week;
- you get more sleepy, cranky, or confused.

What is impetigo?

Impetigo is a very common skin infection that can spread very easily in places where people are close together, such as day care centers and shelters.

What does it look like?

Red blisters that later become crusted can appear anywhere on the body, but most often around your mouth, your nose, or on your arms and legs. It can also look like pus-filled blisters on any part of the body.

How do you get it?

You can get impetigo when you have an open cut on your skin, or when you scratch an insect bite. The sores can quickly spread to other parts of your body.

You can get impetigo if you touch the sores of someone else. If you have impetigo, you can spread it until all your sores get better.

What should you do if you have impetigo?

If you have impetigo, a doctor or a nurse will give you an antibiotic ointment or pills. You must complete the whole recommended treatment in order to keep the infection from coming back.

If you have impetigo, clean your sores with warm water and soap every day, then cover them with clothing or a bandage. Don't share towels or clothing with other people until all your sores go away.

If you have impetigo, wash your hands often with a lot of soap and clean water to keep from spreading the infection. Wash your hands every time you touch impetigo sores or change the bandages or clothing that cover the sores.

Make sure you carefully throw away soiled bandages and keep any clothing or linen that might have drainage on them away from others. Clothing and linen soiled with drainage can be disinfected by washing in a hot water wash cycle with chlorine bleach.

How can you keep from getting impetigo?

Try to avoid scratching insect bites and picking scabs.

Keep any insects bites or cuts clean with soap and water. If it looks like a bite or cut is draining or forming a crust, see a doctor or a nurse.

Flu

What is influenza?

Influenza is the flu, a virus that comes around once a year, usually in the late fall or winter for people in the USA.

When you have the flu, you get a fever, chills, headache, dry cough, and often a sore throat. You feel very tired, and sometimes you have muscle aches and red, watery eyes.

For most people, the flu comes and goes quickly. But the flu can make you very sick, if you have:

- problems with your heart or lungs;
- diabetes;
- anemia (thin or tired blood).

You can also get very sick from the flu if you are infected with HIV, the virus causing AIDS.

How do you get the flu?

The flu is easy to catch where many people live together. You get the flu by breathing germs from someone who is sick or by staying in a shelter where many people are sick.

What should you do if you get the flu?

If you have the flu, you should take it easy and drink plenty of liquids. You can help a sore throat by gargling with warm water and some salt.

Don't use aspirin for your fever or your child's fever.

Use Tylenol™ (acetominophen).

How can you keep from getting the flu?

You can get a flu shot every year so you don't get the flu or give it to other people. Shelters usually give flu shots in November.

You can't get the flu from a flu shot. Most people don't have any side effects from the flu shot. However, sometimes the shot can make you feel achy and tired, or you may have a low fever and chills. This is rare and only lasts for about 2 days. Your arm may be sore for a couple of days after the shot.

If you are allergic to chicken or eggs, you should not get a flu shot.

If you are ill and have a fever, wait until you feel better before you have a flu shot.

You should wash your hands with warm water and soap after blowing your nose or your child's nose to prevent giving the flu to others.

What are lice?

Lice are tiny bugs that live on the human body.

There are three types of lice:

Head lice live on people's hair and make the scalp itch. The eggs often look like dandruff, but you can't pull them off your hair easily.

Head lice spread when a person with head lice comes into contact with another person's hair. They can also spread when people share hats, combs and other things that touch the head or hair. Head lice are very common among children.

Body lice hang from people's clothes, especially in the seams. They do not usually live on the skin. People usually find they have body lice when they get a rash from scratching.

Body lice spread when you touch or come into contact with a person with body lice. They can also spread by sharing things like clothing or bed sheets that have body lice on them.

Pubic lice most commonly spread by close body contact or sexual contact. If you have pubic lice, you should ask a doctor or nurse to exam you for other sexually transmitted diseases.

How do you get rid of lice?

For head lice and pubic lice, ask a doctor or nurse about shampoos or cream rinses that will kill lice in your hair. Usually, you have to leave the shampoo on your hair for 4 to 10 minutes. You then rinse your hair well and dry it with a towel. Once your hair is dry, you may have to comb any remaining eggs out of your hair with a fine-toothed comb. This takes a lot of time. Some people prefer to cut or shave their hair instead of combing.

To keep the lice from coming back, wash all linen and clothing in hot water and dry your laundry in a dryer for 30 minutes before you use it again.

If you can't wash things like stuffed animals and toys, carefully vacuum them.

Soak all your combs and brushes in the lice shampoo diluted with water. A solution of 1 part bleach to 10 parts water or a regular household cleaner with water will also work.

For body lice, all you may have to do is take off your clothing and shower carefully. Body lice live in clothing, not on the skin. Before you put your clothing back on, you should wash your clothes in hot water and dry them in a dryer for 30 minutes. Do not put your clothing back on or sleep in the same bed after you shower until everything is clean.

If you have lice, you should see a nurse or doctor after about a week to make sure the lice are gone. Sometimes you have to get treated again.

How can you keep from getting lice?

The best way to keep from getting lice is not to share clothing, hats, combs and other personal things. Tell people who complain about itching or rashes to see a doctor or nurse.

If you have been close to a person with lice, ask a doctor or nurse to evaluate you for lice.

Measles

What is measles?

Measles is a virus that is easy to get. Measles can make you or your child very sick.

What does measles look like?

Measles often begins like a cold. You can have a cough, high fever, runny nose, and red, watery eyes. Four days later, you get a rash that is red and blotchy. The rash starts on your face and then spreads to your body.

How do you get measles?

When someone who has measles coughs or sneezes, the virus can be spread through the air to other people.

You or your children can get measles if:

- you've never had measles or never been vaccinated;
- you were born after 1957 and you've never had the measles vaccine;
- you were born after 1957 and you had the measles vaccine before 1968;
- your child has never had measles and has not been vaccinated.

If you're near someone who has measles, you should ask a doctor or nurse about the disease.

What should you do if you have measles?

When you see symptoms of measles on yourself or your child, you should go to a doctor immediately. The doctor can tell you if you or your child has measles. There is no medicine to get rid of measles, but you can make sure that others don't get the disease.

If you have measles, don't go into public places like stores, buses, subways, and medical clinics. You could spread the disease to someone who has not yet had it. About 4 days after you get the rash, you can no longer give the disease to anyone else. It is then safe to go out in public.

How do you keep your children from getting measles?

You can prevent your children from getting measles if a doctor gives them a vaccine on or after 12 months of age, and again when they go to kindergarten or first grade or middle school. The vaccine is combined with one for mumps and rubella (MMR) and will protect your child against all three diseases.

What is meningococcal disease?

Meningococcal disease is a serious infection caused by a bacteria. It can lead to meningitis, a swelling of the lining around the brain. It can also cause an infection of the blood.

Meningitis happens most often in children younger than 5 years old, especially in babies 6 to 12 months old.

What are the symptoms of meningococcal illness?

Meningococcal illness can begin as a cold. Or it may start very quickly, with a fever, chills, and tiredness. Often, tiny red or purple splotches show up on your skin.

Older children and adults also get headaches with stiffness or pain in the neck. Very small children may only be cranky and not want to feed. Their cry can sound much higher than normal.

How do you get meningococcal illness?

You can get infected when someone coughs or sneezes the bacteria that cause meningococcal disease into the air you breathe. Your children can get the bacteria when they put objects in their mouths which have been mouthed by other children carrying the germ.

The bacteria can live in the nose and throat of some people who do not get sick. They can still spread it to others.

How do you keep from getting meningitis?

If you or your children spend a lot of time with someone who gets this illness, you can take an antibiotic called rifampin to reduce your chances of getting the disease. It only needs to be taken for two days. Talk to your health provider about this.

You should not take rifampin if you are pregnant, have severe liver disease, or have had previous problems with this medicine.

Rifampin can stain your urine, sweat, saliva, tears, and stool an orange-red color. This goes away once the medicine is finished.

Rifampin can stain soft contact lenses so you should wear glasses until the medicine is finished.

If you have to take rifampin, your birth control pills may not work. You should use another method like a condom or a diaphragm until the end of the birth-control pill cycle.

Rifampin can also interfere with methadone doses. If you are on methadone, have your health provider call your clinic to adjust the dosage.

See a doctor or nurse right away, if you or your family has been around someone with meningococcal illness in the last two weeks and:

- you or anyone in your family develops a fever, headache, or become confused;
- your baby gets a fever, becomes cranky, feeds poorly, or has a funny cry.

Pertussis — Whooping Cough

What is pertussis?

Most people know pertussis by its common name: whooping cough. This disease is very serious in young children. In children under a year old, pertussis can cause serious lung or brain problems.

How do you get pertussis?

You can get pertussis when someone with the disease coughs into the air you are breathing. Also, you can get pertussis by touching the saliva or mucous of someone with the disease.

What does pertussis look like?

Pertussis starts like a cold. You get a runny nose and runny eyes, and you begin to sneeze and cough. The cough goes on for about 2 weeks and gets worse and worse.

Sometimes, especially with children, the coughing fits can end in a big whoop when they take in a breath. They can turn blue while coughing or vomit afterwards. The coughing usually happens at night.

Older people with pertussis may just have a cough that lasts a long time.

If you or your child has a cough that lasts more than 14 days, you may have pertussis. If you or your child have a cough that makes you turn blue or vomit, you may have pertussis. See a doctor or nurse.

What do you do if you have pertussis?

If you have pertussis, see a doctor, drink plenty of fluids, and get lots of rest.

Your doctor or nurse will probably give you some antibiotic pills. The pills can lessen the symptoms and also keep you from spreading germs to other people.

How do you prevent pertussis?

Usually, children get pertussis vaccine several times during their routine checkups between 6 weeks and 7 years. The vaccine is the "P" in the "DTP" shot.

Keep your children's vaccinations up to date. This is the best way to make sure they don't get pertussis.

The pertussis vaccine can wear off. Sometimes, an older child or adult may get whooping cough even though they have had all their shots. These people can give it to small children who haven't had all of their vaccinations.

If you have been near someone who is sick with pertussis, you may need to take antibiotics also. They can prevent you from getting sick.

What are pinworms?

Pinworms are tiny worms that live in people's intestines. Pinworms are very common and very easy to get, even in the cleanest of households.

How do you know when you or your child has pinworms?

It's hard to notice pinworms. The only signs may be an itchy bottom and sometimes a rash from the scratching. Pinworms look like small pieces of white thread. They crawl out of your rectum at night and lay their eggs. This can cause the area to be very itchy.

Pinworms are not very dangerous or harmful. The biggest problem is the itchiness.

How do you get pinworms?

Pinworms spread from one person to another by scratching at the rectal area and then biting nails, sucking thumbs, putting fingers in the mouth, or touching toys or food. The eggs can also get on clothes, bed sheets, or even dust.

People can keep giving themselves pinworms by swallowing the eggs on their hands.

What do you do if you have pinworms?

Pinworms spread easily in places where many people live together. Sometimes everyone in an entire house or shelter may need to take medicine. A single dose of medication (either a pill or liquid) is all that is necessary for the treatment of most cases of pinworm. This may be repeated two weeks later. You can apply Vaseline™ to the buttocks to help the itchiness.

People often get reinfected after treatment for pinworms because the eggs attach to dust that gets into food or onto hands and toys. When you or your children take the pill or liquid for pinworms, you should wash all bed sheets, night toys, clothes and underwear in hot, soapy water. Damp mop or vacuum your floors and wipe down your furniture with a damp cloth.

How do you keep from getting pinworms?

Wash your hands and your children's hands with soap and warm water - especially before eating or preparing food, and after going to the bathroom or changing a diaper.

Eggs can hide in fingernails, so trim your nails and your children's nails.

Ringworm

What is ringworm?

Ringworm is a common infection that can grow on your skin, hair, or nails. It's a fungus, not a worm. Ringworm can appear as small red sores, red circles, or areas of scaling or crusting.

Many children get ringworm on their scalps. Sometimes the small rings get bigger and make your hair fall out. The skin in these areas can get scaly and crusted.

Ringworm on your skin can look like many small circles. Or your skin can just be scaly and very crusted. It can itch a lot.

Ringworm on the feet is common for teenagers and adults. If you have ringworm, your feet will look red and scaly, especially between the toes. These places also itch a lot.

How do you get ringworm?

You or your children can get ringworm of the scalp if you touch another person's ringworm sores and then touch your head. You can also get ringworm on your head if you use an infected person's hat, comb, or anything they had used in or on their hair.

You can get ringworm on your skin and feet by touching another person's sores. You can also get ringworm on your skin or feet by touching something they touched. Often, this happens when you go into the bathroom and walk in your bare feet on a wet floor, or take a bath in a tub that wasn't rinsed out, or sit on a changing bench that wasn't washed.

You can't get ringworm just by being in the same room with someone who has it.

If you have ringworm, you can give it to someone as long as you have sores. Once your sores heal, it can no longer be spread to others.

What do you do if you have ringworm?

If you have ringworm, your doctor or your nurse will give you some pills or a cream. The length of treatment depends on where the infection is and how severe it is.

If you're taking care of someone who has ringworm, wash your hands often. Wash your hands every time you touch infected skin or put lotion on the sores of someone who has ringworm.

Wash in hot water the clothes and linen of anyone with ringworm. Do not let anyone else use these items until they have been washed.

If you or your child has anything on your skin that looks like ringworm, tell someone in the shelter and see a doctor or a nurse. Also, look for the same signs in the rest of your family and in other children who play with your child.

What are scabies?

Scabies are tiny bugs called mites. Scabies burrow under the skin and make you itch and feel uncomfortable, especially at night. They can live anywhere on your body.

How do you get scabies?

Scabies are easy to get, especially in places where a lot of people live or play together. They spread when someone with scabies touches your skin. This can happen when people sleep in the same bed or when you or your children share clothing or bed linen. Scabies can spread until the infected person gets treated.

What do you do if you have scabies?

Scabies may be difficult to treat. A doctor or nurse practitioner can give you a lotion that kills scabies.

If you have scabies:
1) Take a shower.
2) Wait a few minutes for your skin to cool down.
3) Spread the lotion on your body as directed.
4) Do not put on any other cream, ointment, or body lotion.
5) Wait 8 to 12 hours.
6) Take another shower to rinse off the lotion.
7) Wash your linen and bedclothes the morning after the treatment is finished.

For a child with scabies:
1) Bathe or shower the child.
2) Wait a few minutes for the skin to cool down.
3) Spread the lotion on the body as directed.
4) Do not put on any other cream, ointment or body lotion.
5) Wait 8 to 12 hours.
6) Bathe or shower the child again to rinse off the lotion.
7) Wash the linen and bedclothes the morning after the treatment is finished.

Clothing and bed linen should be washed in hot water and dried in a hot dryer for 30 minutes.

Vacuum anything you or your child may have touched if it can't be washed (toys, rugs, and pillows).

Even after treatment, you may continue to itch for a couple of weeks. This is normal. If itching is bad, ask your doctor or nurse about something to help you or your children.

Cut your nails or your children's nails so the scratching doesn't hurt the skin.

How do you keep from getting scabies?

Try not to share your clothing or your children's clothing and bed linen with others.

If you know someone who complains about a rash or itching, urge them to see a doctor or nurse.

If you or your children have been around someone with scabies, see a doctor or nurse.

Streptococcal Pharyngitis

What is streptococcal infection of the throat?

Streptococcal infection of the throat is "strep throat". If you have a strep throat infection that does not get treated with antibiotics, it can make you very sick. It can lead to serious problems in your heart or kidneys.

How do you get strep throat?

You can get strep throat when an infected person coughs or sneezes into the air that you are breathing.

What does strep throat look like?

If you have strep throat:

- your throat is sore, often with gray-white secretions on it;
- you have a fever;
- the glands under your jaw are sore.

Only a doctor or a nurse can tell you if your sore throat is strep throat. They will take a culture of your throat and send it to a laboratory. You must return for the results.

A positive result means that you have strep throat. A negative result means that you do not have strep throat.

What do you do if you have strep throat?

If you have strep throat, your health provider will give you antibiotics. The antibiotics can be pills or a shot.

The shot is only once in the buttocks. You need to take the pills for 10 days. Before you finish the pills, you probably will feel much better. You must take all the pills even if you feel better. If you don't take all the pills, you can get sick again.

If you have a sore throat, put a few pinches of salt in some warm water and gargle. You can also take Tylenol™ and throat lozenges.

What is syphilis?

Syphilis is a sexually transmitted disease or STD, like gonorrhea and chlamydia.

What does syphilis look like?

Syphilis is hard to notice. When you first get syphilis, you may see a sore on your penis, on or around your vagina, in your rectum, or in your mouth. Often, the sore is on a place you can't see, like your vagina or rectum, so you don't notice it. The sore is painless and goes away after a while. But the disease does not.

The disease can go through many stages. The stages can take up to 40 years.

What happens when you get syphilis?

If you have syphilis and you don't treat it, the disease can spread almost anywhere in your body. The disease can cause very serious complications like insanity and blindness.

Syphilis can be very bad for people with HIV infection. If you are infected with HIV, make sure you get a blood test for syphilis.

Babies can be born with syphilis, if the mother is infected. If you are pregnant, make sure you get a test for syphilis on your first prenatal visit and again in the third trimester.

What do you do if you have syphilis?

If you have syphilis, tell your present and past sexual partners that you have the disease. They need to see their doctors even if they don't have any symptoms.

If you have syphilis, your doctor will usually give you penicillin. You will probably get a shot once a week for 2 to 3 weeks.

Penicillin cures syphilis. The earlier you and your partners begin treatment, the better your chances for cure.

If you are being treated for syphilis, your partner must be treated before you can safely have sex together.

If you have syphilis, you should talk to an HIV counselor about HIV testing. HIV is the virus that causes AIDS.

How can you keep from getting syphilis?

Condoms, diaphragms, and spermicides do not keep people from giving syphilis to one another.

People can get syphilis and not know it. If you are sexually active, get a blood test for syphilis every 2 to 3 years at your health center.

TB

What is tuberculosis?

Tuberculosis or TB is a germ that most often infects your lungs. It can also grow in other parts of your body.

How do you get TB?

TB spreads when someone sick with TB in the lungs coughs or sneezes. This puts the germs into the air, and then other people breathe them. If you spend a lot of time near a person who is sick with TB, you can get infected.

How do you know if you have TB?

To make sure you don't have TB, you can take a skin test called the "PPD" every 6 months. This test shows if you have TB germs in your body. If you have TB germs, the test is "positive".

What do you do if you have TB?

If your test is positive, get a check-up and a chest x-ray to see if the germs are making you sick.

Your TB germs may not be making you sick right now. But they can make you sick at anytime in your life. The doctor can give you an antibiotic to kill the germs so they don't begin to grow and make you sick.

If you are infected with TB, but not yet sick, you cannot spread the germs to other people.

If you are sick with TB, it is possible that you can spread the disease to other people. Your friends may need to take a PPD skin test to make sure they are not infected.

If you are sick with TB, you will need to take TB medicine for many months before all the germs are killed. You should take the medicine even if you feel better. TB germs can hide out until the medicine is not around. Then, the germs grow back and make you sick again.

It isn't easy to take medicine in shelters. Ask the shelter staff about a safe place to store the pills. Ask someone to help you to remember to take your pills.

Sometimes, the TB medicine can cause side effects. You may have a fever and a skin rash. You may not want to eat, or your stomach may get upset and you throw up. The right side of your stomach may be sore. Your skin and eyes may turn yellow and your urine may look dark, like tea. This means the medicine is hurting your liver.

If you see any of these signs, stop the pills immediately and see your doctor.

Upper Respiratory Infection

What is an upper respiratory infection?

Upper respiratory infection is a medical term for the common cold. People get colds all the time. An adult can get 2 to 4 colds every year. Children can get as many as 6 to 8 colds every year.

How do you get a cold?

Colds are most likely spread when people cough or sneeze germs into the air, and then other people breathe those germs. Also, people with colds may touch their noses and then put their hands on other people or things like toys.

What are the signs of a cold?

If you have a cold, you have a stuffed and runny nose. You sneeze and your throat is sore. You may feel pressure in your ears.

Adults can sometimes have fevers up to 101° F. Sometimes, children can get a fever up to 102° F.

What do you do if you have a cold?

You should get rest and drink plenty of fluids. If you have a sore throat, mix some salt in warm water and then gargle. You can also use throat lozenges.

If you feel sore everywhere, you can take Tylenol™.

Decongestants may help a stuffed or runny nose.

If you have a high fever, what do you do?

- If you or your children have a high fever (over 102° F), see a doctor or nurse immediately.
- If you have a fever, swollen glands, and a sore throat see a doctor or nurse immediately.
- If you have a fever and cough up yellow or green mucous, see a doctor or nurse immediately.

How do you keep from spreading a cold?

If you or your children have a cold, use tissues (Kleenex™) and throw them away carefully.

If you or your children have a cold you should wash your hands often, especially after blowing noses or wiping secretions. People without colds should also wash their hands a lot with warm water and soap, particularly before preparing, serving or eating food.

Chickenpox

What is chickenpox?

Chickenpox is a virus known as varicella. The same virus causes shingles. Chickenpox spreads easily from one person to another. Once you've had chickenpox, you can never get it again.

What does chickenpox look like?

Chickenpox looks like an itchy rash or bunches of small, red bumps. The bumps grow into blisters, ooze, and then crust over. After about a week, the blister stops oozing and a scab usually forms. People with chickenpox also can have a mild fever.

You can only get chickenpox once. Rashes from other viruses can often look like the one from chickenpox. It is easy to get them confused.

Most people have chickenpox when they are young. Children don't usually get very sick from chickenpox, but some adults do. Some people can get very sick, especially pregnant women or people with bad health.

How do you get chickenpox?

If you've never had chickenpox, you can get it by breathing near someone who has the disease. Children get chickenpox by being in the same classroom and playing or eating with each other. Adults get it by being in the same shelter or by visiting someone who has it.

You can also get chickenpox by touching the fluid on the blisters that come with chickenpox or shingles. Sometimes the fluid gets on clothing and bed sheets, and you can get chickenpox when you touch them.

The rash and fever begin 10 days to three weeks after being near someone who had chickenpox.

If you see a rash on yourself or your children, tell someone on the shelter staff.

What do you do if you have chickenpox?

If you have chickenpox, see a doctor or nurse if you:

- are over 15;
- are pregnant;
- have other health problems.

If you have chickenpox, you need to rest and drink plenty of fluids.

Wash the lesions with soap and cool water to keep them clean. Put on calamine lotion to stop the itching.

Take Tylenol™ (acetominophen) if the fever causes discomfort. Do not take aspirin or medicine with aspirin in it. Aspirin can cause problems when used for the symptoms of chickenpox.

What is viral meningitis?

Viral meningitis is an infection that causes the lining around your brain to swell. The most common symptoms are severe headaches, unusual behavior, fever, vomiting, and excessive tiredness.

What causes viral meningitis?

Viral meningitis can be caused by many different viruses. One of the most frequent causes is a very common virus that also can cause mild diarrhea and colds. Only a few people who get sick with this virus will go on to get meningitis.

How do you keep from getting viral meningitis?

The best way to avoid getting this disease is to wash your hands *often* with warm water and soap. This is very important before preparing, serving, or eating food, or before feeding your child. Handwashing is also important after you or your child go to the bathroom, or you change a diaper.

Wash your hands after blowing or wiping your own or your child's nose. Don't share objects with others that might have been mouthed or chewed.

What if you know someone who has viral meningitis?

Not every type of viral meningitis can spread from one person to another. If you recently spent time with someone who came down with viral meningitis and you get a fever or a severe headache, tell the shelter staff and see a doctor or nurse.

The Vaccine Preventable Diseases:

Measles

Mumps

Rubella

Polio

Diphtheria

Tetanus

Pertussis

Hib

What is a vaccination?

When you get a shot to protect you against a certain disease, you are getting a vaccination.

In the United States, children routinely get shots to protect them against measles, mumps, rubella (German measles), diphtheria, tetanus, pertussis (whooping cough, *Haemophilus influenzae* type b (Hib), and polio.

Certain individuals may also be targeted for other vaccines, such as the hepatitis B vaccine or influenza vaccine. This depends on your health history and your risk for getting these diseases.

Vaccination is very important for you and your children. Children usually receive most vaccines before their seventh birthday. If you didn't get vaccinated in childhood for one of these diseases, you may still be able to receive the vaccine as an adult.

What are the diseases?

Measles is a serious virus that causes a high fever, cold-like symptoms, runny eyes and a body rash. Rarely, measles can lead to pneumonia, inflammation of the brain, deafness, or mental retardation.

Mumps is a virus that causes painful swelling of the glands in the neck and behind the ears. It can lead to inflammation of the lining around the brain (meningitis) and swelling of the testicles in men. Rarely, it causes deafness or sterility.

Rubella is also called German measles. Normally, the symptoms of rubella are mild and include a rash with a low fever. However, pregnant women with rubella can have miscarriages, stillbirths or babies born with serious birth defects.

Polio is a virus that can lead to swelling of the lining around the brain (meningitis) or paralysis. It is extremely rare in the United States due to good vaccination practices. You can get polio if you are not immunized and you are exposed to infected people from other countries where polio is more common.

Diphtheria is an infection that starts in the throat and nose. It causes a thick gray covering over the back of the throat that can make breathing very difficult. This germ can also release a poison that causes paralysis and severe heart problems.

Tetanus is an infection that gets into the body when you get a serious cut, puncture wound, burn, or bite. It leads to stiffness in the muscles, especially those of the jaw ("lockjaw") and the breathing muscles.

Pertussis, or whooping cough, is a serious infection of the upper airway. It begins very much like a cold with a runny nose and cough. The cough may get worse at night, and occur in "fits" that may end in a loud whoop or vomiting. But infants are most at risk for problems including seizures, pneumonia and brain damage from pertussis.

Hib (*Haemophilus influenzae* type b) is a bacteria that can infect the blood, the lining of the brain, and the lungs and airways. It rarely infects adults, but can be a very serious illness in infants and young children.

What are the side effects of these vaccines?

The side effects of these vaccines are usually mild, with some redness and swelling where you get the shot and possibly a fever. Rarely, other more serious side effects can occur with any vaccine. You should talk to your health provider about any concerns you have. Health clinics can also give you information sheets on each vaccine.

What if I don't get my child vaccinated?

If you don't get your children vaccinated, they can get very sick. Also, they may not be able to enroll in a school or day-care center. Massachusetts state law requires all children enrolled in day-care centers, schools, and colleges to be up-to-date with immunizations.

Keep your child's immunization records updated and in a safe place. You will need them as your child grows up.